Wood Pellet Gril Cookbook 2022

400 Recipes For Perfect Smoking On A Wood Pellet Grill

GERARD HOYLES

Table of contents

Introduction

What are Wood Pellets?

Wood pellets are the (fuel) that your smoker requires to create the flavorful (rich) smoke and fire required for great slow and low (BBQ). The majority of (pellet) smokers are formed in the same manner.

What Is a Pellet Smoker?

A pellet smoker (sometimes referred to as a pellet grill) is a (wood-burning device) used to bake, smoke or grill meat.

A pellet grill smoker is a self-contained barbecue that runs on hardwood pellets rather than gas or charcoal. They're easy to use, quick, and provide delicious results.

Pellet smokers use (food-grade compressed wood) pellets, which burned more cleanly and slowly at a lower pressure than conventional (wood) chips. Pellet smokers are ideal for cooking (brisket) fish, turkey, racks of (ribs) and other meats, giving a delicious smokey taste. Furthermore, pellet (smokers) are simple to use: To turn your meat, flip it in the grilled section, or (braise it with a marinade), open the (smoker's) cover.

How Does a Pellet Smoker Work?

A pellet (smoker) consists of heating a (cooking chamber) in which air flows, convectively (heating) food. Food is cooked on (grill) grates at the top of the (cooking) chamber, while hardwood (pellets) and charcoal burn at the bottom (this section is also referred to as a firepot or burn pot). More wood is distributed from a (pellet hopper) positioned just above (cooking chamber) when the fuel supply at low. These pellets are pushed down a (chute) and into the (chamber's) heart by a drill.

Airflow controls the (temperature) settings of a pellet smoker. Heavy-duty (fans) at the bottom of the device pulls air into the lowest (portion) of the cooking (chamber), where the oxygen is used by the burning pellets, raising the temperature. But, when the top cover of the (smoker) is opened, heat may escape.

Types of Wood Pellets for Your Smoker

You may select from a range of (wood) pellet flavors. In reality, there are eight popular flavors and many additional flavor mixes produced by different companies.

The following are the most popular wood (pellet) flavors for your smoker:

Alder – Because alder is a softer wood, I think (alder wood) pellets are the finest for smoking fish. Vegetables, poultry, Beef and seafood all benefit from it.

Apple – Vegetables, poultry and pork all benefit from this seasoning.

Cherry – The finest (wood) pellets for smoking (pulled) pork, in my opinion, are cherry pellets. This taste improves veggies, pork and poultry.

Hickory – Poultry, pork and Beef are the finest meats to combine with this flavor.

Maple – Perfect with Vegetables and pork.

Mesquite –The finest (flavor), best paired with Beef

Oak - Oak (pellets) are, in my view, the finest wood pellets for (smoking) brisket. This is a great way to improve your seafood and Beef.

Pecan – This flavor works well with vegetables, pork and poultry.

How to Use a Pellet Smoker to Smoke Meat

With some experience, using a (pellet) grill becomes easier and easier. First, however, there are a few basic guidelines that every potential (pit boss) should follow:

Keep your smoker clean: Cooking with (wood) pellets has many appeals since they burned clean. Please clean it up after every cooking period by brushing the (grill) grates and discarding any unwanted pellets from the (hopper).

Use your temperature probe: A meat (probe) is included in many modern (pellet) smokers, although it is often one of the (lowest-quality) elements in the system. Investing in a (high-quality digital) thermometer and cook at the exact temperature you require.

Experiment with hardwoods: You may work on building your own unique (hardwood) mix in addition to making a wet brine or (personalized) dry rub. Maybe you're a (purist) who will never combine different types of wood. Alternatively, you might begin with pellets made from a (base) wood such as mesquite, hickory and alder, and then add pellets prepared from (fruitwood) like cherry or apple, except for apple, Beef (smokes) nicely with all woods.

Apart from maple and oak, smoking chicken tastes amazing. Fish that has been smoked with mesquite, alder or oak is especially delicious. When smoked over maple wood, hickory or pecan, vegetables may be delicious. Apart from oak and mesquite, pork goes well with almost everything.

Give yourself plenty of cooking space: Although you don't want your smokers to take up too much space on your (patio), please ensure it has a big enough cooking surface so you can cook your meats properly. A decent (pellet grill) may vary in size from little (over 200 square inches to well over 800 square inches), so consider your goals before making a decision.

Use a sear box: Pellet (grills) do not become as hot as (traditional) charcoal or (gas) barbecues. So consider buying a (pellet) grill with (an add-on sear box—essentially) a tiny grill that can generate temperatures much higher than the smokers themselves—if you're searching for a single machine that can manage both pellet conventional searing and pellet smoking.

Chapter 1: Breakfast

(Image by: debbietingzon)

1.1: Chicken Fajita Omelet

Preparation Time: 30 minutes

Cooking Time: 12 minutes

Servings: 4

Ingredients:

- 1 cup thinly sliced bell pepper

21

- Blackened sriracha rub seasoning to taste
- 2 tbsp. of butter
- 1 cup shredded cheddar jack cheese
- 8 oz. of boneless, skinless chicken breast, thinly sliced
- Six beaten eggs
- 1 tbsp. of thick cream
- One minced jalapeno
- Half a lime
- 1 cup finely chopped red onion
- 1/3 cup Roja salsa
- 2 tbsp. of sour cream
- 1 tbsp. of vegetable oil (distributed)

Steps:

- Pre-heat the Pit Boss Griddle to medium-high heat. Heat a cast-iron skillet use a gas or charcoal grill.

- Drizzle 1 tsp. Oil over cut chicken breasts, then spice with Blackened Sriracha.

- Place the chicken on the grill and drizzle with the remaining oil. After 2 minutes, add the onions and bell peppers to the pan. Continue to sauté for another 2 minutes with more Blackened Sriracha, then deglaze with fresh lemon juice. Take the mixture off the grill and put it aside.

- Reduce the heat to low and whisk together the eggs (3 per omelet) and heavy cream.

- On the griddle, melt 1 tbsp. of the butter. Pour the eggs over the melted butter as soon as possible.

- To make the omelet, fold the egg over. Add some minced jalapeno and more cheese to the mix. Remove the eggs from the pan and top with 1/4 cup of cheese and all but ½ cup of the saved filling.

- Arrange more filling, sour cream, salsa, sour cream, cheese and jalapeno on top of the omelet on a dish. Warm the dish before serving.

1.2: Pulled Pork Eggs Benedict

Preparation Time: 30 minutes

Cooking Time: 300 minutes

Servings: 4

Ingredients:

- 2/3 cup of apple cider vinegar.
- Two sticks of butter
- 6 cups of the chicken broth
- Eight eggs
- Two egg yolks
- 4 English muffins
- 2/3 cup of the ketchup
- 1 tsp of lime juice
- 1 cup maple chipotle rub seasoning
- Salt and pepper according to taste
- 7 lbs. pork shoulder

Steps:

- Preheat the Pit Boss pellet grill to 350 degrees Fahrenheit by smoking it for 10 minutes with the lid open. Preheat the grill to medium/high heat use a charcoal grill or gas.

- Of maple chipotle seasoning in a large mixing basin. Combine the ketchup, apple cider vinegar, chicken broth, and 4 tbsp. Set aside after whisking everything together well.

- Season the pork shoulder well on both sides with the remaining 3/4 cup maple chipotle seasoning, then put on the grill and sear on all sides until brown, approximately 10 minutes.

- Place the pork shoulder in the disposable aluminum pan after removing it from the grill. Over the pork shoulder, pour the chicken broth mixture. It should reach approximately a third to a quarter of the way up the side of the pork shoulder. Aluminum foil should be firmly wrapped around the top of the pan.

- Reduce your Pit Boss grill's temperature to 250°F. Grill the pork in the foil pan for four to five hours, or until it is tender and falling off the bone.

23

- Allow the pork to cool slightly after removing it from the grill. Drain approximately a cup of the liquid from the pan, then shred the pork and top with the saved liquid. Remove from the equation.

- Set up a saucepan of boiling water on the burner and put the two yolks in a dish that will sit on top of the hot water without touching it to create the hollandaise sauce.

- Heat the yolks over boiling water, whisking continuously until they thicken and form a ribbon-like stream when lifted with the whisk.

- In a measuring cup, melt the butter. Place the egg yolk bowl on a level surface that will not slip or shift.

- Slowly pour the butter into the eggs while mixing vigorously and continuously. As additional butter is absorbed into the yolks, the sauce should thicken.

- Lemon juice, pepper and salt to taste.

- Bring 4" of water up the edge of a saucepot to a boil. Poach the eight eggs with salt and vinegar if preferred.

- In a toaster, heat the English muffins and assemble the benedicts.

- Add hollandaise sauce and maple chipotle to the benedicts. Enjoy!

1.3: Cowgirl Steak & Eggs on the Griddle

Preparation Time: 10 minutes

Cooking Time: 15 minutes

Servings: 2

Ingredients:

- Four eggs
- 2 lbs. cowgirl ribeye steak
- ½ minced jalapeño pepper
- 1 tbsp. extra virgin olive oil
- Tt pit boss steak rub pit boss steak rub
- One scallion, thinly sliced
- Yukon gold potatoes, 1 pound

Steps:

- Preheat the (pit boss skillet) to a medium-high setting.

- Generously season steaks the pit boss chop house rub. Drizzle olive oil into a heated pan and sear steaks for 5 - 6 minutes on each side for medium-rare, depending on thickness.

- After the last sear, rapidly sear the edges, then quickly baste the steaks with a tbsp. Or two of butter, rotating with tongs. Transfer the steaks to a chopping board and set aside for 5 minutes to rest.

- Meanwhile, cut the parboiled potatoes in half. Add additional chop house rub to taste.

- While the steaks are resting, sauté the potatoes for 2 minutes on each side in 1 tbsp. of the butter. Finish with the scallions and jalapeno, then removed from the skillet.

- In the center of the skillet, add the rest butter and a drop of olive oil after the first flip of the potatoes. On top, crack four eggs. Cook for an additional minute, just until the yolk is still liquid, but the white is opaque.

- Serve the cut steak with potatoes and two sunny-side-up eggs.

1.4: Pancake Casserole

Preparation Time: 60 minutes

Cooking Time: 60 minutes

Servings: 6

Ingredients:

- Butter (2 tbsp.)
- ½ cup of the chocolate chips
- Eggs 4 beaten
- Syrup (Maple)
- Sugar in powdered form
- Pancakes (12-14)
- Sugar ¼ cup, granulated
- 1 tsp. of the vanilla essence

- Milk 1 ½ cup.

Steps:

- Combine sugar, baking powder, flour and salt in a mixing basin. Then add the egg,

- Melted butter and milk and stir until everything is smooth.

- Preheat the griddle on medium-low heat in the (Pit Boss Platinum Series KC Combo). Preheat a big cast iron pan over medium-low heat if using a gas or charcoal grill.

- Lightly grease the skillet, then spread the mixture onto the griddle, about 1/4 cup each pancake. Cook until golden brown, about 1 to 2 minutes on each side. Allow 15 minutes for cooling before assembling the dish.

How do you put the dish together?

- Lightly grease a metal 9-inch round baking pan. In a baking pan, equally, layer the pancakes.

- Whisk together sugar, milk, eggs, and vanilla in a large measuring cup or bowl. Pour the mixture over the pancakes. Seal with plastic wrap and gently push down with your fingers to immerse the pancakes in the liquid. Refrigerate for at least two hours or up to 24 hours.

Recommendation for wood pellets:

- The mixed wood flavors of apple, maple, and hickory and that make up our competition blend hardwood pellets are hard to beat for this savory and delicious breakfast.

- Remove the plastic wrap from the pan, wrap in foil, and bake for 40 minutes on the top level of the grill. Remove the foil and bake for a further 10 minutes.

- Remove off the grill, slice, and sprinkle with chocolate chips, powdered sugar, and maple syrup (if desired).

1.5: Flank Steak Breakfast Burrito

Preparation Time: 10 minutes

Cooking Time: 30 minutes

Servings: 4

Ingredients:

- 1 cup of the bacon slices, diced

- 2 Avocado
- Butter (2 tbsp.)
- One cup shredded cheddar cheese.
- 2 lbs. of the flank steak
- Four large flour tortillas
- Tt hot sauce
- 2 tsp. of the olive oil
- Chopped onion 1/2 cup.
- Tt pit boss chop (house steak rub)
- Potatoes, 2 cups diced

Steps:

- Pre-heat the (Pit Boss Platinum Series KC Combo) to 425 degrees Fahrenheit. Set the grill to medium-high heat use a charcoal grill or gas. Preheat the skillet to a medium-low temperature.

- For medium-rare, grill steaks for 3 minutes on each side [depend on the thickness of steak]. Remove the steak from the grill and let it rest for about 10 minutes before thinly slicing it against the grain. Drizzle olive oil over the meat and season liberally with (Pit Boss Chop House Steak Rub). Remove from the equation.

- Remove the tortillas from the grill and put them inside to warm.

- Cook for 2 minutes on the skillet with the bacon, add the potatoes and cook for another 2 minutes. Cook until the bacon is crisp, the potatoes have browned, and the onions are transparent. Set aside the mixture.

- Cook scrambled eggs on a skillet with butter. Remove from the equation.

- Sprinkle shredded cheese on tortillas before assembling breakfast burritos. Scrambled sliced steak, eggs, potatoes, and additional cheese on top. To wrap tortillas, fold in the sides and roll from the bottom up.

- Serve with fresh avocado and spicy sauce on the side.

1.6: Smoked Salmon (Lox) Omelet

Preparation Time: 560 minutes
Cooking Time: 270 minutes

Servings: 4-6

Ingredients:

- Brown sugar 1 cup

- Butter 1 tbsp.

- Black pepper crackled

- Cream cheese (2 tbsp.)

- Three eggs

- ¼ tsp dill, chopped

- Garlic in powder form (2 tbsp.)

- 2 tbsp. of the heavy whipped cream

- salt(kosher)

- 2 tbsp. of the onion powder

- One salmon side, approximately 2 lbs.

- 1 tsp chopped scallions.

- 1 tsp powdered white pepper

Steps:

How do you dry brine salmon?

- To make the brine, combine salt, onion powder, brown sugar, garlic powder, and white pepper in a mixing bowl.

- Place a piece of (plastic wrap) on a tray and cover it with half of the dry brine. Place the salmon skin-side down on top of the mixture. Wrap the salmon in plastic wrap after rubbing a large quantity of brine on top. Freeze for 8 hours or overnight in the refrigerator.

- Remove the salmon from the refrigeration and rinse it in cold water to remove the brine.

- Blot with a paper towel, then dry on a cookie sheet at room temp for two hours, just until the salmon has a yellowish sheen.

Recommendation for wood pellets

Our traditional (wood pellet blend's nutty) and delicious smells of mesquite, pecan and (hickory hardwoods) will take this smoked salmon to a new level of taste.

- Set the kc combo to smoke and turn it on. Smoke for 2 hours, then raise the temp to 200 degrees F and smoke for another 1 to 2 hours, just until the interior temperature reaches 145 degrees F.

- Remove off the grill and serve right away, or wrap securely and store in the refrigerator for up to five days.

- Put 2 oz. of smoked salmon on the skillet's bottom right corner to warm. Fresh herbs may be added to the dish.

- Combine the heavy cream and eggs in a mixing bowl. Melt the butter on the griddle, then place the eggs on top. Working quickly, flip, scramble, and then added (smoked salmon) and cream cheese using a high-heat spatula. Pepper and herbs to taste.

- Cooked for 1 min before transferring to a dish and immediately served it.

1.7: Tri Tip Breakfast Sandwich

Preparation Time: 15 minutes

Cooking Time: 10 minutes

Servings: 4

Ingredients:

- Four pieces cooked and sliced bacon
- Four slices of cheddar cheese
- Four eggs
- Four cracked and toasted English muffins
- 1 cup thinly cut tri-tip roast

Steps:

- Get your Pit Boss up and running. The temperature was set to 350°F after it's started.

- Take water to a bare simmer in a heavy pot. Stir the water with a spoon to create a vortex, then break an egg into it. The egg should be poached for 5-7 minutes until the white is set; however, the yolk is still runny. Carry on with the remaining eggs in the same manner.

- Assemble the sandwiches by putting a piece of cheddar cheese, two half of a bacon slice, tri-tip, and a poached egg on each one.

- Grilled for 5 minutes, or until cheese is melted and everything is warmed thoroughly. Serve right away.

1.8: Gluten-Free Chocolate Pumpkin Bread

Preparation Time: 20 minutes

Cooking Time: 75 minutes

Servings: 2

Ingredients:

- 2 cups gluten-free all-purpose flour
- 1/2 tsp of baking powder
- 1 tsp bicarbonate of soda
- 1 ½ stick butter (3/4 cup)
- 1 tsp cinnamon in powder form
- 1 tsp powdered cloves
- 1-2 bars of Lily's dark chocolate
- Two large eggs
- 1 tsp. of powdered nutmeg
- Pumpkin puree 15 oz. (1 can)
- Salt ½ tsp
- Swerve sugar 2 cups.

Steps:

- Pre-heat your grill to 300 degrees Fahrenheit.

- Butter two 8x4 in loaf pans and sprinkle with gluten-free flour (butter works as well).

- Combine all dry ingredients in a medium mixing bowl: salt, cloves, flour, cinnamon, baking soda, baking powder and nutmeg. Stir until everything is well mixed.

- In a large mixing basin, cream the sugar and butter substitutes on medium speed with mixer (electric) until smooth. Now add the eggs, or egg replacements, one by one, and beat thoroughly after each addition. Continue to beat the texture unless it is light and fluffy.

- Combine the sugar, egg, pumpkin puree, sugar and butter in a mixing bowl. At this stage, the mixture will start to appear grainy.

- Mix in the flour mixture with the wet ingredients at low speed until everything is incorporated.

- Crush the choc bar(s) and mix it in with the rest of the ingredients. Mix everything until its smooth.

- Evenly divide the mixture between the two pans and bake for 70-80 minutes, or when a toothpick injected in the center derives out clean. Halfway through the baking time, rotate the pans.

- Remove from the grill and set aside to cool for about 10 minutes before serving.

1.9: Gluten-Free Vegan Apple Pumpkin Muffins

Preparation Time: 15 minutes

Cooking Time: 30 minutes

Servings: 12

Ingredients:

- 1 cup almond milk
- 2 tbsp. of avocado oil
- 1 tsp. of baking powder
- 1/2 tsp. of baking soda
- 1.5 cups all-purpose gluten-free flour
- ½ cup brown sugar
- 1 tsp. of cinnamon, powdered (plus more for apples)
- One batch of flax egg (1 tbsp. of flaxseed meal, 2.5 tbsp. of water)
- 1/3 cup gluten-free oats (plus extra for topping)
- Two granny smith apples, peeled, cored, and diced
- 1 tbsp. of butter vegan
- 3/4 cup of pumpkin puree
- 1/4 tsp salt
- 1 tsp of vanilla essence

31

Steps:

- Heat the grill to 350 degrees Fahrenheit.

- In a large bowl, prepare the flax egg and put it aside.

- In a heated pan, melt vegan butter, then add cinnamon and apples to taste. Cook until the vegetables are tender (3-4 minutes).

- The same dish as the flax egg combines brown sugar, avocado oil, pumpkin puree, almond milk, and vanilla essence.

- Sift together the salt, baking powder, flour, cinnamon, and baking soda. Sift the dry ingredients into the mixing basin slowly. As you gently add the mixture, stir to incorporate it.

- Stir in the oats and apples until well mixed.

- Evenly spoon muffin batter into each pan or liner; top with more oats.

- Bake for about 30 minutes on your grill, or when a toothpick injected the center comes out clean 12 minutes into the cooking time, rotate the pan.

1.10: Gluten-Free Halloweens Pumpkin Bundt Cake

Preparation Time: 15 minutes

Cooking Time: 30 minutes

Servings: 12

Ingredients

- Two gluten-free Funfetti cake mixes

- Orange food coloring

- Flour

- 3/4 cup heavy cream

- Oil

- 1 ½ cup sugar in powdered form.

- 2/3 cup sliced almonds

- 1 tsp of vanilla extract

- One wafer ice cream cone

Steps:

- Heat the grill to 350 degrees Fahrenheit. Close the broiler's flame.

- Set aside two 10-inch fluted pans that have been greased and floured.

- Prepare cake mixes as directed on the box, adding 1 tsp of almond extract and 2/3 cup slivered almond to the batter.

- Divide the batter into two halves and bake according to the package instructions. Allow 10 minutes for cooling. Remove the cakes from the pans and set them aside to cool fully.

- Meanwhile, mix together cream, vanilla, powdered sugar, and 1 tsp of almond extract in a slow, steady stream.

- Add orange food coloring to the frosting until the desired color is achieved.

- Trim the flat side of each frosted cake even if required. Place one cake on a plate, rounded side down. Apply approximately 1/4 cup of the icing to the flat surface. Place the rest of the cake on top, rounded side up. Allow the frosting to run down the sides of the cake. As the stem, use an upside-down ice cream cone.

- If desired, use green icing to cover the ice cream or pipe on leaves.

1.11 Beaver Tails

Preparation Time: 105 minutes

Cooking Time: 2 minutes

Servings: 8

Ingredients

- 2 tbsp. melted butter

- One egg

- 2 ½ cups all-purpose flour

- 12 cups warm milk

- 1 tbsp. of cinnamon, crushed

- 12 tsp salt

- 1 tsp sugar

- ½ tsp vanilla

- 1 l vegetable oil

- 1/4 cup warm water

- 2 ½ tsp of active yeast

Steps:

- Add milk, sugar, water and yeast in a small mixing dish. Allow it to rest for 10 minutes or until it becomes foamy.

- Pour the flour into a separate bowl and create a well in the center. Combine the vanilla, butter, sugar, salt and egg in a mixing bowl. Combine all of the ingredients and stir till the (dough) is smooth. Knead the (dough) for approximately 5 minutes before placing it in an oiled basin. Set aside for approximately an hour until the dough has doubled in size, covered with a towel.

- Pre-heat your oven to 450 degrees F after one hour. Pour 1 liter of veg oil into a (cast iron) pan and put it on your grill's grates. Preheat the oil to 350 degrees Fahrenheit. To avoid grease flare-ups, leave your flame broiler closed.

- While the oil is heating up, punch down the (dough) and divide it into eight tiny balls. Make a flat round out of each piece of dough. Fry the (dough) for approximately 1 minute on each side in the hot oil, or until golden brown.

- Immediately spray with sugar and cinnamon or top with preferred toppings. Enjoy!

1.12: Homemade Blueberry Pancakes

Preparation Time: 5 minutes

Cooking Time: 10 minutes

Servings: 4

Ingredients

- 2 cups of fresh blueberries

- 1 cup of mixed pancake

- Sugar 1 ½ cup

- Warm water ¾ cup

Steps:

Preheat the (cast iron pan) for approximately 10 minutes to create the blueberry sauce. In a (cast iron pan), pour blueberries and cook for a few minutes. Begin crushing and stirring the blueberries, then add the sugar. Stir till the sugar has melted, and the blueberries have reached your desired consistency.

- Preheat the grill to 350 degrees Fahrenheit. Place the (cast iron skillet) on your grill's grates.

- In a large mixing basin, add the water, pancake mix, and 1/2 cup of blueberries.

- Pour the batter into four equal portions onto the griddle. Cook for approximately 6 minutes until the sides of the pancake are slightly cooked, with the lid closed. Cook for a further 4 minutes after flipping each pancake.

- Serve the freshly cooked pancakes with spicy blueberry sauce.

1.13: Blueberry Pie

Preparation Time: 5 minutes

Cooking Time: 30 minutes

Servings: 8

Ingredients:

- One can of pie filling (blueberry)

- Pie shell, DZ 1-9."

Steps:

- Preheat the skillet to 400 degrees Fahrenheit.

- Use a fork to prick the lower of your pie filling. Fill the pie crust with blueberry pie filling.

- Bake for 30 minutes on the grill, turning halfway through.

- Enjoy while it's still warm!

1.14: Basic Crescent Rolls

Preparation Time: 2 minutes

Cooking Time: 12 minutes

Servings: 8

Ingredients:

- One can of crescent dough

Steps:

- Preheat the grill to 375 degrees Fahrenheit.

- Cut the dough into triangles after unrolling it. Place the triangles on a nonstick cookie sheet that hasn't been oiled. On your grill, bake for 10-12 minutes. Whenever the rolls are lightly browned, you'll know they're ready.

1.15: Breakfast Cheeseburger

Preparation Time: 5 minutes

Cooking Time: 10 minutes

Servings: 2

Ingredients:

- Four strips of bacon

- 6 ounces of (lean beef)

- Two buns of the burger

- Eggs (2)

- Cheese, sliced (2)

- Salt and Pepper

Steps:

- Heat your grill on "smoke," with the lid open, until a fire in the burn pot is created (3-7 minutes). Preheat the oven to 400 degrees Fahrenheit.

- Separate the minced beef into two layers of patties using your hands. Brush the grill with oil, then add the patty and cook for 2-5 minutes on each side, or until done to your liking, pushing down to provide a nice sear.

- Take the burger from the grill and start assembling your burger. Begin by placing the patties on the lower bun or bread slice, followed by a piece of American cheese, hash browns, bacon, an over-easy egg, and then the upper bun or bread slice. It's now ready to eat.

1.16: Classic Easter Quiche

Preparation Time: 15 minutes

Cooking Time: 40 minutes

Servings: 6

Ingredients:

- Four chopped bacon strips
- 1/4cup sliced green bell pepper
- Four eggs
- Green onion
- 1 cup half-and-half
- 1 cup shredded mozzarella cheese
- ¼ tsp nutmeg, crushed
- One deep pie crust, at room temperature
- ¼ cup sliced red bell peppers
- 1/8 cup minced red onion

Steps:

- We suggest using our (maple hardwood pellets) for mild smoke with breakfast tastes.
- Turn your (Pit Boss) on to smoke mode and leave the lid open for 10 minutes.
- Heat the grill to 400 degrees Fahrenheit.
- In a pie plate, put the frozen pie crust. Don't forget to use a fork to puncture the bottom! Baked according to the package instructions (approximately 15 minutes @ 400˚F).
- Beat the eggs and half-and-half together in a medium mixing basin until smooth.
- Add the green onion, bacon, onion, bell peppers, nutmeg, and cheese and stir to combine. Combine the egg and half-and-half in a light whisking bowl.
- Pour the mixture into the pie shell and bake for approximately 25 minutes in the Pit Boss. When you can slip a toothpick into it and withdraw it without anything clinging to it, you know it's done.
- Cut into slices and serve immediately. Enjoy!

1.17: Pit Boss Pumpkin Pie

Preparation Time: 5 minutes

Cooking Time: 65 minutes

Servings: 6

Ingredients:

- 1 tsp of powdered cinnamon
- ¼ tsp of powdered cloves
- 1/2 tsp of ginger powder
- Two big eggs
- One evaporated milk
- One deep 9" pie shell
- One can pumpkin pie
- ½ teaspoon salt
- ¾ cup sugar

Steps:

- Preheat the grilling on smoke with the lid opened until a fire in the burn pot has formed (3-7 minutes). Preheat the oven to 400 degrees Fahrenheit.

- In a small bowl, combine the salt, ginger, sugar, cinnamon and cloves. In a large mixing bowl, whisk together the eggs, then add the sugar-spice mixture and pumpkin. Stir in the evaporated milk gradually. Pour the mixture into the pie crust after it has been well combined.

1.18: Maple bacon donuts

Preparation Time: 5 minutes

Cooking Time: 15 minutes

Servings: 8

Ingredients:

- 1 ½ cup sugar (powdered)
- A quarter cup of maple syrup
- 2 tsp of Maple Extract
- 2 tbsp. of cream (heavy)
- 12 Yeast Doughnuts with Glaze

Steps:

•   The temperature was set to high and warm for 15 minutes with the lid covered when ready to cook.

•   Mix powdered sugar, syrup, and maple flavoring in a medium saucepan and simmer over medium-high heat till the mixture comes to a slow boil. Cook for 3-5 minutes, stirring often.

•   Reduce to low heat and whisk in the heavy cream. As required, add additional icing sugar or cream to get the desired texture.

•   Place the bacon strips on the grilled grate immediately. 5-7 minutes on each side on the grill (until crisp).

•   When cool, transfer to a platter and crumble or chop.

•   Place the doughnuts straight on the grilling grate (don't wipe the grate after frying your bacon; the fat will assist the doughnuts not cling). Grilled for 3-5 minutes on each side, or until glaze is bubbling and the doughnuts have grill marks.

•   Transfer the doughnut to a serving dish while they are still hot. Immediately pour the glaze over the top. Serve immediately with the bacon crumbles on top. Enjoy!

1.19: baked candied bacon cinnamon rolls

Preparation Time: 15 minutes

Cooking Time: 35 minutes

Servings: 6

Ingredients:

•   1/3 cup of brown sugar

•   Cinnamon rolls (pre-made)

•   12 slices of bacon, sliced

•   Cream cheese, 2 oz.

Steps:

•   Pre-heat the Traeger to 350°F for 15 minutes with the lid closed when ready to cook.

•   Eight bacon pieces should be dredged in brown sugar, ensuring sure both sides are covered.

- Put the browned sugared bacon pieces on a cookie sheet on top of a huge baking sheet, along with the remaining bacon slices.

- Cook the bacon for 15-20 minutes on the Traeger, or until the fat has rendered, but the bacon is still flexible. Reduce the temperature to 325°F in the Traeger.

- The cinnamon buns should be opened and unrolled. Place one slice of browned sugared bacon on top of one of the unrolled rolls and wrap back up while the bacon is still heated. Carry on with the rest of the rolls in the same manner.

- Preheat the oven to 325°F and bake the cinnamon rolls for 10 to 15 minutes, or until brown. Place the cinnamon rolls in a sprayed 8" × 8" baking sheet or cake pan. Halfway through the cooking period, rotate the pan half a turn.

- Meanwhile, soften the cream cheese and add it to the supplied cream cheese frosting. Cook the bacon and crumble it into cream cheese icing.

- Using a pastry brush, frost the heated cinnamon buns. Warm it up and enjoy it!

1.20: Baked granola

Preparation Time: 20 minutes

Cooking Time: 1 hour

Servings: 6

Ingredients:

- A half-cup of honey
- a half cup of brown sugar
- 1/2 cup melted butter
- 1 tsp of salt
- 2 tsp vanilla bean extract
- 2 tbsp. of cinnamon powder
- A quarter tsp of almond extract
- 5 cup steel-cut oats
- 1 cup sunflower seeds, raw and unsalted
- ½ cup wheat germ, roasted

- 1 cup mixed salted nuts

- 1 pound dried fruit (such as raisins, cherries, blueberries, cranberries, pineapple, etc.)

Steps:

- In a small saucepan, combine the brown sugar, honey, butter, and salt. Over medium-low heat, bring the mixture to a simmer. Cook, stirring periodically, approximately 5 to 8 minutes.

- Remove the pan from the heat and whisk in the vanilla, almond extract, and cinnamon. Allow cooling slightly before serving.

- Using a rimmed baking sheet, lightly grease the bottom and sides.

- In a large mixing plate, combine the sunflower seeds, oats, wheat germ, and roughly chopped nuts.

- Over the oat mixture, pour the heated syrup. Grease your hands and thoroughly combine the ingredients. Place the mixture on the baking sheet that has been prepared.

- When fully cooked, pre-heat the grill to 300°F with the lid covered for 15 minutes.

- Bake for 1 hour or until the granola is gently golden. Allow cooling before chopping into pieces in a large serving bowl.

- Combine the dried fruit and coconut in a mixing bowl. Keep the container sealed. Enjoy!

- 2 cup dried fruit (raisins, cherries, pineapple, cranberries, blueberries, and other dried fruits)

1.21: Baked coffee cake

Preparation Time: 15 minutes

Cooking Time: 45 minutes

Servings: 8

Ingredients:

- ½ cup softened unsalted butter

- 1 cup of sugar

- Two eggs

- 2 quarts flour
- 1 tsp. bicarbonate of soda
- 1 tsp of cinnamon powder
- A half tsp of salt
- 1 cup of sour cream
- 1 ½ tsp of extract de vanilla

Crumbled:

- ½ cup of sugar
- A quarter cup of brown sugar
- 2 tsp of flour
- 1 tbsp. of vanilla bean extract
- ½ tsp. of cinnamon powder
- 1 tbsp. of melted butter

Steps:

- Whenever ready to cook, pre-heat the Traeger to 325°F with the cover sealed for 15 minutes.

- Cooking spray an 8x8-inch cake pan, then line with baking parchment and spray the parchment. Remove from the equation.

- Mix the sugar and butter in the bowl of a stand mixer until light and creamy. Scrape the sides of the dish between each addition as you add the eggs one by one.

- Sift together the baking soda, salt, flour, cinnamon in a medium mixing dish.

- Whisk together the vanilla extract and sour cream in a small bowl.

- In three portions, alternate wet and dry flour and sour cream mix in the sugar mixture, cleaning the dish after each addition.

- To make the crumble topping, combine all of the ingredients in a large mixing bowl. Combine the crumble ingredients in a small mixing dish. Pour half of the batter into the cake pan and top with half of the crumb mixture. Pour in the rest of the batter and top with the remaining crumbs.

- Prepared pan immediately on the grilled grate and bake for 45 to 60 minutes, till a toothpick inserted in the middle of the cake comes out clean.

- Allow cooling after removing from the grill grate. Cut into slices and serve. Enjoy!

1.22: baked Dutch baby

Preparation Time: 5 minutes

Cooking Time: 25 minutes

Servings: 6

Ingredients:

- ¾ cup flour (all-purpose)
- 4 quail eggs
- 1 yolk of an egg
- ¾ gallon of milk
- 1 ½ tsp of sugar
- 1/8 tsp of nutmeg powder
- 1 tsp vanilla bean extract
- 4 tsp of butter
- Fresh Fruit
- Sugar in powdered form

Steps:

- When you're ready to cook, pre-heat the (Traeger) to 500 degrees for 15 minutes with the lid closed.
- Combine eggs, sugar, flour, milk, nutmeg, and vanilla in a food processor or a normal basin with a hand whisk. Blend until completely smooth.
- Melt the butter in the hot Dutch oven. Add the butter to the pan as quickly as the butter has melted (be careful not to burn it).
- Bake for 20 minutes on the Traeger unless the pancakes are brown and puffy.
- Reduce the temperature of the grill to 300 degrees F and bake for a further 5 minutes. Remove the pancake from the grill and slice it into wedges.
- Serve immediately with powdered sugar, preserves, syrup, fresh fruit, or cinnamon sugar. Enjoy!

1.23: Smoked deviled eggs

Preparation Time: 15 minutes

Cooking Time: 30 minutes

Servings: 4

Ingredients:

- 7 cooked and peeled hard-boiled eggs
- Mayonnaise, 3 tbsp.
- 3 tsp. chives, chopped
- 1 tsp of mustard (brown)
- 1 tbsp. of apple cider vinegar
- A spicy sauce
- A pinch of salt and pepper
- 2 tbsp. crumbled cooked bacon
- Paprika

Steps:

- Set the Traeger to 180°F and pre-heat for 15 minutes with the lid covered when you're ready to cook. If Super Smoke is available, use it for the best taste.
- Cook for 30 minutes by setting boiled and peeling egg directly on the grilled grate.
- Remove the eggs from the grill and set them aside to cool. Spoon the yolks into a gallon zip-top bag after slicing the eggs lengthwise.
- Fill the bag with salt, vinegar, mayonnaise, chives, mustard, spicy sauce, and pepper. Close the bag and mix all the ingredients with your hands until totally smooth.
- Squeeze the yolk solution into one of the bag's corners and cut a tiny section off. Fill the hard-cooked egg whites with the yolk mixture. Paprika and crumbled bacon go on top of the deviled eggs. Refrigerate till ready to serve. Enjoy!

1.24: BBQ brisket breakfast tacos

Preparation Time: 10 minutes

Cooking Time: 30 minutes

Servings: 6

Ingredients:

- 4-pound beef brisket that was leftover
- Extra-virgin olive oil, ½ tsp
- 1 diced green bell pepper
- 1 chopped yellow bell pepper
- Ten eggs
- ½ gallon of milk
- A pinch of salt and pepper
- 2 cup shredded cheddar cheese
- Flour tortilla

Steps:

- Start the Traeger grill and adjust the temperature to 375 degrees F when you're ready to cook. Preheat for 10 to 15 minutes with the lid closed.

- Warm leftover beef in the grill with a second layer of foil.

- Pre-heat the skillet for 10 minutes after coating a (cast iron pan) with oil. When the pan is heated, add the diced peppers and cook, occasionally turning, until they are done to your liking.

- Mix all the milk, eggs, salt, and pepper to taste while the peppers are cooking. Scramble the scrambled eggs in the skillet. When the eggs are nearly done, add the cheese to the skillet.

- Remove the eggs and brisket from the grill. Serve egg in a tortilla with beef on top. If desired, top with guacamole or salsa. Enjoy!

1.25: Baked Rustic Country Loaf

Preparation Time: 3 hours

Cooking Time: 30 minutes

Servings: 6

Ingredients:

- 1 ¼ tsp active dry yeast (distributed)
- 1 ¼ cup white flour, unbleached
- ¼ cup flour (whole wheat)
- 1 tbsp. of sugar

- 3 ¾ cup bread flour, unbleached
- Cornmeal
- A half tsp of salt

Steps:

- To make the starter, follow these steps: white flour, 1 cup lukewarm water, 1/2 tsp active dry yeast, and wheat flour should all be combined in the bowl of a stand mixer equipped with the bread hook. Turn off the machine and set aside the bowl for at least 2 hours, covered with a light paper towel. Allow the beginning to rest longer for the greatest taste, preferably overnight or up to 16 hours.

- To make the (dough), combine salt, flour, baking powder in a mixing bowl 1 cup lukewarm water, bread flour, sugar, ¾ tsp of yeast are added to the starter using a spoon. The (dough) will be a clumpy, sloppy mess. Allow it to sit for 12 to 15 minutes before stirring it again. It will become more consistent and fluid.

- Transfer the (dough) to a level surface and mix it for 10 to 12 minutes, adding additional flour as needed.

- Place the (dough) in a lightly oiled dish or plastic container, cover with lightly oiled plastic wrap, and let rise for 1 to 2 hours, or until nearly doubled in size.

- Gently deflate the dough, but don't completely deflate it. Form the (dough) into a round ball for one big loaf. Divide the mixture in half and roll into two balls for two loaves.

- On a baking sheet, place a piece of parchment that has been sprinkled with cornmeal. Place the loaves, seam-side down, on the baking sheet. Cover the bread with lightly oiled plastic wrap and let rise for 45 to 90 minutes, or approximately 40 percent to 50 percent bigger.

- Preheat Traeger to 500°F for 15 minutes with lid closed when ready to cook.

- Raise the loaves and score them with a sharp knife (in one continuous line or a crossed hatch) and a light dusting of flour. Place on the grilling grate immediately.

- Reduce the temperature of the Traeger to 425°F for the first 15 minutes of baking and spray with water in a few minutes. Bake the bread for 25 minutes, or until it's a deep golden brown and an instant-read thermometer reads at least 190°F on the inside. Keep in mind that small loaves will bake faster, so keep an eye on them.

- Remove the bread from the Traeger and set it aside to cool. Cut into slices and serve. Enjoy!

1.26: Avocado Toast

Preparation Time: 5 minutes

Cooking Time: 5 minutes

Servings: 4

Ingredients:

- 1 French loaf of bread
- Olive oil that is extra-virgin
- Avocados (two)
- Juice of lime
- 1 orange zest (as needed)
- 1 glass of orange juice
- 1 tsp of honey
- ½ shallot, cut thinly
- ½ Chile Anaheim
- 1 garlic clove, minced

Steps:

- Pre-heat the oven to 350 degrees F and leave the cover closed for 15 minutes until ready to cook

- Drizzle a little olive oil over the bread pieces (1.5" slices). Lightly sprinkle lemon zest and olive oil over avocado halves.

- Put avocado halves and slice bread on the grate and cook for 5-10 minutes, or until grill marks appear on the avocados. Remove the grill from the heat.

- Cut a cross-hatching pattern across the grilled avocado halves; scoop out the avocado flesh easily. Zest orange and combine with honey, olive oil, juice vinegar in a large mixing dish. Anaheim pepper (minced), Avocado shallots, and garlic clove should all be added. Toss gently.

- Place a liberal amount of avocado mixture on each piece of bread. Enjoy! Season with salt and pepper to taste.

1.27: Smoked oatmeal with coconut milk

Preparation Time: 15 minutes

Cooking Time: 20 minutes

Servings: 4

Ingredients:

- 1 steel-cut oat
- A quarter-tsp of salt
- Coconut milk, 2 c.
- 2 tbsp. of honey
- ½ cup fresh fruit

Steps:

- While ready to cook, pre-heat the grill to 180°F with the lid covered for 15 minutes. If Super Smoke is available, use it for the best taste.

- On a sheet tray, spread out the steel-sliced oatmeal in a single layer. Cook for 10-15 minutes on a baking sheet directly on the barbecue grate. Sprinkle sea salt over smoked oats in a medium mixing bowl.

- Cover the oats with 2 cups boiling coconut milk. Allow for a 5- to the 10-minute recovery period.

- Arrange the oats in individual serving plates or a serving bowl, then garnish with seasonal fruit and honey. Enjoy.

1.28: western breakfast casserole

Preparation Time: 20 minutes

Cooking Time: 35 minutes

Servings: 8

Ingredients:

- 6 cubed bread slices
- 6 eggs, whole
- 1 gallon of milk
- 3/4 tsp mustard powder

- A quarter tsp of salt
- A quarter tsp of black pepper
- Chorizo, 6 oz.
- 6 oz. of turkey minced
- ½ onion, chopped whole
- ½ red bell pepper, whole
- ½ chopped whole Anaheim chili
- 4 cooked and sliced bacon slices
- 1 cup spinach, baby
- 1 cup of Swiss cheese
- 1 cup strong cheddar cheese
- 1 cup grated jalapeno cheddar cheese

Steps:

- Preheat the oven to 350 degrees F then leave the lid covered for 15 minutes when ready to cook.

- Using nonstick cooking spray, coat a 9" by 13" baking pan. In the bottom of the pan, arrange the bread cubes in a single layer. Set aside the eggs, milk, salt, black pepper and powdered mustard that have been whisked together.

- Brown the ground turkey and chorizo in a pan on the heat until fully done.

- Sauté the onion and peppers in the pan until they are soft. Sauté for another minute with the garlic and fried bacon, then add the spinach and simmer until it wilts.

- Half of the meat and vegetable combination, halfway of the egg mixture, and half of the cheeses are layered on top of the toast. Repeat the layering until all of the ingredients are utilized.

- Covered and bake at 350°F for 35-40 minutes, or until well cooked, uncovered for the final 5-10 minutes to allow the cheese to brown lightly on top.

1.29: Grilled ham & egg cups

Preparation Time: 15 minutes

Cooking Time: 25 minutes

Servings: 6

Ingredients:

- 12 ham slices
- A dozen eggs
- Whipped cream, 1 cup
- A pinch of salt and pepper
- 1 cup cheddar cheese, shredded
- Chopped chives

Steps:

- Pre-heat the Traeger to 350°F for 15 minutes with the lid closed when ready to cook

- Coat the muffin tin's wells with cooking spray. Cut the ham into pieces that are just little larger than any muffin well.

- Cooked for 5 to 10 minutes on each side, or until beautiful grill marks emerge, placing the ham slices firmly on the grilled grate. Turn on the grill.

- Combine the heavy whipping cream and eggs in a mixing bowl. Season with salt and pepper to taste.

- Cook for 12 to 15 minutes until the eggs are fully cooked. If preferred, sprinkle with cheese in the final few minutes of cooking.

- Remove the ham and egg cups with care and serve immediately with sliced chives or cilantro. Enjoy!

1.30: Grilled blueberry breakfast sausage

Preparation Time: 45 minutes

Cooking Time: 15 minutes

Servings: 6

Ingredients:

- 2 tbsp. extra virgin olive oil
- ½ cup yellow onion, finely chopped
- 1 tsp of salt
- 2-pound dark meat minced turkey, pork, or a mix of the two

- A half-cup of dried blueberries or cranberries

- 2 tsp fennel seeds

- 2 tsp rosemary, chopped

- 1 gently beaten egg

- 1 tsp lemon juice 1 tsp lemon zest

- ½ tsp of black pepper, freshly in powdered form

Steps:

- In a huge frying pan, warm the olive oil. Place the chopped on top. In a wide fry large frying pan, warm the olive oil. Add a sprinkle of salt and the chopped onion. Cook, stirring continuously, for 5 to 7 minutes, or until onions are transparent. Turn off the heat and set it aside to cool.

- Combine the remaining ingredients in a large baking dish. Toss in the onions. Mix the ingredients with clean hands until they are equally distributed. Freeze for 30 minutes or up to 24 hours after mixing.

- Once ready to cook, pre-heat the Traeger to 325˚F with the cover shut for 15 minutes.

- Erase the sausages from the fridge and form 18 patties out of the meat mixture.

- Place on the grill and cook for 2 to 3 minutes on each side, unless the internal temperature reaches 165˚F to 175˚F. With a bit of salt, enjoy.

1.31: Donut bread pudding

Preparation Time: 15 minutes

Cooking Time: 40 minutes

Servings: 8

Ingredients:

- 16 Donut Cakes

- ½ cup seedless raisins

- Eggs 5

- A quarter cup of sugar

- 1 cup of thick cream

- 2 tsp vanilla bean extract
- 1 tsp of cinnamon powder
- ¾ cup melted butter, slightly chilled
- An ice cream cone

Steps:

- Butter a 9-by-13-inch baking pan lightly. In the pan, layer the doughnuts in an equal layer. If used, scatter the raisins over the top. Drizzle the butter in an equal layer.

- To make the custard, combine all of the ingredients in a mixing bowl and mix the cream, eggs, vanilla, sugar, and cinnamon in a medium mixing basin. Add the butter and whisk to combine. Pour the glaze over the doughnuts. Allow it to rest for 10 to 15 minutes, pressing the doughnuts down into the (custard) as needed. Wrap foil around the dish.

- Begin the (Traeger on Smoke) with the top open till the fire is created when you're ready to cook (4 to 5 minutes). Preheat the oven to 350°F and bake for 10 to 15 minutes with the lid covered.

- 30–40 minutes, unless the custard is set, bake the bread pudding. Erase the foil and bake for another 10 minutes, or until the top is gently browned.

- Allow it cool for a few minutes before slicing into squares. If desired, drizzle with melting ice cream. Enjoy!

1.32: Baked breakfast sausage casserole

Preparation Time: 15 minutes

Cooking Time: 1 hour

Servings: 8

Ingredients:

- ½ gallon of milk
- 1 tsp black pepper, freshly 1 tbsp. extra virgin olive oil or vegetable oil
- 2 medium chopped red or green bell peppers
- 1 medium diced yellow onion
- 3 tsp. kosher salt, divided, plus more salt as required
- 1 pound bacon, thick-cut

- 1 pound breakfast sausage, ground
- 2 pound defrosted shredded hash browns or tater tots
- 3 cup medium cheddar shredded cheese, split
- A dozen large eggs
- ground, plus more as required

Steps:

•   Set the Traeger to 350°F and heat for 15 minutes with the lid covered when you're ready to cook. Put a (cast iron pan) on one side of the grill and let it warm with the lid covered while the grill put a (cast iron pan) on one side of the grill and let it warm with the lid covered while the grill.

•   Of olive oil and combine the onions, chopped peppers, and 1 tsp of salt in a mixing bowl. Add 1 tbsp. Cook until soft, approximately 20 minutes, mixing every 5 to 7 minutes with the lid covered.

•   Place the bacon on the grill simultaneously and cooked until crispy, approximately 25 to 30 minutes. Bacon should be drained on paper towels before being chopped into bite-size pieces.

•   Remove the onions and peppers from the pan after they're done cooking and pour the sausage. Cook the sausage until it is crumbled and just cooked through, approximately 8 to 10 minutes total, raising the grill cover to mix it every few minutes.

•   Combine the bacon, onions, salt, pepper, hash browns or tater tots, cooked sausage, cooked peppers and 1-1/2 cup cheese in a large mixing dish. Mix well and pour into a 9x13-inch baking dish.

•   Whisk together the milk, eggs, 2 tsp of salt, and 1 tsp of cracked black pepper in a separate dish. Allow 5 minutes for the eggs to soak into the other ingredients after pouring the egg mixture equally over the other components in the baking dish. The remaining cheese should be sprinkled on top.

•   Wrap the dish in foil and place it on the grill. Remove the cover and cook for yet another 15 minutes, just until the mixture is set, the potatoes are browned, and the cheddar is bubbling. Enjoy!

Chapter 2: Lunch Recipes

(Image by: Mokeneco)

2.1: Smoked Paleo Beef Jerkey

Preparation Time: 8 hours

Cooking Time: 5 hours

Serving: 6

Ingredients:

- 1/4 cup of (Worcestershire) sauce
- 1 tbsp. of garlic powder
- 1/2 cup of Tamari Sauce
- 1 tbsp. of onion powder
- 1 tsp. of freshly (ground) black pepper

55

- 2 1/2 Pound of (flank) steak
- 1/2 tsp. of cayenne pepper

Steps:

- In a mixing bowl, add the garlic powder, black pepper, Worcestershire sauce, tamari sauce, onion powder and cayenne pepper. To combine the ingredients, stir them together.

- Remove any (connective tissue) and excess fat from the meat. With a (sharp) knife, cut it into 1/4-inch thick slices against the grain. Place the pieces in a large, resalable plastic bag.

- Spread the marinade mixture over the beef pieces and compress the bag so that the marinade is evenly distributed. Cover the bag and refrigerate for several hours or overnight.

- When you're ready to cook, preheat the oven to (180°F) and prepare food for 15 minutes with the top covered.

- Take out the beef from the marinade and discard it. Place the meat in a (single) layer on the (grill) grate. Smoked for 4 to 5 hours, just until the jerky is dried but still pliant and chewy, or when you (bend) a piece.

- Place it to a (refrigeration) rack and let to rest for 1 hour. Refrigerate any (remaining) jerky by sealing it in a (plastic zip) top bag.

2.2: Cowgirl Cut Smoked Steak

Preparation Time: 15 minutes

Cooking Time: 1 hour

Serving: 2

Ingredients:

- As Needed (Winemaker's Napa Valley) Rub
- 1 New York or Rib (Eye Steak), 1" or more

Steps:

- When you're ready to cook, preheat the oven to (180°F) and prepare food for fifteen min with the top covered. Use (Super) Smoke if it's available for the best flavor.

- Season both sides of the steak generously with (Winemaker's) Rub.

- Start smoking the steak for 60 minutes on the (barbecue) grill. Remove it from the grill and allow it to rest.
- Raise the temperature and preheat the oven to 500 degrees Fahrenheit with the top covered.
- When the grill is heated, place the (steak) back on the (grill) grate. Cook until steaks reach the ideal (internal) temperature of (125-130 ° F) for medium rare.
- Enjoy with a bold red wine, rich and bourbon rocks.

2.3: Smoked Beef Tenderloin

Preparation Time: 10 minutes

Cooking Time: 45 minutes

Servings: 4

Ingredients:

- 1 - 4 pound of (beef) tenderloin
- 3 tbsp. of (steak) rub of your choice
- 1 tbsp. of salt kosher

Steps:

- Fire your (pellet grill) to high setting, as directed by the manufacturer.
- Remove any extra fat from the tenderloin and cut into equally sized pieces if the tenderloin is tapering. Season the tenderloin with salt and steak rub before placing it on the hot grill.
- Cook for 10 minutes with the top closed. Close the cover for the next 10 minutes after flipping the tenderloin.
- Reduce the heat and keep the grill top open for 2-3 minutes to bring the heat down to about (200-225 degrees). Close the cover and smoked until the (interior temperature) reaches (130 degrees Fahrenheit).
- Remove the steak from the grill and set aside for 15 minutes before cutting.

2.4: Easy Beef Garlic and Broccoli

Preparation Time: 10 minutes

Cooking Time: 15 minutes

Serving: 1

Ingredients:

- 1.5-2 lb. of iron steak (flat)
- 2 tsp. of chunky garlic (Mix in paste)
- 2 tbsp. of canola oil
- 2 tbsp. of mirin
- 1 tsp. of sesame oil
- 4 tbsp. of water
- 2 tbsp. of honey
- 1 1/2 tbsp. of cornstarch
- 3-4 cups of broccoli florets (fresh)
- 1/2 tsp. of (ground) ginger
- 4 tbsp. of soy sauce

Steps:

- Place the steak on a cutting board and cut it against the grain.
- Heat half of the oil in a big wok over high temperature until the oil and wok become hot, (nearly) smoking.
- Gently place 1/3 - 1/2 part of a meat in the pan and constantly cook for 1 minute. Pour a couple of broccoli and cook for another 1-2 minutes.
- Cooked before the sauce has thickened, coating the broccoli and meat.
- Put it aside and covers to stay warm while you prepare the rest of the meal.
- Served the white rice with sesame seeds as a garnish.

2.5: Texas Style Smoked Brisket

Preparation Time: 30 minutes

Cooking Time: 480 minutes

Servings: 12

Ingredients:

- 10-12 (pound whole) beef brisket

- 1/2 (any brand) beer, can
- 1 cup of (apple cider) vinegar
- brisket rub and Pit boss beef
- 2 tbsp. of Worcestershire sauce

Steps:

- Take out the brisket from the fridge. Cutting a (cold) brisket is simpler than cutting a brisket that is at room temp.

- Turn the brisket so that the (pointy) end is on the inside. Trim and remove any (silver) skin or (extra) fat from the flat muscles.

- On the (flat) of the meat, there will be a big, (crescent-shaped) fat portion. Cut the fat until it is soft against the beef, resulting in a (smooth) transition from (point to flat).

- Turn the (brisket) over and cut the (fat cap) to a thickness of 1/4 inches.

- To prepare (mop) sauce, combine the (Worcestershire) sauce, beer and (apple cider) vinegar in a bowl.

- Prepare your Smoker to (225 degrees Fahrenheit).

- Set the (brisket) in the smoker, attach a (thermometer) probe, and cook for approximately 8 hours, or until the (internal) temperature reaches (165°F).

- For keeping the brisket juicy, basting it with (mop) sauce every (2 hours).

- Take out the brisket from the smoker once it hits (165°F), cover it in (butcher) paper, fold the corners over to create a leak-proof cover, and place (seam-side) down in the smoker for a further 5-8 hours.

- Take out the brisket from the (smoker) and set aside for an hour to (settle) before cutting.

2.6: Grilled Salmon Burger with Chipotle Mayo

Preparation Time: 10 minutes

Cooking Time: 10 minutes

Servings: 4

Ingredients:

- 1 Medium jalapeño pepper (seeded and minced)

- brioche buns (as required)
- 2 Whole scallions (minced)
- 1/2 tbsp. of Chicken Rub
- Black pepper (pinch)
- 1/2 tbsp. of (minced) cilantro leaves
- Butter lettuce (as required)
- 1 Clove of (minced) garlic
- Pickled red onion (as required)
- 2 Whole chipotle peppers in (adobo sauce), minced, plus 1 tbsp. of sauce
- 1/2 Cup of mayonnaise
- 1/2 lime (juiced)
- Dill pickles (as required)
- Salt and pepper (according to your taste)

Steps:

- In a (food) processor, mix cilantro, garlic, scallions, jalapeno, Chicken Rub, pepper and salt. Blend well until smooth. Blend once or twice more after scraping down the (edges) of the bowl.
- Removed the (salmon) mixture from the (food processor) and divide it into 5 patties.
- Refrigerate the patties for 10 to 15 minutes after placing them on a sheet pan.
- Preheat the grill to (500°F) for 15 minutes with the lid covered.
- Grill the (salmon) patties for 4 minutes on each side, turning once, (directly) on the (grill) grate.

For the Chipotle Mayo:

- Mix together the pepper and salt, lime juice, adobo sauce, mayonnaise and chipotles in a small bowl. Put in fridge for some time.
- To prepare the burgers, put the (salmon burger) on the lower bun and cover with pickles, red onion, lettuce and chipotle mayo. Serve immediately.

2.7: Smoked Peppered Chicken

Preparation Time: 10 minutes

Cooking Time: 1 hour

Serving: 6

Ingredients:

- 4 chicken legs (as Needed)
- 1 cup of Jalapeno Jelly
- Chili powder
- 1 cup of water
- Chicken Rub (as Needed)

Steps:

- Combine the water and jelly in a sauce pan and cook over medium heat for about 10 minutes.
- Season the chicken (parts) with the chili powder and chicken rub.
- Preheat the grill to 300 degrees F for 10 to 15 minutes with the top covered.
- Place the chicken on the (grill) and cook for 15 minutes with the lid covered.
- Brush the chicken (legs) with the pepper (syrup). Every 15 minutes, flip your legs over and (baste) them for 30 minutes.
- Set the timer for 1 hour on Smoker and (Smoke).
- Cook for another 15 minutes, just until the chicken reaches (165 degrees).

2.8: Smoked Baby Back Ribs

Preparation Time: 15 minutes

Cooking Time: 3 hours

Serving: 6

Ingredients:

- 3 rack (baby back) ribs
- Black pepper (crushed as needed)
- Salt kosher (as required)

Steps:

• Remove the (membranes) from behind the (ribs) and season both sides with salt and pepper.

• When ready to cook, preheat the grill to 225°F and cook for 15 minutes with the lid covered. Use (Super Smoke) if it's available for the best flavor.

• Cook the meat (side up) for two hours. Cook for a further hour after flipping the (ribs) so that the (beef side) is down. Enjoy your meal.

2.9: Smoked Rib-Eyes with Bourbon Butter

Preparation Time: 20 minutes

Cooking Time: 45 minutes

Serving: 4

Ingredients:

• 4 (1 inch thick) (rib-eye) steaks

• 2 tbsp. of bourbon

• 1/2 cup of butter (room temperature)

• 1 tbsp. of (minced) chives or green onions

• 2 cloves of (minced) garlic

• 1/2 tsp. of (ground) black pepper

• Prime Rib Rub (as required)

• 1 tbsp. of (minced) parsley

• 1/2 tbsp. of salt

Steps for the Bourbon Butter:

• Add the pepper, salt, garlic, chives, butter, bourbon and parsley, to a small size mixing bowl and whisk with a (wooden) spoon. Butter may be made (ahead of time) and kept refrigerated until ready to use.

• Preheat the grill to 180°F and cook for 15 minutes with the lid covered. Use (Super Smoke) if it's available for the best flavor.

• Gently season the steaks with Prime (Rib Rub).

• Place the steaks (directly) on the grill grate and smoke for 1 hour.

• Immediately transfer the steaks to a plate and preheat your grill to 500° F.

- When the grill is heated, return the (steaks) to it and cook, rotating once, until they reach an internal temp of 135 ° F for (medium-rare), about 6 to 8 minutes on each side.

- Transfer the steaks to a serving plate and coat each with a pat of (bourbon) butter straight away.

- Allow the meat to settle for 3 minutes before serving.

2.10: Smoked Venison Soft Tacos

Preparation Time: 15 minutes

Cooking Time: 30 minutes

Serving: 2

Ingredients:

- 1 Pound of Venison (back strip steaks)
- 2 tbsp. of (Big Game) Rub
- 1 Medium jalapeño
- 1/2 Pound of Tomatillos
- 2 cloves of garlic
- 1/4 Cup of Quest fresco (crumbled)
- 3 Chiles (Anaheim)
- 2 (Whole) limes
- 1 Medium (yellow) onion
- 4 flours (tortillas)
- 1 (Whole) avocado
- 1/4 Cup of cilantro leaves
- 1/2 Cup of cilantro (finely chopped)
- Salt (according to your taste)

Steps:

- (Traeger seasoning) Set aside for 20 minutes at room temperature with the (big game) rub for the steaks.

- Start the Traeger and set the temperature to (185F) for 10 to 15 minutes to preheat.

- Place the steaks (directly) on the grill and cooked for 30 to 45 minutes at (185F), or until the (internal temperature) reaches 110 degrees F.

- While the steaks are cooking, roast the onion, chili, garlic tomatillos and jalapenos in the oven until browned. Add salt, lime juice and chopped coriander to a mixer with roasted (salsa Verde) components. Purée the (mixture) until it is smooth. Set aside until the (tacos) are ready to be assembled.

- Remove from the grill when the (internal temperature) of the steaks reaches 110 degrees F. Raise the grill temperature to (500°F) and preheat it for 10 to 15 minutes with the lid covered.

- Set the steaks again on the grill at the temperature of the grill and (sear) for 2 to 4 minutes on each side, just until the (internal temperature) reaches 130 degrees F for medium rare. Remove the steaks from the grill. They can (continue to cook) after being removed from the grill and should achieve a final (internal temperature) of 135 degrees F. Allow 10 minutes for resting before cutting.

- Serve the tortillas with (sliced) venison, sliced avocado, salsa Verde and cheese fresco, as well as (cilantro) leaves. Enjoy your meal.

2.11: Smoked Bologna

Preparation Time: 5 minutes

Cooking Time: 4 hours

Serving: 4

Ingredients:

- 1 tbsp. of yellow mustard
- 1/4 cup of brown sugar
- 1 tsp. of soy sauce
- 1 pound of bologna log
- Worcestershire sauce

Steps:

- Split the (bologna) file, being cautious not to chop too deeply.

- Combine the mustard, Worcestershire sauce, brown sugar and soy sauce in a mixing bowl.

- Spread it all over the bologna.
- Set the grill temp to 225°F and cook for 15 minutes with the cover closed.
- Smoked the bologna for 3 to 4 hours.
- Take out from the (grill) and set aside to cool.
- Slice the sandwiches in half and serve.

2.12: BBQ Rib Sandwich

Preparation Time: 15 minutes

Cooking Time: 3 hours

Serving: 2

Ingredients:
- Black pepper (cracked as required)
- 1/2 cup of Qu BBQ Sauce
- 3 rick (baby back) pork ribs
- Salt kosher (as needed)

4 hoagie rolls:
- 1 yellow onion (thinly sliced)
- 1/2 Cup of Qu BBQ Sauce
- 1 Jar of Pickles

Steps:
- On the back of the ribs, there is a peeling membrane. Season gently with salt and ground black pepper.
- Preheat the grill to (225°F) for 15 minutes with the lid closed.
- Grill for two hours on the (meaty) side, then turn the ribs and cook for another hour on the (meaty) side.
- Take out the ribs from the grill and flip them over so that the bone side is facing up on a (cutting) board. Utilizing a (sharp) knife, cut (each bone) along the center and extract the bones with your fingers.
- Rotate the ribs back over and cover with half of the '(Que BBQ) sauce. Cook the sauce back for 5 to 10 minutes on the grill. Take out from the barbecue and put aside.

- Slice (rib) racks to fit the (length of the hoagie) rolls. Half-open the (hoagie rolls) and place the (bottom) bun on the ribs.

- Add pickles, onions and additional (BBQ) sauce to the (top bun).

2.13: Pork Loin with Sauerkraut and Apples

Preparation Time: 15 minutes

Cooking Time: 2 hours

Serving: 4

Ingredients:

- 2 tbsp. of butter
- 1 sweet onion (thinly sliced)
- 2 1/2 Pound of Pork (Loins)
- 1 Pound of Sauerkraut
- Sweet rub (as required)
- 2 Granny Smith Apples (Peeled and Diced)
- 1 Cup of dark beer
- 1/3 Cup of brown sugar
- 2 bay Leaf

Steps:

- Preheat the grill to (180 degrees F) for 15 minutes with the lid covered.

- Season the (pork) loin on both sides with salt and pepper or (sweet) rub. Arrange the roast (directly) on the pan grill, cover, and cook for 1 hour.

- In a large size (Dutch) oven or glass (baking dish), add the bay leaves, butter, apple sauerkraut, onions, brown sugar and beer. Place the (smoked) pork loin immediately on top of the (sauerkraut) mixture. Wrap the pan with a piece of foil.

- Preheat the grill to (350 degrees Fahrenheit) and placed the pan back on the grill. Close the lid and roast the (pork) for a further hour, just until an (instant-read meat thermometer) hit to (160 degrees F).

- Transfer the roast to a chopping board and set it aside to rest. Meanwhile, gently swirl the (sauerkraut) mixture and arrange it on a serving platter. Sliced the pork (roast) and place it on the apple and sauerkraut.

2.14: Smoked Pork Loin

Preparation Time: 5 minutes

Cooking Time: 3 hours

Serving: 6

Ingredients:

- Rub (as required)
- 1 Pork (Loins)

Steps:

- Seasoned pork loin with (Traeger) Rub.
- Preheat the grill to 180°F for 15 minutes with the lid covered.
- Arrange the (pork) loin on the grill (grates) in a diagonal pattern and cook for 3 to 4 hours.
- Raise the grill temp to 350 (degrees Fahrenheit) and cook for 20 to 30 minutes.
- Take out from the grill and the "slice into 1-1/2" steaks and serve.

2.15: Smoked Burgers

Preparation Time: 15 minutes

Cooking Time: 2 hours

Serving: 8

Ingredients:

- 1 tbsp. of Worcestershire sauce
- 2 Pound of (ground) beef
- 2 tbsp. of Beef Rub

Steps:

- Add the Beef Rub, and Worcestershire sauce and ground beef in a mixing bowl.
- Make 8 (hamburger) patties out of the meat mixture.
- Preheat the grill to 180°F and cook for 15 minutes with the lid covered. Use (Super Smoke) if it's available for the best flavor.

- Place the patties (directly) on the grill for 2 hours and smoke them. Eat. Have fun.

2.16: Smoked Sausage

Preparation Time: 30 minutes

Cooking Time: 3 hours

Serving: 4

Ingredients:

- 3 Pound of (ground) pork
- Hog casings (soaked and rinsed in cold water)
- 1 tbsp. of onion powder
- 1 tbsp. of garlic powder
- 1 tsp. of (pink curing) salt
- 1/2 tbsp. of (ground) mustard
- 4 tsp. of black pepper
- 1/2 cup of ice water
- 1 tbsp. of salt

Steps:

- In a medium size (mixing) bowl, add the seasonings and meat and mix thoroughly.

- Pour ice water in the meat and mix until smooth with (quick-moving) hands.

- Pour the mixture in a sausage (stuffer) and following the manufacturer instructions.

- Consider the length of attachment you want, then twist and squeeze it a (few) times or knot it off once all of the meat is filled. Repeat for each connection.

- Preheat the grill to (225°F) and cook for 15 minutes with the lid covered. Use (Super Smoke) if it's available for the best flavor.

- Put the (connections directly) on the grill and cooked for 1 to 2 hours, or until the internal temperature reaches 155 degrees Fahrenheit. Allow the sausage to settle for a few minutes before slicing.

2.17: Smoking' Thai Curry Chicken

Preparation Time: 4 hours

Cooking Time: 20 minutes

Serving: 6

Ingredients:

- 2 tbsp. of (extra-virgin) olive oil
- 3 pounds of Chicken Brest
- 1/4 cup of soy sauce
- 3 tbsp. of brown sugar
- 1/2 tsp. of Cardamom
- 2 cloves of (minced) garlic
- 2 tsp. of curry powder
- 1 tsp. of (freshly grated) ginger
- 1 jalapeño (seeded and diced)
- 1 tsp. of Lemon Grass
- Cilantro
- Thai Red Curry Rub (as needed)
- Coconut
- 2 tbsp. of lime (juice)

Steps:

- Mix all of the (ingredients) for the marinade in a bowl (oil, cloves, pepper, ginger, curry powder, soy sauce, brown sugar, lime juice, cardamom, red pepper and lemon zest or (Thai) curry paste). Fill a large size (resalable) bag with chicken breasts and the marinade.

- Marinate the chicken for a minimum of four hours.

- Increase the temperature to high and preheat for 15 minutes with the lid covered.

- Take out the chicken from the (marinade) and place it on the grill immediately. Cooked for 10 minutes on (each) side just until an (instants read) thermometer indicates a temperature of (165 degrees F).

- Allow the (chicken) to rest for around 5 minutes before serving.
- Serve with coconut flakes and fresh cilantro.

2.18: Traditional Smoked Thanksgiving Turkey

Preparation Time: 15 minutes

Cooking Time: 45 hours

Serving: 8

Ingredients:

- 1/2 Pound of butter
- 20 Pound Turkey Whole Birds, (18-20 lbs.)
- 8 (Sprig fresh) thyme
- 6 Cloves of (minced) garlic
- 1 (Sprig fresh) rosemary
- 1 tbsp. of (cracked) black pepper
- 1/2 tbsp. of salt kosher

Steps:

- Set the grill to 300 degrees Fahrenheit and preheat for 15 minutes with the lid covered.
- In a small size bowl, mix the minced garlic, salt kosher, black pepper, melted butter, thyme leaves and chopped rosemary.
- Remove the (skin) from the breast of the turkey to make a (pocket) in which to fill the (butter-herb) mixture. Using a (1/4-inch thick butter) mixture, coat the whole breast.
- Season the (entire) turkey with black pepper and kosher salt.
- Preheat the grill to (300°F) for 15 minutes with the lid closed.
- Cook the turkey for 3 to 4 hours on the barbecue. Examine the internal temperature; the (ideal temperature) in the (thigh near the bone) is 175 degrees Fahrenheit, and (in the breast) is 160 degrees Fahrenheit. Cook the turkey continuously after being removed from the grill until it reaches a (final breast) temperature of (165° F).
- Set aside for 10-15 minutes and serve immediately.

2.19: Roasted Ham

Preparation Time: 15 minutes

Cooking Time: 2 hours 15 minutes

Servings: 4

Ingredients:

- ¼ cup of horseradish
- 2 tbsp. of mustard (Dijon)
- 8-10 pounds of ham (bone-in)
- 1 bottle BBQ (Apricot Sauce)

Steps:

- Fire the smoker to (325 degrees) Fahrenheit.
- Wrap a (roasting) pan with foil and put the ham in it. Set it in the smoker for 1 hour and 30 minutes.
- Mix the horseradish, sauce and mustard in a small skillet over medium heat and simmer for a few minutes.
- Place it to the side.
- Glazed the ham after 1 hour 30 minutes of smoking and continue to smoke for another 30 minutes before the inner (Smoke Temperature) rises 135 degrees F.
- Allow 20 minutes for resting before slicing and serving.

2.20: Honey Garlic Salmon

Preparation Time: 5 minutes

Cooking Time: 20 minutes

Servings: 6

Ingredients:

Sauce

- 3 tbsp. of butter
- 2 tbsp. of (minced) garlic
- 3 tbsp. of (balsamic) vinegar

- 1/3 cup of honey

- 3 tbsp. of soy sauce

- 2 tbsp. of (white) wine

Salmon

- Olive oil

- 6 (small wild) salmon filets

- Garlic powder

- Pepper (as required)

- Onion powder

- Salt (as required)

Steps:

- Fire your grill to 350 degrees Fahrenheit.

- In a small size (nonstick grill) pan, combine all of the (sauce) ingredients. To ensure that all of the (ingredients) are spread equally, stir them together.

- Prepare a (nonstick foil) pan with side using a (pre-made foil) pan that has been coated with olive oil. Arrange the salmon within, coat with (olive) oil, and add pepper and salt for seasoning.

- Set the saucepan and salmon on the grill for 10 to 20 minutes, just until the salmon is cooked to your liking. Salmon should be cooked to a temperature of (145˚F).

- Maintain a close eye on the sauce. It only takes about 10 minutes to boiling. Make sure it isn't placed over a hotspot.

- Before presenting, turn of the heat and spread the (sauce over) the salmon.

2.21: Chili Pepper Grilled Halibut Fillets

Preparation Time: 10 minutes

Cooking Time: 30 minutes

Serving: 6

Ingredients:

- 1 cup of (virgin) olive oil

- 4 (halibut) fillets

- 2 cloves of garlic (cut into quarters).

- 2 (large) red chili peppers (chopped).

- 2 lemons

- 1 (twig) of rosemary

- 4 tbsp. of (white) vinegar

- 1 (bay) leaf

Steps:

- Combine lemon juice, white vinegar, bay leaf, olive oil, (chopped) red chili, garlic, and rosemary in a big container.

- Submerge the (halibut) fillets in the sauce and mix well to incorporate.

- Put in the fridge for a few hours or overnight.

- Drain the (anchovies) from the marinade and wipe them dry with (paper) towels for 30 minutes.

- Preheat the grill by turning it on to medium heat. For 10 to 15 minutes, keep the top closed.

- Grilled the anchovies for approximately 10 minutes, (skin side) down, just until completely done.

- Rotate the halibut once while cooking to prevent it from falling apart.

- Move to a wide serving plate and drizzle with (lemon) juice.

- Serve the fish with a rosemary.

2.22: Homemade Grilled Trout in White Wine

Preparation Time: 10 minutes

Cooking Time: 30 minutes

Serving: 4

Ingredients:

- ¼ cup of olive oil

- 4 trout fish (cleaned).

- 1 tsp. of (fresh) basil (finely chopped).

- ½ cup of (white) wine

- 1 lemon (juice)

- 1 tsp. of (fresh) basil (finely chopped).

- 2 cloves of (minced) garlic.

- Lemon (slices for garnish)

- Salt and (freshly ground) black pepper (according to your taste).

Steps:

- Combine freshly ground black pepper, salt, garlic, wine, basil, olive oil, lemon juice and parsley in a large size (mixing) bowl.

- Toss the fish in the sauce to thoroughly coat it.

- Wrap and (marinate) overnight in the fridge. When you're ready to cook, fire up the (grill. For 4 to 5 minutes, smoked with the cover open. Preheat the oven to 400 degrees Fahrenheit with the lid covered for 10 to 15 minutes.

- Take out the fish from the marinade and wipe it dry with a (paper towel); set aside the marinade.

- Grilled the trout for 5 minutes on each sides. Spread the (marinade) over the fish and immediately serve with (lemon) slices.

2.23: Oysters with Tequila Butter Skillet

Preparation Time: 10 minutes

Cooking Time: 15 minutes

Serving: 6

Ingredients:

- 7 tbsp. of (unsalted) butter

- 3 dozen (scrubbed medium) oysters.

- ½ tsp. of (fennel) seeds

- 2 tbsp. of tequila

- ¼ tsp. of (crushed) red pepper

- 1 tsp. of (dried) oregano

- Rock salt (for serving)

- 2 tbsp. of lemon (juice)

- ¼ cup of sage leaves (plus 36 small leaves for the garnish)
- Salt kosher (according to your taste)

Steps:

- Roast the crushed red pepper and fennel seeds in a pan over medium heat for 1 minute.
- Transfer to a mortar and set aside to cool. Pound the (spices to a coarse powder) using a pestle, then transfer to a bowl.
- Melt 3 1/2 tbsp. of butter in the same pan over medium heat until it turns (dark) brown, approximately two minutes.
- Stir in 1/4 cup of (sage) and simmer for another 2 minutes, stirring regularly. Transfer the (sage) to a dish.
- Combine the spices and butter in a (mixing) dish. Using the leftover butter and sage leaves, continue the process. Set aside a portion for garnishing.
- Squash the (cooked sage leaves) in the mortar with the pestle. Season with pepper and salt after adding the tequila, oregano, crushed sage and lemon juice to the butter.
- Get the grill ready. Using (rock salt), cover a plate. Grilled the oysters over high temperature for 1 to 2 minutes.
- Discard the (top shell) and carefully place the oysters on the (rock salt).
- Pour the warm (tequila sauce) over the oysters and garnished with a (fresh) sage leaf.

2.24: Traeger Cajun Broil

Preparation Time: 30 minutes

Cooking Time: 1 hours

Serving: 8

Ingredients:

- 2 tbsp. of olive oil
- 3 Pound of (large) shrimp with tails (deveined)
- 2 Pound of (red) potatoes
- 2 Pound of (smoked kielbasa) sausage

- 6 Corn Ears (each cut into thirds)
- 2 tbsp. of butter
- Old Bay (for seasoning)

Steps:

- Preheat the Traeger to (450° F) for 15 minutes with the lid covered when ready to cook.
- Drizzle half of the (olive) oil over the potatoes, then season gently with pepper and salt. (seasoning of the Old Bay)
- Place it right on the grill. Cook for 20 minutes just until the potatoes are tender
- Toss the corn with the (remaining) olive oil and season gently with pepper and salt. (seasoning of the Old Bay)
- Arrange the kielbasa and corn (next to the potatoes) directly on the grill (grate). Allow fifteen minutes for roosting.
- Seasoning shrimp with (Old Bay) seasoning. Arrange the shrimp on the side of the plate.
- Place the remainder of the ingredients on the grill (grates) and cook for 10 minutes.
- Remove everything from the grill and place it in a large size mixing bowl and with (more vintage) Season with pepper and salt, then put butter and (season) again.
- Serve immediately.

2.25: Smoked Buffalo Fries

Preparation Time: 15 minutes

Cooking Time: 30 minutes

Serving: 4

Ingredients:

- Oil as needed (for frying)
- 4 chickens (breast)
- 1/2 cup of (frank's red) hot sauce
- 6 (russet) potatoes

- 1 celery (stalks)

- Black pepper (as needed)

- 2 cups of (blue) cheese (for dressing)

- Salt (as required)

Steps:

- When you're ready to cook, fire the grill to (325°F) and cook for 15 minutes with the lid down.

- Rub the chicken (breasts) with pepper and salt. Smoke for 25 to 30 minutes, or until the temperature reaches 165 degrees. Pull and set aside.

- Combine the hot sauce and (blue cheese) dressing in a cup and put aside.

- Soak the chopped (celery) (2' long sticks) in (cold) water.

- Cut the potatoes into 1/4 sticks, similar to how you would cut (French) fries.

- Preheat the oil to 375 degrees in a deep pot or (Dutch) oven, then carefully pour it over the potatoes. Drain on a paper (towel-lined sheet) pan. Fried before lightly browned, about 5 minutes. Add salt kosher or sea salt for seasoning.

- Continue the process just until (all of the potatoes) are fried. Warm (them in the oven) until you're prepared to eat.

- Assemble the fries on a plate or a (wooden) board coated with (butcher) paper.

- Pour the (sauce) over the crisps before adding the (pulled) chicken. Serve immediately after garnishing with celery. Enjoy your meal.

2.26: Cowgirl Cut Smoked Steak

Preparation Time: 15 minutes

Cooking Time: 1 hour

Serving: 2

Ingredients

- (winemaker's Napa Valley) Rub (as needed)

- 1 (New York or Rib Eye) Steak (1" or more)

Steps:

- When you're ready to cook, set the oven to (180°F) and cook for 15 minutes with the lid covered. Utilize (Super Smoke) if it's present for the best flavor.

- Season all sides of the steak gently with (Traeger Winemaker's) Rub.

- Smoke the steak for 60 minutes on the (barbecue) grill. Take out it from the grill and allow it to rest.

- Raise the temperature and preheat the oven to 500 degrees Fahrenheit with the lid covered.

- When the grill is warm, place the (steak back on the grill) grate. Sear (medium rare steaks) until they reach the (ideal internal temperature) of 125 to 130° F.

- Represent with delicious bourbon rocks, a glass of rich and robust red wine.

2.27: Smoked Classic Borchetta

Preparation Time: 8 hours

Cooking Time: 3 hours

Serving: 8

Ingredients

- 6 Pound of Pork Belly (skin on)
- 4 Cloves of (minced) garlic
- 3 Pound of Pork Loin (boneless, center cut)
- 2 tsp. of salt
- 1 tsp. of black pepper
- 1 tsp. of red pepper flakes
- Salt (according to your taste)
- Black pepper (as required)
- Salt and black pepper (as required)
- 2 tbsp. of rosemary (chopped)
- Black pepper and salt (as needed)

Steps:

- To prepare the garlic mix, in a medium cup, add the red pepper flakes, salt, pepper, minced garlic and rosemary.

- Place belly (skin side up) on a clean (work surface) and score skin in a (crosshatch pattern). Turn the (stomach) over and coat the (flesh) side with ½ of garlic mixture, salt and pepper.

- Place the (trimmed pork) loin in the center of the belly and brush with the leftover garlic (mixture), seasoning with pepper and salt.

- Roll the (pork) belly around the loin and knot firmly with (kitchen twine) at 1' intervals to create a (cylindrical) shape. Season the skin pepper and with salt, then place it in the refrigerator, uncovered, to dry overnight.

- When you're ready to cook, set the oven to (180°F) and cook for 15 minutes with the lid covered.

- Place the (porch Etta) on the grill grille (seam side) down and smoke for 1 hour.

- After an hour, raise the grill temperature to (325°F) and cook for another 2-1/2 hours, just until the (internal temperature) reaches (135°F). If the outside begins to burn before the (target interior temperature) is reached, tent with (foil).

- Turn off the heat and set aside for 30 minutes before cutting.

2.28: Smoked Pico De Gallo

Preparation Time: 10 minutes

Cooking Time: 30 minutes

Serving: 4

Ingredients

- Olive oil (as needed)
- 1 jalapeño (diced)
- 3 Cup of (diced Roma) tomatoes
- 1/2 red onion (diced)
- 2 limes (juiced)
- Salt (as required)

Steps:

- Prepare the (Traeger to 180°F) when ready to cook and warm for 15 minutes with the lid down. Utilize (Super Smoke) if it's provided for the best flavor.

- Spread the (diced) tomatoes in a thin layer on a small sheet pan. Place the (sheet pan) directly on the grill and smoked for 30 minutes.

- When the tomatoes are fully cooked, combine all of the (ingredients) in a medium size bowl and season with olive oil, lime juice and salt. Serve immediately

2.29: Smoked Olives

Preparation Time: 10 minutes

Cooking Time: 20 minutes

Serving: 6

Ingredients:

- 1 Quart of (extra-virgin) olive oil
- 4 (Whole) rosemary sprigs
- 1 Pound of (mixed) olives
- 1 (Whole lemon) zest
- 1/2 tbsp. of red pepper (flakes)
- 1 (Whole orange) zest
- 3 (Whole dried) bay leaves
- 1/2 tbsp. of (dried) fennel seed
- 4 (Whole) thyme sprigs

Steps:

- When ready to cook, set the (Traeger) grill on Smoke and adjust the temperature to the smoke setting.

- Arrange the olives in a (roasting) pan and cook them. Start smoking for 20 to 30 minutes, just until the olives have a smoky flavor.

- When the olives have reached the appropriate level of smokiness, remove it from the grill and let it to cool.

- Combined olive oil, smoked olives, orange, and lemon zest, red pepper flakes, fennel, bay leaves, thyme, and rosemary until cold. To ensure that all of the olives are submerged, store in an (airtight) jar.

- Serve it and enjoy your meal.

2.30: Grilled Zucchini Squash Spears

Preparation Time: 5 minutes

Cooking Time: 10 minutes

Serving: 6

Ingredients:

- 2 tbsp. of olive oil
- 4 (medium) zucchinis
- 2 springs thyme (leaves pulled)
- 1 tbsp. of (cherry) vinegar
- Pepper and salt (as required)

Steps:

- The zucchini must be cleaned and (each end) of the zucchini should be sliced off. Cut each of them into (thirds after breaking them) into halves.

- Combine the leftover ingredients in a medium (Ziploc container) and put the lances. To cover the (zucchini), turn it over and mix well.

- When you're ready to cook, preheat the oven to 350 degrees Fahrenheit and cook for 15 minutes with the lid covered.

- Take out the spears from the bag and place the (cut side down) on the (grill) grate.

- Cook for 3 to 4 minutes on (each) side just until the grill lines emerge and zucchini is soft.

- Take out it from the grill and top with (additional thyme) leaves if desired.

Chapter 3: Dinner Recipes

(Image by: ilovebutter)

3.1: Marinated Grilled Chicken Kabobs

Preparation Time: 45 minutes

Cooking Time: 12 minutes

Servings: 6

Ingredients:

Marinade:

- 1/2 cup of olive oil
- 1 tsp. of lemon juice

- 2 tbsp. of white vinegar
- 1 tbsp. of (minced) garlic
- 2 tbsp. of fresh chives (chopped)
- 1 1/2 tsp. of fresh thyme (chopped)
- 1/2 tsp. of (coarse ground) pepper
- 2 tbsp. of fresh Italian parsley (chopped)
- 1 1/2 tsp. of salt

Kabobs:

- 1 1/2 pounds of (boneless, skinless) chicken breasts (cut into 2 inch chunks)
- 1 (red, orange, and yellow) bell pepper
- 10-12 (medium cremini) mushrooms

Serve with:

- Nan (bread)

Steps:

- Combine all of the (marinade) ingredients in a mixing bowl, then add the mushrooms and chicken. Put in refrigerate for 30 minutes. Put the kabob (skewers) in boiling water while the marinade is cooking.
- Take out the kabobs from the refrigerator and begin assembling them. Fire your grill to 450 (degrees Fahrenheit).
- Cook the kabobs for 6 minutes on one side, then turn and cook for another 6 minutes. Removed the steaks from the grill and put them aside.
- Set the (Nan) bread on the grill for a few minutes to warm them up.
- Served with a side of fresh (Caesar) salad.

3.2: Traeger Tri-Tip

Preparation Time: 5 minutes

Cooking Time: 1 hour 30 minutes

Servings: 6

Ingredients:

- 3 pounds of tri-tip

- 1 tsp. of paprika
- 1 tsp. of black pepper
- 1 tsp. of onion powder
- 1/2 tsp. of cayenne
- 1 tsp. of garlic powder
- 1 1/2 tsp. of salt kosher

Steps:

- Prep your wood pellet grill to 250 (degrees Fahrenheit).
- Add the spices all over the meat. Put on the grill to cook.
- Grill for 30 minutes on one side, then turn and cook for (another) 30 minutes.
- Preheat the grill to (350°F) and cook for another 20-30 minutes. Remove the meat at 125°F for (medium-rare) wait for 10 minutes, then sliced across the (grain) and immediately serve.

3.2: Beer Can Chicken

Preparation Time: 10 minutes

Cooking Time: 1 hour 15 minutes

Servings: 6

Ingredients:

- 1 can beer
- 1 4-5 (pound) of chicken
- 1/2 cup of (dry) chicken rub

Steps:

- Prepare your grill for 4 to 5 minutes on (smoke) with the cover opened. Preheat the oven to high temp, then cover the lid and cook for another 10 to 15 minutes, just until it hits 450 degrees.
- Put (half of the beer into your mouth), then bury the (open can in the chicken) where the sun is not shining. (Move it down there and prop it up with the legs like a tripod).
- Cook until the inner (temperature) reaches 165 degrees Fahrenheit.

- Take out the chicken from the grill with care and set aside to rest for 15 minutes. Slice and immediately serve!

3.3: Lime shrimp and Grilled coconut with Caribbean rice

Preparation Time: 2 hours

Cooking Time: 25 minutes

Servings: 4

Ingredients:

- 1 tbsp. of olive oil
- 2 Limes (zested and juiced)
- 1 lb. of Shrimp (peeled, deveined, and tails removed)
- 1/4 cup of Pineapple juice
- 2 tbsp. of Soy sauce
- 1 tbsp. of Brown sugar
- 2 tbsp. of Hot Sauce
- 1/2 cup of Coconut milk
- 2 tbsp. of (minced) Garlic
- Cilantro (for garnishing)

Caribbean Rice:

- 1 1/3 cups of Chicken broth
- 2 cups of Jasmine rice
- 14 oz. of Coconut milk
- 1/2 cup of Pistachios (chopped, salted and roasted)
- 1 cup of Mango (diced)
- 1 tsp. of Salt

Steps:

- Toss all (marinade) ingredients together in a large size bowl. Place the marinade and shrimp for at least 4 hours in the refrigerator, turning them for several times to ensure they are uniformly seasoned.

- In a large skillet, put salt, coconut milk and chicken broth. Add the rice and mix well. Cover, and cook for around 15 minutes, or until water has been evaporated and rice is soft. Turn off the heat and let aside for 5 minutes. Combine the pistachios and mangoes carefully.

- Lightly coat your (Memphis Wood Fire Grill) with vegetable oil and use (fruitwood) pellets to adjust the temperature to (500°F).

- Put shrimp onto skewers, pierce the tail and head of (each) shrimp. Grill the shrimp for 2-3 minutes (each side), or until they become pink. Serve with (chopped) cilantro and Caribbean rice.

3.4: Steak Fajitas

Preparation Time: 40 minutes

Cooking Time: 30 minutes

Servings: 12

Ingredients:

- 3 tbsp. of avocado oil
- 6 pounds of steak
- 1 (large size) onion
- 2 tbsp. of the Spice guy (Fajita seasoning)
- 1/2 tsp. of pepper
- 3 bell peppers (multi-colored)
- 1 small can of (El Pato Jalapeno) Salsa
- Tortillas (as your choice)
- 2 tsp. of salt

Steps:

- Against the (grain), cut the meat into small pieces. Add pepper, salt, pepper, and 1 1/2 tsp. of (Fajita) spice. Put it in a (plastic baggie) or a container. Allow 30 minutes for the (El Pato Jalapeno Salsa) to soak in.

- Cut your veggies and add with the (remaining Fajita spice).

- Fire your wood pellet grill for 10-15 minutes on high temperature. Place your oil on the grill and brush it before placing your meat on (one side) and vegetables on the other.

- Grill the steak, turning it periodically, until it is cook to your liking. When the veggies are tender)-crisp, remove them from the grill.

- Before serving, cook your (tortillas) quickly on the griddle with almost all of your favorite (fajita) ingredients.

3.5: Crab Scampi Recipe

Preparation Time: 10 minutes

Cooking Time: 15 minutes

Servings: 4

Ingredients:

- 1 cup of (melted salted) butter
- 6 pounds of (pre-cooked) crab
- 2 tbsp. of (minced) garlic
- 2 tsp. of salt kosher
- 1 cup of (dry white) wine
- 1 tbsp. of Old Bay (for seasoning)

Steps:

- Prepare the grill to medium-high heat.

- Rub the crab with (Old) Bay and salt and put it on the grill to coat. The garlic should be poured on first, then add the butter. Grill for a minute, moving the garlic butter and crabs on the grill with the tones.

- Covered, and cook for 2-3 minutes after pouring the (wine) over the crab.

- Continue spooning and scraping the (wine/garlic) butter sauce over the surface of the crabs with a (bench scraper).

- Turn off the heat and serve immediately!

3.6: Espresso Brisket Rubbed Pork Chops

Preparation Time: 5 minutes

Cooking Time: 55 minutes

Servings: 4

Ingredients:

- 2 tbsp. of yellow mustard
- 1 (12-pound/5.4 kg) full packer brisket
- Worcestershire Mop and Spritz (for spritzing)
- 1 batch of (Espresso Brisket) Rub

Steps:

- Fill your smoker with (wood pellets) and fire it up according to the (manufacturer's) instructions. Preheat the grill to (180°F) 82° C with the lid covered.
- Cover both sides of the pork chops with pepper and salt.
- Smoked the chops for 30 minutes by placing them (directly) on the grill grate.
- Preheat the grill to (350 degrees Fahrenheit) 177 degrees Celsius. Grill the chops until they reach an (internal) temperature of 145°F (63° C).
- Take out the (pork) chops from the grill and let them aside for 5 minutes to rest before presenting.

3.7: Easy Baked Bacon

Preparation Time: 5 minutes

Cooking Time: 25 minutes

Servings: 6

Ingredients:

- 1lb. (454 g) bacon

Steps:

- Set the oven to 375 (degrees) Fahrenheit (191 degrees Celsius). Place the (thick-cut bacon) in a thin layer on a (baking) sheet lined with (parchment) paper.
- Cook the bacon for 20 minutes in the oven. Cook for another 20 minutes on the other side.
- Immediately serve.

3.8: Peppery Tri Tip Roast

Preparation Time: 5 minutes

Cooking Time: 35 minutes

Servings: 8

Ingredients:

- 1 (1.3 kg) (tri tip) roast, trimmed
- 1 tbsp. of (granulated) garlic
- 1 tbsp. of (granulated) onion
- Freshly ground black pepper and salt (according to your taste)

Steps:

- Combine all (ingredients) in a mixing bowl, except the roast, and stir thoroughly.
- Gently (coat) the meat in the (spice) mixture.
- Allow it to rest at room temperature until the grill is ready to use.
- Fire the grill to (250 degrees F) 121 degrees C with the lid covered for 15 minutes.
- Cooked for approximately 25 minutes on the grill with the roast.
- Prepare the grill to (350 degrees F) 177 degrees C with the lid covered for 15 minutes. And cook (each side) for approximately 3 to 5 minutes.
- Removed the roast from the grill and let aside for 15-20 minutes on a chopping board before cutting.
- Slice the (roast across the grain) with a (sharp) knife and immediately serve.

3.9: Crispy and Spicy Grilled Lamb Chops

Preparation Time: 10 minutes

Cooking Time: 6 minutes

Servings: 6

Ingredients:

- 2 tbsp. of olive oil
- 2lb. (907 g) of lamb (chops)
- ½ tbsp. of black pepper
- ¼ cup of (distilled) white vinegar

- 1 tbsp. of minced garlic

- 1 onion (thinly sliced)

- 2 tbsp. of salt

Steps:

- Whisk together the oil, garlic, pepper, salt, vinegar and (chopped) onion, and oil in a (resalable) bag just before the salt is dissolved completely.

- Toss in the (lamb chunks) until thoroughly coated. Put in the refrigerator for 2 hours for marinating. Prepare the (wood pellet) grill to its highest setting.

- Take out the lamb from the fridge. Any (exposed) bones should be wrapped with foil.

- Cook the lamb for 3 minutes on (each) side on the grill. For additional crispiness, simmer the chicken in a broiler. Immediately serve.

3.10: Peppery Smoked Brisket

Preparation Time: 5 minutes

Cooking Time: 2 hours

Servings: 8

Ingredients:

- 2 tbsp. of (yellow) mustard

- 1 (12-pound/5.4 kg) full (packer) brisket

- Freshly (ground) black pepper and salt according to your taste

Steps:

- Fill with (wood pellets) and following the detailed instructions.

- Set the grill to (225°F) 107°C and close the cover.

- Gently remove all but about 1/2 inch of the thick layer of (fat) covers one side of the brisket with a (boning) knife.

- Spread mustard all over the brisket and add pepper and salt for seasoning.

- Arrange the brisket (directly) on the grill grate and cook until the temperature reached 160 degrees Fahrenheit (71 degrees Celsius) and the brisket has developed a (dark) bark.

- Take out the brisket and cover it in (aluminum) foil thoroughly.

- Put the (wrapped) beef to the grill and raise the temperature to (350°F) 177°C. Cooked until it achieves an (internal) temperature of (190°F) 87°C.

- Place the (wrapped) brisket in a cooler, cover it, and set it aside for 1 to 2 hours to rest.

- Take out the brisket from the fridge and uncover it.

- Serve immediately.

3.11: Poultry Rubbed Pork Belly

Preparation Time: 5 minutes

Cooking Time: 3 hours 30 minutes

Servings: 8

Ingredients:

- Pork and poultry rub (as needed)

- 3 pounds (1.3 kg) of pork belly (skin removed)

- ½ tsp. of (ground) black pepper

- 4 tbsp. of salt

Steps:

- Warm the grill by turning it on, filling the hopper with (apple-flavored) wood pellets, to use the control panel to turn it on, selecting ('smoke') or setting the temperature to 275 degrees F (135 degrees C) and allowing it to ready for at least 15 minutes.

- In the meanwhile, ready the (pork belly) by coating both sides of the pork belly with poultry rub and pork, black pepper and salt.

- Once the grill has heated, open the cover, put the (pork) belly on the (grill) grate, and close the grill for 3 hours and 30 minutes, just until the (internal) temperature hits 200 degrees F (93 degrees C).

- When the pork belly is cooked, move it to a chopping board and set it aside for 15 minutes before cutting it into pieces and immediately serve.

3.12: Big Game Rubbed Smoked Pulled Pork

Preparation time: 5 minutes

Cooking time: 6 hours

Servings: 4

Ingredients:

- (Big Game) Rub
- (Que) BBQ Sauce
- 2 cups of apple cider
- 2 pounds (907 g) of (bone-in) pork shoulder

Steps:

- Remove the extra fat from the pork shoulder and mix the (Big Game Rub) in a dish.
- Preheat the grill to (250°F) for 15 minutes and close the cover. When cooking, utilize maple (wood pellets).
- Cook the pork for 5 hours on the (grill grate), just until the (internal) temperature hits (160° F) 71° C.
- Leave the pork to rest after removing it from the grill.
- Place four sheets of (aluminum) foil on a (baking sheet) and (stack) them on top of each other. Arrange the pork in the middle of the foil and fold the edges up to form a (sleeve) around the meat.
- Put the (apple cider) on top.
- Cook the 9foil-wrapped) pork for another 3 hours at (204° F) 95°C on the grill.
- Take out the meat from the grill and set it aside to cool. Removed the pork from the (foil sleeve) and place it on a dish; shred the meat with help forks.
- Drizzle the (BBQ sauce) over the meat after it has been shredded.
- Serve immediately.

3.13: Yummy Pulled Beef Roast

Preparation Time: 5 minutes

Cooking Time: 2 hours

Servings: 8

Ingredients:

- 2 tbsp. of (yellow) mustard

- 1 (4-pound/1.8 kg) top round roast
- ½ cup of (beef) broth
- 1 batch of (espresso brisket) rub

Steps:

- Set your (wood) pellets and following the setup instructions.
- Set the grill to (225°F) 107°C and cover it.
- Rub the mustard on roast and mix it with the rub.
- Arrange the roast directly on the grill grate and smoked until the temperature reached 160 degrees Fahrenheit (71 degrees Celsius) and a dark bark has developed.
- Take out the roast from the grill and wrap it in enough (aluminum foil) to fully cover it. Raise the temperature of the grill to (350°F) 176°C.
- Wrap the roast in foil on (three sides) and pour in the (beef) broth. Fold in the final side, enclosing the liquid and roast entirely. Put the (covered) roast again to the grill and cook until it reaches an (internal) temperature of 195 degrees Fahrenheit (91 degrees Celsius).
- Removed the roast from the grill and store it in the refrigerator. Allow 1 to 2 hours for the roast to rest in the (cooler).
- Take out the roast from the fridge and uncover it. Immediately serve.

3.14: Homemade Pork Ribs

Preparation Time: 5 minutes

Cooking Time: 4 hours

Servings: 4

Ingredients:

- 1 cup of (homemade) BBQ rub
- 2 (racks) back ribs
- 2 12-oz (340 g) hard apple cider
- 2 batches of (homemade) BBQ sauce
- 1 cup of (dark brown) sugar

Steps:

- Preheat the smoker and cut any (membranes) from the meat.

- Smoke the pork for 5 hours, just until the (internal) temperature hits (175°F) 79°C.

- Preheat the grill to (225 degrees Fahrenheit) 107 degrees Celsius. Place the meat in a pan that has been coated with cooking oil.

- Put one (bottle of strong) apple cider into the pan and coat the ribs with brown sugar.

- Return the pan to the grill, covered with (tin foil). 4 (hours) in the oven

- Take out the (tin foil) from the ribs, raise the temperature to (300°F) 149°C, and put them on the (grill) grates.

- Cooked for 1 hour, coating the ribs (three times) with (BBQ) sauce.

- The ribs must be (falling off) the bone at this point. Allow for a 5-minute as rest period before eating.

3.15: Beef Rubbed Grilled Tri-Tip

Preparation Time: 5 minutes

Cooking Time: 3 hours

Servings: 7

Ingredients:

- ⅛ Cup of coffee, (ground)

- 3 lb. (1.4 kg) (tri-tip) roast

- ¼ cup of beef rub

Steps:

- Fire the grill to (180°F) 82°C for 15 minutes with the lid covered.

- In the meanwhile, coat the roast with a (mixture) of beef rub and coffee. Smoked the roast for (three) hours on the (grill) grate.

- Take out the roast from the grill and cover it in (foil) twice.

- Raise the temperature to (135 degrees Fahrenheit) 275 degrees Celsius.

- Put the meat to the grill and cooked for 90 minutes, or until it hits 135°F (57°C) internal temperature.

- Take out it from the grill, uncover it, and set it aside to settle for 10 minutes before serving. Enjoy your meal.

3.16: Lamb Chops in Soy Sauce

Preparation Time: 15 minutes

Cooking Time: 17 minutes

Servings: 4

Ingredients:

- ¼ Cup of onion, (chopped roughly)
- 2 tbsp. of soy sauce
- 2 garlic cloves, (chopped roughly)
- 2 tbsp. of balsamic vinegar
- ½ Cup of extra-virgin olive oil, (divided)
- 1 tsp. of Worcestershire sauce
- 2 tsp. of Dijon mustard
- 1 tbsp. of chopped fresh rosemary
- Freshly (ground) black pepper according to your taste
- Salt according to your taste
- 4 (5-oz/142 g) (lamb) chops

Steps:

- Pour 1 tbsp. of olive oil in a small saucepan over (medium) heat and cook the garlic and onion for approximately 4 to 5 minutes.

- Take out the pan from the heat and pour the ingredients into a blender.

- Mix the black pepper, rosemary, soy sauce, vinegar, Worcestershire sauce and mustard until thoroughly mixed in a blender.

- Slowly drizzle in the (remaining) oil while the (motor is running) and pulsed until soft.

- Pour the sauce into a mixing dish and put it aside.

- Fire the grill to (500 degrees F) 260 degrees C with the lid covered for 15 minutes.

- Drizzle the remaining oil over the (lamb) chops and add black pepper and salt for seasoning.

- Place the chops on the grill and cook for 4 to 6 minutes on each side.

- Take out the chops from the grill and serve immediately with the sauce.

3.17: Smoked Lamb Meatballs

Preparation Time: 15 minutes

Cooking Time: 1 hour

Servings: 20

Ingredients:

- 1 lb. (454 g) of lamb shoulder (ground)
- ¼ cup of (panko) breadcrumbs
- 3 tbsp. of shallot (diced)
- 3 garlic cloves (finely diced)
- ½ tbsp. of pepper
- ½ tbsp. of cumin
- 1 egg
- ¼ tbsp. of red pepper (flakes)
- ½ tbsp. of (smoked) paprika
- ¼ tbsp. of cinnamon
- 1 tbsp. of salt

Steps:

- Preheat oven to 250 degrees Fahrenheit (121 degrees Celsius). In a small mixing bowl, combine all of the (ingredients) and thoroughly combine with (your) hands.

- Roll the meatballs into (golf ball-sized) balls and put them on a (baking) pan.

- Smoke the (baking) sheet just until the inner temperature rises 160 degrees Fahrenheit (71 degrees Celsius).

- When the meatballs are cooked, remove them from the smokers and serve immediately.

3.18: Grilled Bacon Strips

Preparation Time: 5 minutes

Cooking Time: 30 minutes

Servings: 4 to 6

Ingredients:

- 1 (1-pound / 454-g) package (thick-sliced) bacon

Steps:

- Fill your smoker with (wood pellets) and fire it up according to the package recommendations. Prepare the grill to (275°F) 135°C and cover it.

- Arrange the (bacon) strips directly on the (grill) grate and smoked for 20 to 30 minutes, until crispy. Immediately serve.

3.19: Maple and Honeyed Bacon

Preparation Time: 5 minutes

Cooking Time: 2 hours

Servings: 4 to 6

Ingredients:

- 1 (1-pound / 454-g) package (thick-sliced) bacon

- 2 tbsp. of honey

- 1 cup of (pure maple) syrup

- 1 cup of (packed light brown) sugar, divided

Steps:

- In a large sealed jar, thoroughly combine the ½ cup of brown sugar, maple syrup and honey. Toss in the bacon and coated well. Put it in the fridge for a night and cover it.

- Fill your smoker with (wood pellets) and fire it up according to the package recommendations. Fire the grill to (200°F) 93°C with the lid covered.

- Removed the bacon from the marinade and put it straight on the (grill) grate, keeping it away from the (drain) pan.

• Finish by sprinkling the (remaining) 1/2 cup of (brown) sugar over top. Smoked the bacon for approximately 2 hours, or just until it's done to your taste. Serve immediately.

3.20: Cajun Rubbed Honeyed Ham

Preparation Time: 5 minutes

Cooking Time: 1 hour 10 minutes

Servings: 10 to 16

Ingredients:

• 1 batch of (Cajun) Rub

• 1 (5- or 6-pound / 2.3- or 2.7-kg) (bone-in smoked) ham

• 3 tbsp. of honey

Steps:

• Fill your smoker with (wood pellets) and fire it up according to the manufacturer's instructions. Prepare the grill to 225°F (107°C) and cover the lid.

• Coat the ham well with the rub and cook it in a pan.

• Alternatively, you may cook directly on the (grill) grate. It should be smoked for 1 hour.

• Pour the honey over the ham and cook it until it's done.

• The (internal) temperature of the ham hits (145°F) 63°C.

• Take out the ham from the grill and set it aside for 5 to 10 minutes before serving and cutting (thinly).

3.21: Coriander Spiced Pork Loin Roast

Preparation Time: 15 minutes

Cooking Time: 3 hours

Servings: 8

Ingredients:

• 1 (1½- to 2-pound / 680- to 907-g) pork loin roast

• ¼ cup of paprika

- ¼ cup of garlic powder

- ¼ cup of (finely ground) coffee

- 1 tbsp. of (packed light brown) sugar

- 2 tbsp. of chili powder

- 1 tbsp. of (ground) coriander

- 1 tbsp. of (freshly ground) black pepper

- 2 tsp. of (ground) mustard

- 1 tbsp. of (ground) allspice

- 1½ tsp. of (celery) seeds

Steps:

- Fill your smoker with wood pellets and fire it up according to the package recommendations. Set the oven to (250°F) 121°C and cover it.

- Make a rub with the garlic powder, pepper, coriander, celery seeds, ground coffee, paprika, chili powder, brown sugar, allspice and mustard in a small dish. Rub the pork loin roast gently.

- Arrange the (pork loin fat-side) up on the grill, cover, and cook for 3 hours, just until a meat (thermometer) placed into the (thickest) portion of the meat reaches (160°F) 71°C.

- Set aside for 5 minutes before serving and slicing the pork.

3.22: Garlicky Pork Pineapple Kebabs

Preparation Time: 15 minutes

Cooking Time: 1 to 4 hours

Servings: 12 to 15

Ingredients:

- 2 tbsp. of canola oil

- 2 pounds (907 g) of (thick-cut) pork chops or pork loin (cut into 2-inch cubes)

- 1 (20-ounce / 567-g) bottle (hoisin) sauce

- 10 ounces (284 g) of fresh pineapple (cut into chunks)

- ¼ cup of honey

- ¼ cup of (apple cider) vinegar
- ½ cup of Sriracha
- 2 tsp. of (minced) garlic
- 12 (metal or wooden) skewers (soaked in water for 30 minutes if wooden)
- 2 tsp. of onion powder
- 1 bag mini sweet peppers (tops removed and seeded)
- 1 tsp. of (ground) ginger
- 1 tsp. of (freshly ground) black pepper
- 1 red onion (cut into wedges)
- 1 tsp. of salt

Steps:

• Combine the vinegar, oil, onion powder, black pepper and salt, hoisin, Sriracha,

• honey, chopped garlic and ginger in a small size (mixing) bowl to make the marinade. 1/4 cup is set aside for (basting).

• Mix the leftover marinade with the (pork) cubes, tiny peppers, pineapple pieces and onion wedges. Put it in the fridge for at least 1 hour or up to 4 hours, covered.

• Fill your smoker with (wood pellets) and fire it up according to the package recommendations. Set the oven to (450°F) 232°C and closed the cover.

• Drain the vegetables, pork and pineapple from the marinade but do not (rinse) them. Remove the marinade and toss it out.

• Prepare the kebabs using the (double-skewer) method. Thread a piece of pineapple, a piece of onion, a piece of pork and a sweet (little pepper) onto each of the (6 skewers), ensuring that skewer passes through (left hand side) of the ingredients.

• Thread each (skewer) two more times with the threading. Stick additional (6 skewers) into the right side of the (ingredients) to (double-skewer) the kebabs.

• Arrange the kebabs on the grill (directly), cover it, and smoked for 10 to 12 minutes, rotating once. When a meat (thermometer) placed in the pork hits (160°F) 71°C, it's ready.

3.23: Garlic Spiced BBQ Tenderloin

Preparation Time: 10 minutes

Cooking Time: 15 minutes

Servings: 4

Ingredients:

- ¼ cup of olive oil
- 1 pork tenderloin (silver skin removed and dried)
- (Fresh) herb sauce
- BBQ (for seasoning)
- ¼ tbsp. of garlic powder
- 1 handful basil (fresh)
- ½ tbsp. of salt kosher

Steps:

- Prepare the (wood pellet) grill to medium-high temperature.
- Rub the pork with BBQ spice and cooked it on the grill over indirect heat. Stir well.
- Cooked until the (internal) temperature reaches 145 degrees Fahrenheit (63 degrees Celsius). Take out the steak from the grill and set it aside to cool for 10 minutes.
- In the meanwhile, blending all of the sauce (ingredients) in a (food processor) making the (herb) sauce.
- Cut the pork into diagonal slices and serve with the sauce on the side.

3.24: Sriracha Hot Sauce Spiced Candied Bacon

Preparation Time: 5 minutes

Cooking Time: 35 minutes

Servings: 6

Ingredients:

- 1 lb. (454 g) of (Centre cut) bacon

- ½ cup of maple syrup
- ½ cup of (dark brown) sugar
- ½ tbsp. of (cayenne) pepper
- 1 tbsp. of (sriracha) hot sauce

Steps:

- Mix together the cayenne pepper, maple syrup, sugar and sriracha sauce in a mixing bowl.
- Prepare the (wood pellet) grill to 300 degrees Fahrenheit (149 degrees Celsius).
- Place the bacon in a baking sheet lined with (parchment) paper.
- There is just one layer. Spray the bacon with the (sugar) mixture until it is well coated.
- Grill for 20 minutes using the (baking) pan.
- Cook for another 15 minutes with the bacon.
- Take out the bacon from the grill and set aside for 10 minutes to cool before serving.

3.25: Greek Seasoned Grilled Lamb Chops

Preparation Time: 10 minutes

Cooking Time: 20 minutes

Servings: 8

Ingredients:

For the Lamb:

- 2 tbsp. of Greek Freak (for seasoning)
- 16 lamb chops (fat trimmed)

For the Mint Sauce:

- 1 cup of olive oil
- 12 cloves of garlic (peeled)
- 1 tbsp. of (chopped) parsley
- ¼ tsp. of dried oregano
- 1 tbsp. of (chopped) mint

- ¾ cup of lemon juice
- ¼ tsp. of (ground) black pepper
- 1 tsp. of salt

Steps:

- To make the (mint) sauce, combine all of the ingredients in a (food) processor and process for 1 minute.

- Pour 1/3 cup of the (mint) sauce into a (plastic) bag, pour the (lamb) chops, close the bag, flip it (upside) down to cover the (lamb) chops in the sauce, and refrigerate for at least 30 minutes.

- When you start cooking, turn on the grill, load the grill (hopper) with (apple-flavored wood) pellets, turn on the grill with the (control) panel, choose ("smoke") or adjust the temperature to 450 degrees F (232 degrees C) and let it warm for at least 15 minutes.

- Removed the (lamb) chops from the marinade and (season) with Greek (spice).

- Once the grill is hot, open the cover, put the (lamb) chops on the grill (grate), close the grill, and smoked for 4 to 5 minutes (each) side.

- When the (lamb chops) are cooked, move them to a serving plate and serve.

3.26: Teriyaki Pineapple Rubbed Pork Tenderloin

Preparation Time: 10 minutes

Cooking Time: 2 hours

Servings: 6

Ingredients:

- 8 oz. (226 g) of (teriyaki) sauce
- 1½ lb. (680 g) of pork (tenderloin)
- 1 can of pineapple (rings)
- 1 tbsp. of paprika
- 1 tbsp. of onion powder
- ½ tbsp. of garlic powder
- 1 pack of (Kings Hawaiian) rolls
- ½ tbsp. of cayenne pepper

- Salt (according to your taste)

Steps:

- Preheat oven to 325 degrees Fahrenheit (163 degrees Celsius). Combine all of the rub (ingredients) and coat the pork (tenderloin) evenly.

- Arrange the pork on the (prepared) grill and cook for 4 minutes, rotating once. Cook until the (beef) reaches an (internal) temperature of (145°F) 63°C.

- In the meanwhile, roast the (pineapple) rings on the grill until well browned.

- While the (pineapples) are cooking, split the (Hawaiian) rolls in half and cook them until (golden) brown.

- Removed the pork from the pan and set aside to (rest) for 5 minutes.

- Make the (sliders) by layering a bottom bun pineapple ring, (pork) tenderloin, teriyaki sauce, and a (top) roll on top.

- Serve immediately.

3.27: Cinnamon and Cloves spiced Ham

Preparation Time: 10 minutes

Cooking Time: 5 hours

Servings: 12

Ingredients:

- 1 (12- to 15-pound/6.8 kg) (whole bone-in) ham, fully cooked
- ½ tsp. of (ground) cloves
- ½ cup of (packed light brown) sugar
- ¼ cup of (yellow) mustard
- 1 cup of pineapple (juice)
- 1 tsp. of (ground) cinnamon

Steps:

- Fill your smoker with (wood pellets) and fire it up according to the package recommendations. Set the oven to (275°F) 135°C and close the lid.

- Remove the (extra) fat and skin from the ham leaving a 1/4-inch border, a thick coating of fat.

- Place the ham in a (roasting) pan lined with (aluminum) foil.

- In a medium skillet over moderate flame. Mix together the pineapple juice, salt and pepper, brown sugar, mustard and cinnamon in a mixing bowl and boil for 15 minutes, just until thickened and decreased by half.

- Brush half of the pineapple (brown sugar) syrup on the ham.

- The remainder will be used for brushing (later) in the oven.

- Set the (roasting) pan on the grill, cover, and cook for 4 minutes.

- Brush the leftover (pineapple–brown) sugar syrup over the ham then keep smoking for another hour with the top covered, or until when a meat (thermometer) is put into the thickest section of the ham, it shows 165°F (60°C)

- Take out the ham from the grill, cover with (foil), and set aside for 20 minutes to rest. Serve immediately.

3.28: Sesame Oil Grilled Lamb Shank

Preparation Time: 10 minutes

Cooking Time: 10 hours

Servings: 2

Ingredients:

- 2 (1¼-lb/566g) lamb (shanks)

- 1 tbsp. of (dark) sesame oil

- ¼ cup of brown sugar

- 2 (3-inch long) cinnamon (sticks)

- ¼ cup of rice wine

- 4 (1½x½-inch) (orange zest) strips

- 1-2 cup of water

- ¼ cup of soy sauce

- 1½ tsp. of Chinese (five-spice) powder

Steps:

- Fire the grill to 250 degrees F (121 degrees C) with the lid covered for 15 minutes, using coal and (soaked apple) wood chips.

- Pierce each (lamb shank) many times with a (sharp) knife.

- In a mixing bowl, combine the other (ingredients) and stir until the sugar is dissolved.

- Arrange the (lamb shanks) in a large (foil pan) and equally cover with the (sugar) mixture.

- Set the (foil) pan on the grill for 8 to 10 hours, turning every 30 minutes.

- Take out the pan from the grill and immediately serve.

3.29: Delicious Prime Rib Roast

Preparation Time: 10 minutes

Cooking Time: 3 hours 50 minutes

Servings: 10

Ingredients:

- 5 tbsp. of olive oil
- 1 (5-lb/2.2 kg) (prime rib) roast
- 2 tsp. of garlic powder
- 1 tsp. of paprika
- 1 tsp. of onion powder
- 4 tsp. of dried rosemary (crushed)
- ½ tsp. of cayenne pepper
- (Freshly ground) black pepper (as required)
- Salt (according to your taste)

Steps:

- Rub the roast well with salt.

- Wrap the roast in (plastic) wrap and place it in the refrigerator for approximately 24 hours.

- Combine rest of the ingredients in a mixing dish and leave aside for (1 hour).

- Cover the roast on (both sides) equally with the (oil) mixture.

- Place the roast on a large size (baking) sheet and place in the refrigerator for 6 to12 hours.

- Preheat the grill to 230 degrees Fahrenheit (110 degrees Celsius) with the lid covered for 15 minutes, utilizing (pecan wood) chips.
- Set the roast on the grill and cook for about 3 1/2 hours.
- Meanwhile, set the oven to 500 degrees Fahrenheit (260 degrees Celsius).
- Take out the roast from the grill and put it on a large size (baking) pan.
- Set the (baking) sheet in the oven and bake for 15 to 20 minutes.
- Removed the roast from the oven and set it aside on a chopping board for 10 to15 minutes before presenting.
- Slice the roast into (desired-sized) pieces with a (sharp) knife and immediately serve.

3.30: Pigs in a Blanket

Preparation Time: 10 minutes
Cooking Time: 30 minutes
Servings: 1
Ingredients:
- 1 pack of Biscuit (dough)
- 1 pack of Pork (sausages)

Steps:
- Set your (pellet) grill to 350 degrees Fahrenheit.
- Divide the dough and sausages into thirds.
- Cover the sausages in the dough. Lay them out on a (baking) pan.
- Close the cover and grill for 20 to 25 minutes, or just until fully cooked.
- Once they are light brown, remove them from the oven.
- Serve with your favorite sauce.

3.31: Beefy Bolognese

Preparation Time: 25 minutes
Cooking Time: 1 hour 30 minutes

Servings: 4

Ingredients:

- 1 tbsp. of Olive oil
- (2-lbs, 0.9-kgs) ground beef
- 1 tbsp. of (salted) butter
- (8-ozs, 227-gms) spaghetti
- 3 cloves of (minced) garlic
- 2 cups of tomato sauce
- 1 yellow onion (peeled and diced)
- Parmesan cheese (grated)
- 3 large tomatoes (chopped)
- 1 tsp. of dried basil
- 2 tsp. of Paprika
- 2 tsp. of dried oregano
- Black pepper and salt (according to your taste)

Steps:

- First, warm the (oil) in a large saucepan. In the pan, combine the onion, meat and garlic.
- Cook until the meat has browned and the onion has softened.
- Put the (tomatoes), then the paprika, basil, black pepper, salt, tomato sauce and oregano. To mix, stir everything together.
- Cook for 5 minutes, stirring periodically.
- Remove the pan from the heat and place it in the smoker. Smoke for a total of 1 1/2 hours, stirring periodically. Meanwhile, boil the spaghetti according to the package instructions, then strain.
- When the meat (sauce) is done, remove it from the smoker and whisk in the butter until it dissolves.
- Distribute the sauce over the hot pasta.
- Serve topped with (grated) Parmesan.

3.32: Brunch Burger

Preparation Time: 10 minutes

Cooking Time: 20 minutes

Servings: 2

Ingredients:

- Olive oil
- (6-ozs, 170-gms) (lean ground chuck) beef
- 2 burgers (buns)
- 4 rashers bacon (cooked until crispy)
- 2 medium eggs (fried)
- 2 slices of (American) cheese
- 2 hash browns (cooked and kept warm)
- Black pepper and salt (as required)

Steps:

- Split the meat into two (equal halves) and shape into thin, even burgers. Add pepper and salt for seasoning.
- Before putting the burger on top, spray the (grate) with oil. Grilled for 3 to 4 minutes on each side, just until done to your liking.
- Take out the burgers from the grill and put each one on a bun. Place a (piece) of bacon, hash brown, cheddar and a fried egg on top of each burger.
- Serve immediately.

3.33: Classic Pastrami

Preparation Time: 6 Hours

Cooking Time: 29 hours 20 minutes

Servings: 4-6

Ingredients:

- (6-lbs, 2.7 -kgs) beef brisket (cut from the point)
- 2 tsp. of onion powder

- 6 tbsp. of brown sugar
- 6 cups of warm water
- 1 tbsp. of (curing) salt
- 1 tbsp. of honey
- ¼ tsp. of coriander seeds
- 3 bay leaves (chopped)
- ¼ tsp. of cayenne pepper
- 1 tsp. of garlic (peeled and chopped)
- 1 tbsp. of brown sugar
- ¼ cup of (whole black) peppercorns
- ¼ cup of coriander seeds
- 1 tbsp. of paprika
- 2 tsp. of garlic powder
- 6½ tbsp. of kosher salt

Steps:

- To begin, make the brine. In a large size mixing bowl, mix together the salt kosher, cayenne pepper, honey, garlic, brown sugar, coriander seeds, curing salt and bay leaves. Melt the salt and sugar, stir in the heated water. Allow for an hour of relaxation. Place the meat in the brine and (weigh down) with a platter.

- Allow the meat to (marinate) for one week. Every day, rotate the meat in the (brine).

- Refrigerate the brisket on a (wire) rack for 24 hours to allow the meat to (dry out).

- Boil the brisket for 12 hours in water, changing the water every 3 hours.

- To make the seasoning, put the onion powder, paprika, garlic powder, black peppercorns, brown sugar and coriander seeds in a mixing dish. The mixture should be applied evenly on the (outside) of the meat.

- Grill the beef for 4 hours on the (grill) grate.

- Remove the meat from the grill and let aside for 60 to 90 minutes before serving and slicing.

3.34: Fully Loaded Beef Nachos

Preparation Time: 10 minutes

Cooking Time: 25 minutes

Servings: 6

Ingredients

- (1-lbs, 0.45-kgs) ground beef
- ½ cup of red onion (peeled and diced)
- 1 large (bag tortilla) chips
- ½ cup of scallions (sliced)
- 1 green bell pepper (seeded and diced)
- 3 cups of cheddar cheese (shredded)
- Guacamole, sour cream, salsa (for serving)

Steps:

- Place the (double layer of tortilla) chips in a (cast-iron) pan. Sprinkle with the bell pepper, scallions, cheddar cheese, ground beef and red onion.
- Set the (cast-iron) skillet on the grill for about 10 minutes, just until the cheese is fully (melted).
- Remove from the grill and serve immediately with salsa, sour cream and guacamole on the side.

3.35: Garlic, Lemon, and Goat Cheese Mashed Potatoes

Preparation Time: 1 hour and 15 minutes

Cooking Time: 20 minutes

Servings: 6-8 servings

Ingredients:

- 1 tsp. of olive oil
- 3 lbs. of Yukon gold potatoes (peeled and roughly chopped)
- 1/4 cup of (melted) butter (plus more for drizzling)
- 3/4 cup of (crumbled Goat) cheese

- 3/4 cup of (heavy whipping) cream
- 1 head of garlic
- 2 tbsp. of fresh chives (finely diced)
- Sea Salt & (freshly cracked) black pepper

Steps:

- Adjust the smoke temperature to (350°F) and warm for 10 to 15 minutes with the lid down when ready to cook.

- Slice approximately 1/8" from the (top of the garlic) head with a (sharp) knife (keeping the root intact), exposing the single garlic cloves. Add pepper and salt for seasoning and pour the olive oil over the (exposed) garlic.

- Cover the bulb tightly in (aluminum) foil and cook for 30 to 35 minutes before the cloves are tender. Cut the (garlic) cloves and mix them with a fork to make a paste.

- Meanwhile, over medium flame, carry a big (stockpot of salted) water on the stove. Simmer for 15 to 20 minutes, just until the potatoes are hash able and softened.

- Remove and return to the saucepan, stirring (constantly) until it is fully d

- Removed the (preferred wood) pellet from the oven and add the goat cheese, garlic mash, cream, lemon zest, and 1/4 cup of butter.

- Add pepper and salt for seasoning. Extra chives and a (liberal spray) of melted butter are optional toppings.

3.36: Easy Pork Chuck Roast

Preparation Time: 15 minutes

Cooking Time: 4-5 hours

Servings: 4

Ingredients:

- ¼ cup of olive oil
- 1 (whole) 4-5 pounds of chuck roast
- 2 tbsp. of paprika
- ¼ cup of (firm packed) brown sugar

- 2 tbsp. of (cayenne) pepper
- 2 tbsp. of Cajun (for seasoning)

Steps:

- Use (oak Preferred Wood) Pellet to fire your smoker to 225 degrees Fahrenheit.
- Pour olive oil all over the (chuck) roast.
- In a small size bowl, combine cayenne pepper, brown sugar, paprika and Cajun spice.
- Rub the roast completely with the (spice) mixture.
- Smoking the (chuck) roast for 4 to 5 hours on the (smoker) rack.
- Remove the meat and slice it after the (internal) smoke temperature rises 165 degrees Fahrenheit.
- Serve immediately.

3.37: Jalapeno-Bacon Pork Tenderloin

Preparation Time: 25 minutes

Cooking Time: 2 hours and 30 minutes

Servings: 4 to

Ingredients:

- 1 tbsp. of (unsalted) butter (melted)
- 2 (1-pound) pork tenderloins
- ¼ cup of (Our House) Dry Rub
- 8 ounces of cream cheese (softened)
- 1 cup of (grated Cheddar) cheese
- 2 jalapeño peppers (seeded and diced)
- 1 tbsp. of (minced) garlic
- ¼ cup of yellow mustard
- 1½ pounds of bacon

Steps:

- Spread the mustard all over the (pork) tenderloins, then gently cover them with the dry rub.

- Fill your smoker with wood pellets and read the directions.

- Set the oven to (350°F) with the lid down.

- Arrange the tenderloins immediately on the grill, cover, and smoke for 2 hours.

- Take out the meat from the grill and raise the smoke temperature to (375°F).

- Mix the garlic powder, cheddar cheese, cream cheese and melted butter, and garlic powder in a small size mixing bowl.

- Garlic and (jalapenos) are two of the ingredients.

- Starting at the top, make a deep cut along the middle of (each) tenderloin, resulting in a cavity.

- Fill the cavity of one tenderloin with half of the (cream cheese) mixture. Continue with the remaining piece of meat and rest of the mixture. Fold half of the bacon around one (tenderloin) carefully. Continue the procedure with the other piece of meat and the rest of the bacon.

- Close the cover of the grill and smoke the (bacon-wrapped) tenderloins for approximately 30 minutes, just until a meat (thermometer) placed into the thickest part of the meat reaches (165°F).

- A portion of the beef has a temperature of (160°F), and the bacon has been fried and cooked thoroughly. Allow for 5 to 10 minutes resting time before serving and slicing the tenderloins.

3.38: Smoked Brats

Preparation Time: 10 minutes

Cooking Time: 1 hour and 30 minutes- 2 hours

Servings: 10

Ingredients:

- 2 tbsp. of (unsalted) butter (plus more for the rolls)

- 10 brats (uncooked)

- 4 (12-ounce) cans of beer

- 10 hoagie rolls (split)

- 2 onions (sliced into rings)

- 2 tbsp. of red pepper (flakes)

- 2 green bell peppers (sliced into rings)
- Mustard (for serving)

Steps:

- Bring the onions, butter, beer, onions, peppers and red pepper (flakes) to a boil in a big saucepan over high temperature in your kitchen.

- Preferred (Wood pellets) should be used in your smoker, and the maker's specified start-up method should be followed. Warm the oven to (225°F) with the lid down.

- Set a (disposable) pan on one side of the grill and put the hot (beer mixture) into it to make a ("brat tub").

- Close the cover and smoked for 1 hour, rotating 2 or 3 times, with the brats on the (opposite side) of the grill, on the grate.

- Place the brats to the pan with the peppers and onions, cover well with (aluminum foil0, and smoke for 30 minutes to 1 hour, just until a meat (thermometer) placed into the brats reaches (160°F).

- Butter the (cut sides of the hoagie) buns and toast them on the grill, (cut side) down.

- Removed the peppers, brats and onions from the (cooking liquid) using a (slotted) spoon and dispose the liquid.

- Represent the brats on (toasted) buns with the mustard, onions and peppers (ketchup if required).

3.39: Country Pork Roast

Preparation Time: 20 minutes

Cooking Time: 3 hours

Servings: 8

Ingredients:

- (Extra-virgin) olive oil (for rubbing)
- 1 (2- to 2½-pound) pork (loin roast)
- 1 (28-ounce) jar or 2 (14.5-ounce) cans of (sauerkraut)
- ¾ cup of (packed light) brown sugar
- 3 Granny Smith apples (cored and chopped)

- 2 tsp. of (dried) basil leaves
- 3 tbsp. of greek (for seasoning)

Steps:

- Preferred Wood Pellet pellets should be used in your smoker, and the maker's specified start-up method should be followed. Set the oven to (250°F) with the lid down.
- In a large size mixing bowl, combine the brown sugar, sauerkraut and apples.
- Fill a (9-by-13-inch) baking dish halfway with the (sauerkraut-apple) mixture.
- For the rub, combine the dried basil and Greek seasoning in a small size dish.
- Spread the rub on the (pork) roast and put it (fat-side up) in the baking dish on top of the sauerkraut.
- Close the cover on the grill and cook the pork for 3 hours, just until a meat (thermometer) placed into the thickest portion of the flesh reaches (160°F).
- Take out the (pork) roast from the oven and set aside for 5 minutes before cutting.
- Split the (sauerkraut-apple) mixture among dishes and serve with the (sliced) pork.

3.40: Pickled-Pepper Pork Chops

Preparation Time: 15 minutes

Cooking Time: 45-50 minutes

Servings: 4

Ingredients:

- 4 (1-inch-thick) pork (chops)
- ¼ cup of (chopped roasted) red peppers
- ½ cup of pickle juice or pickled jalapeño juice
- ¼ cup of (canned diced) tomatoes (well-drained)
- ¼ cup of (chopped) scallions
- ¼ cup of (chopped) pickled (jarred) jalapeño pepper (slices)
- 2 tsp. of (freshly ground) black pepper
- 2 tsp. of poultry (for seasoning)

- 2 tsp. of salt

Steps:

- Fill a (big) container with a cover halfway with (jalapeno) juice. Covered and refrigerate the (pork) chops for minimum 4 hours or overnight.

- To create a relish, put the chopped (pickled jalapenos), tomatoes, poultry spice, roasted red peppers, tomatoes and scallions in a small size mixing bowl. Set aside.

- Take out the pork (chops) out of the marinade and brush off any excess.

- Remove the marinade from the pan. Add the pepper and salt on both sides of chop.

- Preferred (wood pellet) should be used in your smoker, and the maker's specified start-up method should be followed. Set the oven to (325°F) with the lid covered.

- Place the (pork) chops directly on the grill, cover the lid, and smoked for 45 to 50 minutes, just until a meat (thermometer) inserted into the flesh reaches (160°F).

- Split the chops among plates and serve with the pickled (pepper).

3.41: Smoked Plum and Thyme Fizz Cocktail

Preparation Time: 15 minutes

Cooking Time: 1 hours

Serving: 1

Ingredients

- 1 thyme sprigs
- 3 fresh Plums
- 1 cup of (smoked) simple syrup
- 3/4 Fluid ounce (lemon juice)
- Fluid ounce vodka

Steps:

- Prepare the grill to (180° F) and warm for 15 minutes with the lid covered when ready to cook.

- Halve three plums and removing the (pit). Arrange the plum halves in a bowl.

- Smoked for 25 minutes straight on the (grill grate).

- To make the thyme (simple syrup) and pulm, combine all of the (ingredients) in a small (mixing) bowl. Remove after 25 minutes.

- Take out the plums from the grill and slice them into quarter's pieces. Add thyme and plums with thyme, 1 cup of smoked simple syrup + sprigs 45 minutes of

- The mixture should be smoked. Take out the steaks from the grill and set aside to cool.

- Combine thyme syrup, 2 oz. of vodka, 0.75 oz. of fresh lemon juice, and 1 oz. of smoked salmon to the (cocktail's mixing) glass, and don't forget the ice.

- Finish with a slice of lemon, a piece of smoked plum, club soda and a thyme sprig.

- Put over a (clean ice cube) tray.

3.42: Hawaiian Pulled Pig

Preparation Time: 15 minutes

Cooking Time: 5 hours

Serving: 4

Ingredients:

- 7 Pound of (bone-in) pork shoulder

- 2 (Whole) Banana Leaves

- Ground black pepper (as required)

- 3 tbsp. of (Jacobsen) Salt or Pure Kosher Sea salt

Steps:

- Season the pork (shoulder) with pepper and (Jacobsen) salt.

- Place a (banana) leaf on your work surface. Place the (pork) shoulder in the center at (right angles) to the first, lay the (second) banana leaf, and (draw up the ends to enclose the meat Wrap the whole package with aluminum foil). Refrigerate overnight.

- Prepare the grill to 300 degrees F for 15 minutes with the lid covered.

- Place the (wrapped) pork directly on the grill and cook for 5 to 6 hours, just until the internal temperature reaches 190 degrees F.

- Transfer the pork to a chopping board and set aside for 20 minutes to rest while still wrapped. Carefully unwrap the (pork) and preserve any juices that have accumulated in the (foil).

- Cut the pork into pieces and (shreds), removing any bone lumps or fat. Enjoy your meal.

Chapter 4: Fish and Seafood

4.1: Candied Smoked Salmon with Orange Ginger Rub

Preparation Time: 1hour

Cooking Time: 2 Hours 10 Minutes

Servings: 10

Ingredients:

- Salmon fillet (4-lbs., 1.8-kg.)

The Marinade

- ½ tsp. of salt
- ¼ cup of brown sugar

The Rub

- 1 tsp. of grated fresh ginger

- 2 tbsp. of (minced) garlic
- 2 tsp. of grated orange zest
- ½ tsp. of cayenne pepper
- ½ tsp. of chili powder

The Glaze

- 2 tbsp. of dark rum
- 1 cup of honey
- 2 tbsp. of red wine
- 1 ½ cups of brown sugar

Steps:

- Apply a (mixture) of brown sugar and salt to the fish (salmon) fillet. Allow it to settle for about an hour, just until the sugar has dissolved. Meanwhile, add fresh ginger, cayenne paper, minced garlic, orange zest and chili powder in a mixing bowl. Continuous stirring.

- Set aside the (salmon fillet) after rubbing it with the spice (mixture).

- Filling the (hopper) with pellets after plugging in the (Pellet) smoker. Turning it on.

- Preheat the Smoker on (indirect) heat and then reduce the (smoke) temperature to 107 degrees Fahrenheit (225 degrees Fahrenheit).

- Smoke the marinated fish for 2 hours in a (Pellet) smoker.

- Combine honey, black rum, red wine, black and brown sugar, and honey until smooth.

- During the (smoking) procedure, cover the salmon (fillets) with the (honey) mixture.

- Remove the (smoked) salmon from the Pellet smoker after it has flaked.

- Place it on a serving platter. Immediately serve.

4.2: *Juicy Lime Smoked Tuna Belly*

Preparation Time: 30 minutes

Cooking Time: 2 Hours 10 minutes

Servings: 10

Ingredients:

- Tuna belly (3-lb., 1.4-kg.)

The Marinade

- 2 tbsp. of white sugar
- 3 tbsp. of brown sugar
- 2 fresh limes
- ½ tsp. of pepper
- 2 tbsp. of sriracha sauce
- 1 tbsp. of soy sauce

Steps:

- Sprinkle the lime juice over the (tuna belly) after cutting the limes in half.
- For about 10 minutes, marinade the (tuna belly) in the juice.
- Next, whisk together sriracha sauce, white sugar, pepper, brown sugar and soy sauce.
- After washing and rinsing the tuna belly dry it.
- Filling the (hopper) with pellets after plugging in the (Pellet) smoker. Turning on the light.
- Set the (smoke temperature) to 225°F (107°C) after adjusting the smoker for (indirect) heat.
- Put the (seasoned) tuna belly in the (pellet) smoker after it has reached the appropriate smoke temperature.
- Removed the (tuna belly) from the smoker after 2 hours and until it (flakes).
- Present and have fun.

4.3: Lemon Butter Smoked Mackerel with Juniper Berries Brine

Preparation Time: 15 minutes

Cooking Time: 2 Hours 10 minutes

Servings: 10

Ingredients:

Mackerel (fillet) (4-lbs., 1.8-kg.)

The Brine

- 1 tbsp. of mustard seeds
- 4 cups of cold water
- 3 bay leaves
- 1 tbsp. of (dried) juniper berries
- 1 tbsp. of salt

The Glaze

- 2 tbsp. of lemon juice
- 2 tbsp. of butter

Steps:

- Fill a jar halfway with cold water and sprinkle with mustard seeds, salt, bay leaves and dried juniper berries, stirring well.

- Soaking the mackerel (fillet) in the (brine) mixture for about 20 minutes before washing and rinsing it. Dry the mackerel with a paper towel.

- Filling the (hopper) with pellets after plugging in the (Pellet) smoker. Turning on the light.

- Modify the smoke temperature to 225°F (107°C) after setting the smoker for (indirect) heat.

- Put the salted (mackerel) on a piece of aluminum foil and brush it with butter.

- Sprinkle the mackerel (fillet) with lemon juice and cover it in aluminum foil.

- Take out the (wrapped mackerel) from the smoker after 2 hours of smoking or until it (flakes).

- Present the (smoked) mackerel (unwrapped).

4.4: Smoked Crab Paprika Garlic with Lemon Butter Flavor

Preparation Time: 15 minutes

Cooking Time: 30 minutes

Servings: 10

Ingredients:

- Fresh crabs (7-lb., 3.2-kg.)
- The Sauce
- 1 ½ tsp. of cayenne pepper
- ½ cup of lemon juice
- 2 cups of salted butter
- 1 tbsp. of salt
- 1 tbsp. of (Worcestershire) sauce
- 2 tsp. of (smoked) paprika
- 2 tsp. of garlic powder
- **Steps:**
- Melt the butter in a pot set at low flame. Allow enough time for it to cool.
- Add the salt with (melted), garlic powder, cayenne pepper and Worcestershire sauce and (smoky) paprika, and then add the lemon juice. Set aside after stirring until everything is well combined.
- Filling the (hopper) with pellets after plugging in the (Pellet) smoker. Turning on the light.
- Modify the (smoke) temperature to 350°F (177°C) after setting the smoker for indirect heat.
- Place the crabs on a (disposable aluminum) pan and sprinkle with the sauce.
- Take out the crabs from the (smoker) after 30 minutes of smoking.
- Place the (smoked) crabs on a serving platter and present.

4.5: Cayenne Garlic Smoked Shrimp

Preparation Time: 15 minutes

Cooking Time: 15 minutes

Servings: 10

Ingredients:

- Fresh (shrimps) (3-lb., 1.4-kg.)
- The Spices

- 2 tbsp. of olive oil
- ¾ tsp. of salt
- ½ tsp. of pepper
- 2 tsp. of smoked paprika
- 2 tbsp. of garlic powder
- 1 tsp. of dried thyme
- 2 tbsp. of onion powder
- 2 tbsp. of lemon juice
- 2 tsp. of cayenne pepper

Steps:

- Whisk together the garlic powder, cayenne pepper, onion powder, salt, smoked paprika, pepper, garlic powder and dried thyme, and cayenne pepper.

- After that, (peel) the shrimps and take out the heads. Fill a (disposable aluminum pan) halfway with water.

- Shake the shrimps to cover them with lemon juice and olive oil. Allow the shrimps to rest for about 5 minutes.

- Filling the (hopper) with pellets after plugging in the (Pellet) smoker. Turning on the light.

- Modify the (smoke) temperature to 350°F (177°C) after setting the smoker for (indirect) heat.

- Drizzle the (spice) mixture over the shrimps and mix until they are evenly coated.

- Set the shrimps in the (disposable) aluminum pan in the (pellet) smoker and cook for 15 minutes. The shrimp would be opaque and pink.

- Place the (smoked) shrimps to a serving plate after removing them from the (pellet) smoker.

- Serve immediately and have fun.

4.6: Cinnamon Ginger Juicy Smoked Crab

Preparation Time: 10 minutes
Cooking Time: 30 minutes

Servings: 10 servings

Ingredients:

Fresh Crabs (7-lb., 3.2-kg.)

The Spices

- 3 tbsp. of (ground) celery seeds
- ½ tsp. of cayenne pepper
- 1 tbsp. of salt
- 2 tsp. of (ground) mustard
- ½ tsp. of black pepper
- A pinch of (ground) clove
- 1 ½ tsp. of smoked paprika
- 1 tsp. of (ground) ginger
- ¾ tsp. of (ground) allspice
- ½ tsp. of (ground) cardamom
- 2 bay leaves
- ½ tsp. of (ground) cinnamon

Steps:

- In a cup, mix together the entire spices black pepper, salt, clove, ginger, cinnamon, mustard, crushed celery seeds, cayenne pepper, smoked paprika, allspice and cardamom.
- Wrap the crabs in aluminum foil after sprinkling the (spice) mixture over them.
- Filling the (hopper) with pellets after plugging in the Pellet smoker. Switch on the light. Modify the (smoke) temperature to 350°F (177°C) after setting the smoker for (indirect) heat.
- Smoke the (wrapped crabs) for 30 minutes in the (Pellet) smoker.
- Take out the (wrapped) smoked carbohydrates from the (Pellet) smoker after it is ready and set aside for 10 minutes to cool.
- Move the (smoked) crabs to a serving plate after unwrapping them.
- Present and have fun!

4.7: Garlic Asiago Oysters

Preparation Time: 10 minutes

Cooking Time: 5 minutes

Servings: 12

Ingredients:

- 1 tbsp. of minced garlic
- 1 lb. of (sweet) cream butter
- 2 dozen of fresh oysters
- French bread, (warmed)
- ½ cup of (grated) Asiago cheese
- ¼ cup of diced chives

Steps:

- Preheat the (pellet) grill to medium heat.
- Melt the butter in a (skillet) over medium-high heat. Reduce the heat and add the garlic.
- Cooked for 1 minute before turning off the heat.
- Arrange the oysters on the (pellet grill). Remove the shells from the grill as soon as the (pop) open.
- Connective muscle should be cut and each oyster should be returned to its shell.
- Pour 2 tbsp. of butter (mixture) over each oyster and top with 1 tsp. of cheese. Cook it for 3 minutes on (high) heat, or until cheese begins to brown.
- Serve with chives on top.
- Remove off the (pellet) grill and present right away with the remaining butter and bread.

4.8: Wasabi Oysters

Preparation Time: 20 minutes

Cooking Time: 5 minutes

Servings: 6

Ingredients:

- 8 oz. of white wine
- 2 tbsp. of wasabi mustard
- 12 (small) Pacific oysters, raw in shell
- ¼ cup of minced shallots
- 1 tbsp. of soy sauce
- 1 cup of chopped cilantro leaves
- 2 tbsp. of (white wine) vinegar
- 1 cup of unsalted butter
- Black pepper and salt according to your taste

Steps:

- Mix the shallots, white wine vinegar and wine in a small saucepan at low heat. Cook until the water has been reduced somewhat. Drain and discard the shallots, then put the water into the pan. Reduce the heat to a low setting. Stir in the soy sauce and wasabi mustard.

- Stir in the butter gently over low heat. Whisk in the cilantro and turn off the heat after all of the butter has been absorbed.

- Put the mixture in a small bowl and put it aside.

- To keep the oyster (shells) in place, make a dish of (coarse) salt.

- Oysters should be properly cleaned. Close the cover on the oysters and put them flat (side up) on the pellet (grill) that has been heated to moderate. Cook oysters until the (shells) are just beginning to open for (5-6 minutes). Removed the oysters from the (pellet grill) and remove the (connective) muscle off the top shell (carefully, as the liquid will leak.) Return the oyster to the cup (half of the shell) by turning it over. Remove the cover.

- To maintain each oyster (upright), coat it into the (coarse) salt, then pour 1-2 tbsp. Of wasabi-butter (sauce) over each and immediately serve.

4.9: Pacific Northwest Salmon with Lemon Dill Sauce

Preparation Time: 5 minutes

Cooking Time: 15 minutes

Servings: 8

Ingredients:

- 1 cup of melted butter, melted
- Salt to taste
- 6 lb. of Chinook salmon fillets
- 4 cups of (plain) yogurt
- 4 tbsp. of (dried) dill weed
- 1 cup of lemon juice
- 1 tbsp. of garlic salt
- Black pepper as per your taste

Steps:

- Fill a (baking dish) halfway with salmon fillets. In a small dish, combine the 1/2 lemon juice and butter, and pour over the salmon. Sprinkle with pepper and salt.
- Whisk the pepper and salt, dill, yoghurt and garlic powder in a mixing bowl. Distribute the sauce evenly over the fish.
- Arrange fillets on heated pellet (grill grate), cover with foil, and cover lid immediately with a towel soaked in a little olive oil.
- Grill the fish for 6 minutes at medium heat.
- Serve with additional sauce on the side.
- Present with (wild) rice.

4.10: Seared Wasabi Tuna

Preparation Time: 5 minutes

Cooking Time: 3 minutes

Servings: 8

Ingredients:

- 1 1/4 cup of white wine
- 1 cup of unsalted butter
- 6-ounce tuna steaks
- 1 cup of cilantro leaves

- 1/4 cup of minced shallots
- 1 tbsp. of wasabi paste
- 2 tbsp. of (white wine) vinegar
- 1 tbsp. of soy sauce
- Pepper and salt to taste
- 1 tbsp. of olive oil

Steps:

- In a medium saucepan, whisk together the shallots, wine and wine vinegar.
- Reduce to approximately 2 tsp. of by simmering. Remove and (discard) the shallots.
- Reduce (Preferred Wood Pellet) by adding soy sauce and wasabi to the mixture.
- Gently pour in the butter while stirring constantly until completely combined. Remove from heat and stir in the cilantro.
- Fire the pellet (grill) to the highest setting possible. This one requires a lot of heat.
- Olive oil should be brushed on tuna steaks. Put on the (grill) and season with pepper and salt.
- Grilled for 90 seconds, then flip and grill for another 90 seconds. Take out the tuna from the grill immediately.
- Present with sauce.

4.11: Sweet Grilled Lobster Tails

Preparation Time: 10 minutes

Cooking Time: 7 minutes

Servings: 12

Ingredients:

- ½ cup of olive oil
- ¼ cup of fresh lemon juice
- 1 tbsp. of crushed garlic
- 12 lobster tails

- ½ cup of butter

- 1 tsp. of sugar

- ½ tsp. of black pepper

- 1/2 tsp. of salt

Steps:

- Combine salt and pepper, garlic, lemon juice and butter and stir until thoroughly combined

- Rub the (meat) side of the lobster tails with (olive) oil, put them on the grill, and cooked for 5-7 minutes, based on their size.

- During the cooking (process), be sure to flip the pan at once.

- Baste the meat with (garlic) butter for 2-3 times after it has been turned.

- When completed, the shell must be (bright) red. Removed the tails from the grill and cut the top portion of the shell with help of big (kitchen) shears.

- Warm (garlic) butter is served alongside for dipping.

4.12: Seasoned Smoked Oysters

Preparation Time: 20 minutes

Cooking Time: 1½-2 hours

Servings: 2 dozen

Ingredients:

- ½ cup of soy sauce

- 1-gallon cold water

- 1 cup of salt

- 2 tbsp. of Worcestershire sauce

- 1 cup of (firmly packed) brown sugar

- 2 cloves of garlic (minced)

- 2 (dried) bay leaves

- 2 tsp. of (freshly ground) black pepper

- 1 tbsp. of onion powder

- 1 tbsp. of hot sauce

- 2 dozen raw, shucked oysters, shells discarded
- ½ cup of (1 stick) unsalted butter, (at room smoke temperature)
- ¼ cup of olive oil
- 1 tsp. of garlic powder
- Cocktail sauce, for serving
- Crackers or toast points, for serving

Steps:

- Combine the sugar, salt, onion powder, water, garlic, soy sauce, Worcestershire, bay leaves, pepper and spicy sauce in a big container.
- Refrigerate the (raw) oysters after submerging them in the brine and covering the container overnight.
- Preheat the oven according to the package recommendations.
- Preheat the smoker to 225°F and put a preferred (wood pellet) of alder, oak or hickory.
- Take out the oysters from the fridge and rinse them or discarding the (brine).
- Drizzle the olive oil over the oysters and place them on a nonstick grill mat.
- In the smoker, put the mat.
- Oysters should be smoked for 1 /2 to 2 hours, or until crisp.
- Combine the garlic powder and butter in a mixing bowl.
- Take out the oysters from the (preferred wood) pellet and sprinkle them with the butter or balsamic vinegar.
- Garnish the oysters with cocktail sauce and crackers or (toast points).

4.13: Caribbean Smoked Rockfish

Preparation Time: 10 minutes

Cooking Time: 50 minutes

Servings: 2

Ingredients:

- 2 tbsp. of (extra virgin) olive oil (garlic flavored)
- 4 Ounces of Pacific Rockfish fillets (fresh, wild)

- 1 tbsp. of Caribbean seafood (seasoning)

Steps:

- Rub the rockfish fillets with olive oil on both sides.

- Coat the salmon fillets gently with the seasoning.

- Fire the smoker (grill) to 225 degrees Fahrenheit and adjust it to (indirect) cooking.

- Arrange the fillets immediately on the (grill) grates, skin side down.

- Allow the salmon (fillets) to rest for 5 minutes in the smoker until the inner Smoke temperature reaches 140°F.

- Present and have fun!

4.14: Smoked Brined Tuna

Preparation Time: 35 minutes

Cooking Time: 5 Hours

Servings: 2

Ingredients:

- 2 Cups of (fresh) fish Brine

- 3 Pounds of salmon fillets (farmed)

Steps:

- Preparing the Grill

- Slice the fillets into 4 (inch) pieces so that they cook at the same time.

- Place the (pork) chops in a sealed plastic (container) and put the sauce into it.

- Refrigerate it overnight after covering it.

- Removed the (pork) chops after this time and rub them with (paper) towels. Drying the salmon fillets with air.

- Preheat the grill to (indirect) cooking on the smoker.

- Fill a Teflon-coated (fiberglass) mat halfway with salmon fillets.

- Set the smoker to 180°F and smoke the salmon fillets until the inner Smoke temperature reaches 145°F.

- Allow 10 minutes for resting after removing them from the grill.

- Present and have fun!

4.15: Easy Grilled Mahi-mahi

Preparation Time: 5 minutes

Cooking time: 20 minutes

Servings: 4

Ingredients:

- 2 tbsp. of olive oil
- 4 mahi-mahi fillets
- Black pepper and salt

Steps:

- Preheat the (grill) to 350 degrees F (176 degrees C) with the lid covered for 15 minutes.
- Drizzle olive oil over the fish fillets and (season) equally with black pepper and salt.
- Grill the fish (fillets) for approximately 5 minutes on each side.
- Take out the fish (fillets) from the grill and serve immediately.

4.16: Grilled Lobster Tails with Citrus Butter

Preparation Time: 5 minutes

Cooking Time: 40 minutes

Servings: 4

Ingredients:

- ½ cup of melted butter
- Salt and freshly ground black pepper, to taste
- 2 cloves of garlic, (minced)
- 4 lobster tails
- 2 tsp. of fresh lemon juice

Steps:

• Preheat the (grill) to 450 degrees F (232 degrees C) with the lid covered for 15 minutes.

• Combine all (ingredients) in a metal pan, except the lobster tails, and stir thoroughly.

• Cook for approximately 10 minutes on the (grill) using the pan.

• Meanwhile, cut the heads of the lobster (shell) to (expose) the meat.

• Take out the butter (mixture) pan from the grill.

• Using the butter mixture, cover the (lobster) meat.

• Arrange the lobster tails on the grill and cooked for approximately 15 minutes, brushing halfway through with the (butter) mixture. Removed from the (grill) and serve immediately.

4.17: One Pan Citrusy Catfish

Preparation Time: 15 minutes

Cooking Time: 30 minutes

Servings: 4

Ingredients:

Spice blend

• ½ cup of Cajun seasoning

• ¼ tp. of cayenne pepper

• 1 tsp. of (ground) thyme

• 1 tsp. of onion powder

• 1 tsp. of granulated garlic

• 1 tsp. of (ground) oregano

• 1 tbsp. of smoky paprika

• 1 tsp. of pepper

• 4 catfish fillets

• ½ cup of butter

• Salt, to taste

Steps:

- To make the spice blend, put all of the ingredients in a mixing dish.

- Season the fish on both sides with the spice mixture and salt. Preheat your (wood pellet) grill to 450 degrees Fahrenheit (232 degrees Celsius).

- Melt the butter in your (cast iron) pan. Fill the pan with the fillets.

- Grill each side for 5 minutes. Serve with lemon (slices) as a garnish.

4.18: Grilled Tender Rainbow Trout

Preparation Time: 10 minutes

Cooking Time: 2 hours

Servings: 4

Ingredients:

- 1 tbsp. of (ground) black pepper

- ¼ cup of salt

- 2 tbsp. of soy sauce

- ½ cup of brown sugar

- 16 cups of water

Steps:

- Make the brine by combining all of the (ingredients) in a big jar, stirring until the sugar has mixed, then adding the fish and allowing to (soak) for 1 hour in the fridge.

- When you start cooking, turn on the grill, load the grill hopper with (oak-flavored wood pellets), turn on the grill with the (control center), choose '(smoke)' on the temperature dial, or adjust the temperature to 225 degrees F (107 degrees C) and allow it to warm for at least 15 minutes.

- Remove the fish from the (brine) and dry it.

- After the grill has heated up, open the cover and put the fish on the (grill) grate. Close the grill and smoked for 2 hours, or until the trout is fully tender and cooked.

- When the trout is cooked, move it to a serving dish and enjoy.

4.19: Moms Special Grilled Lingcod

Preparation Time: 5 minutes
Cooking Time: 15 minutes
Servings: 6
Ingredients:

- ½ tbsp. of salt
- 2 lb. of (lingcod) fillets
- Lemon wedges
- ¼ tbsp. of cayenne
- ½ tbsp. of white pepper

Steps:

- Fire the (wood pellet) grill to 375 degrees Fahrenheit (191 degrees Celsius).
- Season the lingcod with cayenne pepper, salt and white pepper on parchment paper, then garnish with the lemon.
- Grill the fish for 15 minutes, or until it hits an internal temperature of 145°F (63°C).
- Present and have a good time.

4.20: Grilled Garlicky Salmon with Avocado Salsa

Preparation Time: 10 minutes
Cooking Time: 20 minutes
Servings: 6
Ingredients:

- 3 lb. of (1.36 kg) salmon fillet
- 4 cups of avocado, (sliced into cubes)
- Garlic salt and pepper
- 1 chopped onion
- 1 tbsp. of lime juice
- 1 jalapeño pepper, (minced)

- 1 tbsp. of olive oil
- Salt, to taste
- ¼ cup of chopped cilantro

Steps:

- Season the salmon on both sides with pepper and garlic salt.
- Fire the (wood pellet) grill and allow it to smoke.
- Cook the salmon for around 7 to 8 minutes on each side on the grill.
- In the meanwhile, make the salsa by mixing together the other (ingredients) in a container.
- Toss the salmon with the (avocado) salsa and serve.

4.21: Grilled Citrusy Scallops

Preparation Time: 5 minutes

Cooking Time: 15 minutes

Servings: 4

Ingredients:

- ½ tbsp. of garlic salt
- 2 lb. of (907 g) sea scallops, (dried with a paper towel)
- 2 tbsp. of salt kosher
- Squeeze lemon juice
- 4 tbsp. of salted butter

Steps:

- Fire the (cast pan) inside the wood (pellet) grill to 400°F (204°C).
- Season all side of the scallops with pepper and salt.
- Melt the butter in a (cast iron) skillet and then put the scallops. Cook for 8 minutes with the lid closed.
- Turn the scallops and closed the cover again. Cook for a further 8 minutes.
- Take out the (scallops) from the grill and squeeze a lemon over them. Serve right away and enjoy.

4.22: Garlic Spiced Shrimp Skewers

Preparation time: 10 minutes

Cooking Time: 25 minutes

Servings: 4

Ingredients:

- 6 cloves of garlic
- 6 oz. of (170 g) chili
- 3 tbsp. of olive oil
- 2 tbsp. of chicken dry rub
- 1 ½ tbsp. of (white) vinegar
- 2 lb. of (907 g) shrimp, deveined and peeled
- 1 ½ tsp. of sugar

Steps:

- In a food processor, combine the garlic, chili, sugar, olive oil dry rub and vinegar.
- Combine until completely soft.
- Pour the mixture into a container. Add the shrimp and mix well.
- Put it in the fridge for 30 minutes after covering.
- While the lid is covered, pre - heat the wood (pellet) grill for 15 minutes.
- Using skewers, put shrimp onto the skewers. Cook for 3 minutes each side on the grill.
- Serve immediately.

4.23: Delicious smoked Halibut

Preparation Time: 15 minutes

Cooking Time: 2 hours

Servings: 6

Ingredients:

- ¼ cup of (extra-virgin) olive oil

- ¼ cup of (finely chopped) sweet onion
- 4 (6-ounce/170 g) halibut steaks
- 1 tsp. of (freshly ground) black pepper
- ½ cup of sweet pickle relish
- ¼ cup of (finely chopped) tomato
- ½ cup of mayonnaise
- ¼ cup of (finely chopped) cucumber
- 2 tbsp. of Dijon mustard
- ¼ cup of (chopped roasted) red pepper
- 1 tsp. of minced garlic
- 2 tsp. of salt kosher

Steps:

• Drizzle the olive oil over the (halibut) steaks and season all sides with pepper and salt. Put it in the fridge for 4 hours after transferring to a platter and covering with plastic wrap.

• Fill your smoker with (wood pellets) and fire it up according to the package recommendations. Set the oven to 200°F (93°C) and keep cover on it.

• Take the halibut out of the fridge and coat it with mayonnaise.

• Place the fish (directly) on the grill grate, cover, and cook for 2 hours, or until the salmon is opaque.

• In a medium size mixing bowl, mix together the onion, tomato, pickle relish, roasted red pepper, cucumber, garlic and Dijon mustard while the fish is smoked. Keep the mustard relish refrigerated until ready to be served.

• Toss the (halibut) steaks with the mustard relish and serve immediately.

4.24: Dijon mustard Tuna Steaks

Preparation Time: 5 minutes

Cooking Time: 1 hour

Servings: 3

Ingredients:

• 2 pounds (907 g) yellow fin tuna

- ¼ cup of Dijon mustard

- 2 tbsp. of peppercorn

- (Freshly ground) black pepper, according to your taste

- Salt, according to your taste

Steps:

- In a big container, absorb the salt in warm water.

- Place tuna in (brine), covered, and chill for 8 hours.

- Using your wood pellet, preheat your (smoker) to 250 degrees Fahrenheit (121 degrees Celsius).

- Take out the tuna and dry it.

- Place tuna on grill pan and apply Dijon mustard all over it. Add pepper and salt and top with peppercorns.

- Place tuna in (smoker) for around 1 hour. Enjoy your meal.

4.25: Peppery Prawn Skewers

Preparation Time: 5 minutes

Cooking Time: 10 minutes

Servings: 6

Ingredients:

- 2 tbsp. of oil

- 2 lb. of spot prawns

- Pepper and Salt, as required

Steps:

- Set oven to 400 degrees Fahrenheit (204 degrees Celsius).

- Using skewers, (skewer your prawns), then gently season with pepper, oil and salt.

- Arrange the skewers on the (grill) and cooked for around 5 minutes and cover it.

- Take out from the skewers and serve immediately while still hot.

4.26: Grilled Pink Shrimp Kabobs

Preparation Time: 10 minutes

Cooking Time: 10 minutes

Serving: 4

Ingredients:

- 2 tbsp. of oil
- 6 skewers
- 1 lb. colossal shrimp (peeled and deveined)
- ½ tbsp. of Garlic salt
- ⅛ tbsp. of pepper
- ½ tbsp. of Salt

Steps:

- Set the oven to 375 degrees Fahrenheit (191 degrees Celsius). Using a paper towel and dry the shrimp
- Combine the vegetables in a mixing dish with the pepper and salt, oil or garlic salt.
- In a large size mixing bowl, toss the shrimp in the mixture until thoroughly mixed.
- Skewer the (shrimps) and cooked for 4 minutes with the top covered.
- Grill for another 4 minutes after opening the lid and flipping the skewer.
- Immediately serve.

4.27: Delicious Tuna Patties

Preparation Time: 10 minutes

Cooking Time: 30 minutes

Servings: 6

Ingredients:

- 1 white onion (chopped)
- 2 lb. tuna steak

- 2 eggs
- 1 tbsp. of Blackened Saskatchewan rub
- 1 tsp. of soy sauce
- 1 green bell pepper (seeded and chopped)
- Salt and freshly ground black pepper, according to your taste

Steps:

- Preheat the grill to 500 degrees Fahrenheit with the lid covered for around 15 minutes.
- Put all of the (ingredients) in a mixing dish and stir until completely mixed.
- Shape patties from the (mixture) using oiled hands.
- Arrange the patties on the grill and cooked for 10-15 minutes, turning halfway through.
- Serve immediately.

4.28: Grilled Prosciutto Scallops

Preparation Time: 5 minutes

Cooking Time: 40 minutes

Serving: 4

Ingredients:

- 8 (extra-thin) prosciutto slices
- 8 large scallops (cleaned and shelled).

Steps:

- Set the (wood pellet) grill to medium-high flame. The temperature should be between 225 and 250 degrees Fahrenheit (121 degrees Celsius).
- Using a flat surface, place the prosciutto pieces.
- Fold one prosciutto (slice) up with one scallop on the side.
- Using the leftover prosciutto pieces and scallops, repeat the process.
- Set the scallops covered in foil on a (small) wire rack.
- Grill for approximately 40 minutes on the (wire) rack on the grill.
- Serve the scallops immediately after removing them from the grill.

4.29: Citrusy Garlic Clams

Preparation Time: 5 minutes

Cooking Time: 8 minutes

Serving: 6

Ingredients:

- ½ cup of cold butter (chopped).
- 1 tsp. of (fresh) lemon juice
- 24 littleneck clams
- 3 cloves of (minced) garlic.
- 2 tbsp. of (minced) fresh parsley.

Steps:

- Set the wood pellet grill to 450˚F (232˚C). Using cold running water, clean the clams.
- Combine rest of the (ingredients) in a large size (casserole) dish. Preheat the grill and put the (casserole) dish on it.
- Place the clams (directly) on the grill and cooked for around 5 to 8 minutes.
- Move the (opened clams) to the (casserole) dish with tongs and removed from the grill. Serve immediately.

4.30: Citrusy Clams with Chickpeas and Tomatoes

Preparation Time: 15 minutes

Cooking Time: 25 minutes

Serving: 4

Ingredients:

- 2 tbsp. of olive oil
- 2 large shallots (chopped).
- 1 tbsp. of tomato paste
- 4 thinly (sliced) garlic cloves
- 6 tbsp. of unsalted pieces of butter

- 1 cup of cherry tomatoes
- 1 cup of beer
- 2 tbsp. of sambal oiled.
- 1 ½ ounce (42 g) of chickpeas (rinsed).
- 4 (thick slices) of country-style bread
- 1 tbsp. of (fresh) lime juice
- ½ cup of cilantro leaves
- 24 scrubbed littleneck clams
- Lime wedges
- Salt Kosher

Steps:

- Preheat the grill to medium heat using (indirect) heat. Melt 4 tbsp. of butter in a large pan on the grill over (direct) heat.

- Pour the garlic and shallots and continue to cook, stirring often, just before the garlic and shallots are soft.

- It takes approximately 4 minutes for soften.

- Add the (tomato) paste and continue to simmer, stirring constantly, until it has thickened. Toss in the beer and tomatoes.

- Cook for approximately 4 minutes, or until the beer has almost been reduced by half.

- After the sambal and chickpeas have been oiled, add the clams.

- Cook, covered, until the clams have (opened), about 5 to 10 minutes.

- Depending on the size of the (clams) and the temperature, it may take up to 10 minutes. Discard any clams that refuse to open. Stir in the (lime) juice and 2 tbsp. of leftover butter.

- While the clams are cooking, brush the toast with oil and season with salt. Cook until crispy and golden brown for about 5 minutes.

- Arrange the toasts on plates and top with the (clam) mixture.

- Serve with (lime) wedges on the side.

4.31: Oregano Herbed Salmon Kebabs

Preparation Time: 10 minutes

Cooking Time: 25 minutes

Serving: 4

Ingredients:

- 2 tbsp. of olive oil
- 1 ½ pounds (680 g) of (skinless) salmon fillets (cut into 1" pieces).
- 2 tsp. of sesame seeds
- 2 tbsp. of (chopped) fresh oregano.
- ¼ tsp. of (crushed) red pepper flakes
- 1 tsp. of ground cumin
- 16 bamboo skewers (soaked in water for one hour)
- 2 lemons thinly sliced into rounds.
- 1 tsp. of salt kosher

Steps:

- Preheat the grill to medium. In a small size bowl, combine the sesame seeds, cumin, red pepper flakes, oregano and salt. Set aside the (spice) mixture.
- Make 8 (kebabs) by threading the lemon (pieces) and fish onto 8 pairs of similar (skewers).
- Season with the (spice) mixture and drizzle with olive oil.
- Cook the fish on the grill, turning it frequently, until it is done.
- Immediately serve.

4.32: Grilled Citrusy Butter Cod

Preparation Time: 10 minutes

Cooking Time: 15 minutes

Serving: 4

Ingredients:

- 1 tbsp. of (extra virgin) olive oil

- ¼ cup of butter
- 4 (6ounce/ 170 g) cod fillets
- 1 (finely chopped) small onion.
- ¼ cup of white wine
- ½ tsp. of black pepper
- Lemon wedges
- ½ tsp. of salt (according to your taste)

Steps:

- Preheat the grill to moderate temperature.
- Melt the butter in a small skillet. Sauté for 1 or 2 minutes after adding the onion.
- Pour in the (white) wine and cook for a further 3 minutes. Remove it from the oven and set it aside to settle for 5 minutes.
- Drizzle (extra virgin) olive oil over the fillets and use salt and pepper for seasoning. Cook fish for 8 minutes on a (well-oiled) rack.
- Season it with sauce and turn it carefully. Cooked for another 6 to 7 minutes, flipping once more, or until the fish reaches an internal temperature of (145°F) 63°C.
- Take out from the grill and serve with (lemon) wedges on top.

4.33: Grilled Sweet Mustard Calamari

Preparation Time: 10 minutes

Cooking Time: 20 minutes

Serving: 6

Ingredients:

- 2 cups of milk
- 8 Calamari, (cleaned)
- Sauce as needed
- Lemon juice (from 2 lemons)
- 4 tsp. of (sweet) mustard
- ½ cup of olive oil

- Freshly ground pepper
- 2 tbsp. of fresh oregano (finely chopped)
- ½ bunch of parsley (finely chopped)

Steps:

- Thoroughly clean the calamari and split it into pieces.
- Arrange calamari in a (big metal bow) and covered with milk (overnight).
- Drain the (calamari) thoroughly after removing them from the milk. Lightly brush the fish with olive oil.
- Whisk the lemon juice and mustard in a mixing dish.
- Lightly beat and gently drizzle the olive oil, stirring constantly until all of the (ingredients) are well mixed.
- Mix pepper and the oregano well. Preheat wood pellet grill and adjust the temperature to moderate; warm for 10 to 15 minutes with the (lid) covered.
- Arrange the calamari on the grill and cooked for 2-3 minutes. Take out from the grill.
- Put the calamari on a serving dish and serve with chopped parsley and the mustard sauce.

4.34: Oregano Herbed Cuttlefish with Spinach

Preparation Time: 10 minutes

Cooking Time: 20 minutes

Serving: 6

Ingredients:

- 1 tsp. of oregano
- 1 tbsp. of lemon juice
- ½ cup of olive oil
- Pinch of salt
- Spinach, pine nuts, vinegar and olive oil for (serving)
- 8 large cuttlefish, (cleaned)

Steps:

- Combine oregano, olive oil and lemon juice and a sprinkle of pepper and salt for making a marinade.

- Toss the cuttlefish in the (marinade) to evenly coat it. Covered and let aside for 1 hour to marinate.

- Take out the cuttlefish and wipe with a (paper) towel.

- Fire the grill on high temp for 10 to 15 minutes with the lid covered.

- Cook the (cuttlefish) for around 3 to 4 minutes on each side on the grill.

- Toss with vinegar, pine nuts, spinach and olive oil and serve immediately.

4.35: Grilled Paprika Catfish Fillets

Preparation Time: 10 minutes

Cooking Time: 10 minutes

Serving: 6

Ingredients:

- ½ tsp. of salt

- 2 tbsp. of Dijon mustard

- 1 tsp. of paprika

- Juice of 4 lemons

- 4 (6- to 8-oz/227 g) (catfish) fillets

- ½ cup olive oil

- Fresh chopped rosemary

Steps:

- Preheat the oven to Medium temp, with the lid covered, for 10 to 15 minutes.

- In a mixing dish, combine the salt, lemon juice, mustard, olive oil, paprika and (chopped) rosemary.

- Spread half of the (olive oil-lemon) mixture on one side of each (fish fillet); add pepper and salt to taste.

- Cover and (grill) the fillets for 4 to 5 minutes. Brush the leftover (olive oil-lemon) mixture over the fillets.

- Cook for another 4 to 5 minutes on the grill (do not cover it).
- Transfer the (fish fillets) to a serving dish and top with rosemary.

4.36: Parsley Herbed Fish Stew

Preparation Time: 15 minutes
Cooking Time: 30 minutes
Serving: 8
Ingredients:
- 2 tbsp. of Butter
- 2 oz. (56 g) of Tomato paste
- 1 jar (28oz/794 g) of (Crushed) Tomatoes
- ¼ cup of Chicken (Stock)
- 2 cloves of (minced) Garlic.
- ¼ cup of White wine
- ½ lb. (226 g) of Shrimp (divined and cleaned).
- ¼ Onion (diced).
- ½ lb. (226 g) of Halibut
- Parsley
- ½ lb. (226 g) of Clams
- Bread

Steps:
- Set the grill to 300 degrees Fahrenheit with the lid closed. Melt the (butter) in a (Dutch) oven over moderate temp. For 4 to 7 minutes, cook the onion. Garlic should be added now. Cook for another minute.
- Add the (tomato) paste to the pan. Cook until it becomes a rusty red color. Put in the stock and wine. Cooking for ten minutes. Boil the tomatoes after adding them.
- Slice the halibut and place it in the (Dutch) oven with the other fish. Cover it with a lid and set it on the grill.
- Allow for 20 minutes for cooking. Set aside after seasoning with salt and black pepper. Serve the (chopped) parsley and toast on top. Enjoy your meal.

4.37: Delicious Butter Roasted Snapper

Preparation Time: 5 minutes

Cooking Time: 15 minutes

Serving: 4

Ingredients:

- Pepper and salt according to your taste
- 4 snapper fillets
- 2 tsp. of (dried) tarragon
- 2 lemons, (sliced)
- Olive oil, as required

Steps:

- Preheat the grill to high temperature. Close the cover and warm it for 15 minutes. On highest point of a (foil) sheet, place 1 fish fillet.
- Season with tarragon, salt and pepper. Pour some oil on top. Add lemon (slices) on the top. Fold the packets and cover it.
- Preheat the grill and place the (foil packs) on it. Cook for 15 minutes in the oven.
- Before serving, drizzle with (melted) butter

4.38: Pesto Fish Fillets with Basil

Preparation Time: 10 minutes

Cooking Time: 20 minutes

Serving: 6

Ingredients:

- ½ cup of walnuts
- 1 cup of chopped parsley, chopped.
- ½ cup of olive oil
- 4 (white) fish fillets
- 2 cups of fresh basil

- Pepper and salt according to your taste
- 1 cup of grated Parmesan cheese

Steps:
- Set the grill for 15 minutes on high heat with the lid covered.
- In a (food processor), except fish combine all of the (ingredient).
- Blend until the mixture is smooth.
- Season the (fish) with pepper and salt before serving.
- Cook for around 6 to 7 minutes each side on the grill.
- Toss with (pesto) sauce and serve. Serve with fresh (basil leaves) as a garnish.

4.39: Garlic Pesto Halibut with Pine Nuts

Preparation Time: 20 minutes

Cooking Time: 10 minutes

Serving: 4

Ingredients:
- 1 cup of olive oil
- 4 halibut (fillets)
- ¼ cup of garlic (chopped).
- ¼ cup of (pine) nuts
- Pepper and Salt, according to your taste

Steps:
- Fire up the grill and let it smoke. Set the timer for 5 minutes to start the fire.
- Increase the temperature to a high setting. On a grill, set a (cast iron) skillet.
- Season the fish with pepper and salt before serving. Toss the fish into the pan. Sprinkle a little oil on top.
- Pulse the other (ingredients) in the (food) processor to make the (garlic) pesto.
- Blend until fully smooth in a (food) processor.
- Toss the fish with (garlic) pesto and serve.
- Before serving, garnish with (fresh) herbs.

4.40: Grilled Citrusy Vermillion Snapper

Preparation Time: 10 minutes

Cooking Time: 25 minutes

Serving: 6

Ingredients:

- 4 Garlic cloves (chopped, peeled)
- 1 Lemon (thinly sliced).
- 2 Rosemary (springs)
- Black pepper, according to your taste
- 1 Vermillion (Snapper gutted and scaled)
- Sea Salt, according to your taste

Steps:

- Set the grill to high temperature with the lid closed.
- Put the garlic inside the fish. Stuffed with (lemon) slices and season with sea salt, rosemary and black pepper.
- Cook for 25 minutes on the grill.

4.41: Thyme Herbed Smoked Sea Bass

Preparation Time: 15 minutes

Cooking Time: 30 Minutes

Serving: 4

Ingredients:

Marinade

- ¼ cup of oil
- 1 tbsp. of Thyme (fresh)
- 1 tsp. of Blackened Saskatchewan
- 8 cloves of Garlic (crushed).
- 1 lemon, (the juice)

- 1 tbsp. of Oregano (fresh)
- Chicken Rub (for Seasoning)
- 4 Sea bass fillets (skin off)
- Seafood (for seasoning) (like Old Bay)
- 8 tbsp. of Gold Butter
- Sea Bass

For garnish:

- Lemon
- Thyme

Steps:

- To prepare the marinade, put all of the ingredients in a (Ziploc bag) and stir well. Put the marinade and fillets in the refrigerator for 30 minutes. Flip.

- Set the grill to 325 degrees Fahrenheit with the lid covered.

- Place the butter in a (baking) dish. Take the fish out of the marinade and place it in a (baking) tray. Sea food rub and chicken are used to season the fish. Put it on the grill in a baking dish. Cook time is 30 minutes. 1 – 2 times each

- When the (inner temperature) reaches 160 degrees Fahrenheit, take out from the grill.

- Serve with thyme and lemon (slices) and thyme as garnish.

Chapter: 5 Vegetable Recipes

5.1: Yummy Honey Glazed Carrots

Preparation Time: 10 minutes

Cooking Time: 35 minutes

Servings: 5

Ingredients:

- 2 tsp. of olive oil
- 1 bunch of asparagus (trimmed ends)
- Sea salt, according to your taste
- 1 lb. of carrots, (peeled)

- Lemon zest
- 2 tbsp. of honey

Steps:

- Drizzle the asparagus with olive oil and season with pepper and sea salt. Pour salt and honey over the carrots.

- Pre - heat the (wood pellet) to 165 degrees Fahrenheit (74 degrees C) and closed the cover for fifteen mints.

- In the wood pellet cook the carrot for 15 mints. Put the asparagus and Continue to cook for another 20 minutes, just before the asparagus is cooked completely.

- Sprinkle lemon zest over the asparagus and carrots.

5.2: One Pan Baked Pork Beans

Preparation Time: 10 minutes

Cooking Time: 3 hours

Servings: 12

Ingredients:

- 3 jalapenos
- ¾ cup of barbeque sauce
- 56 oz. of (1.58 kg) pork and beans
- ¼ cup of apple cider vinegar
- 2 tbsp. molasses
- ½ cup of dark brown sugar
- 1 medium size yellow onion diced
- 2 tbsp. of Dijon mustard

Steps:

- Prepare the smoker to 250 degrees Fahrenheit (121 degrees Celsius). In a pan, combine the all of the liquid and beans. Molasses, brown sugar, Dijon mustard, barbecue sauce and apple cider vinegar should all be added at this point.

• Combine all ingredients in a mixing bowl. Put (one of the racks) on top of the pan. Start smoking for 3 hours, just until the sauce has hardened. After 3 hours, take it out and then serve.

5.3: Cheesy Split Pea with Mushrooms

Preparation Time: 15 minutes

Cooking Time: 35 minutes

Servings: 4

Ingredients:

• 2 tbsp. of olive oil

• 2 finely chopped carrot

• 9 cups of water

• ½ tsp. of dried thyme

• 3 cloves of garlic, finely chopped

• 1lb. of (454 g) Portobello mushrooms

• ⅓ cup of green Peas

• 1 onion (quartered)

• 3 tbsp. of parsley, chopped and fresh

• 2 tsp. of salt

• ¼ tsp. of black pepper

• 1 bay leaf

• 2 celery Ribs, finely chopped

• 6 tbsp. of grated parmesan cheese

Steps:

• In a blender pitcher, combine the garlic, oil and onion. Then press the ('sauté') option.

• Add the remaining of the ingredients, except the cheese and parsley, once they've been sautéed. And then pressing the ("hearty soup") icon.

• To serve, add soup in serving dishes and top with cheese and parsley.

5.4: Smoked Carrots and Potatoes Bowl

Preparation Time: 5 minutes

Cooking Time: 35 minutes

Servings: 6

Ingredients:

- 2 large size peeled and chopped carrots
- 5 tbsp. of olive oil
- Pepper and salt, as per your taste
- 2 large size Yukon Gold potatoes, wedged and peeled
- 5 tbsp. of balsamic vinegar

Steps:

- Preheat the grill to 400 degrees Fahrenheit (204 degrees Celsius). When cooking, use the wood pellets of your choice. Preheat for fifteen minutes with the lid closed.
- Toss all of the ingredients in a dish and coated the veggies with spice.
- Set on a foil-lined baking sheet.
- Arrange on the (grill grate) and cover with the lid. Cooking time is 30 minutes.

5.5: Baked Mayo Mushrooms

Preparation Time: 10 minutes

Cooking Time: 15 minutes

Servings: 8

Ingredients:

- 8 mushroom caps
- ½ cup of grated Parmesan cheese, grated
- Salt
- ¼ cup of mayonnaise
- Hot sauce
- Pinch of paprika

Steps:

- In a (baking pan), put the mushroom caps.
- In a mixing dish, combine the rest of the ingredients.
- Place the mushroom on top of the mixture.
- Preheat the grill and placed the (baking pan) on it.
- Preheat the (wood pellet grill) to 350°F (176°C) and cook for 15 minutes with the cap covered.
- You may also toss in some diced sausage to the batter.

5.6: Smoked Garlicky Brussels sprouts

Preparation Time: 5 minutes

Cooking Time: 45 minutes

Servings: 6

Ingredients:

- 2 cloves of garlic (minced)
- Sea salt and cracked black pepper
- 1-½ pounds of (680 g) Brussels sprouts
- 2 tbsp. of (extra-virgin) olive oil

Steps:

- Clean the sprouts by rinsing them.
- Cut the sprouts' brown bottoms and outer leaves.
- Put the sprouts in a large size mixing dish and drizzle with olive oil.
- Place it to the saucepan and then put salt, pepper and garlic.
- Fill the smoker's top rack with woodchips and water.
- Start smoking for 45 minutes just until temperature hits 250°F (121°C).
- Dish out

5.7: Grilled Mayo Street Corn

Preparation Time: 15 minutes

Cooking Time: 25 minutes

Servings: 6

Ingredients:

- 6 ears of corn on the cob, shucked
- Salt kosher and pepper, to taste
- 1 tbsp. of olive oil
- Salt kosher and pepper, to taste
- ¼ cup of mayo
- 1 tbsp. of garlic paste
- 6 ears of corn on the cob, shucked
- ¼ cup of sour cream
- ½ tbsp. of chili powder
- ½ cup of cotija cheese, crumbled
- 6 lime wedges
- Pinch of (ground) red pepper
- ¼ cup of cilantro, chopped

Steps:

- Drizzle some oil over the corn and season it with salt.
- Arrange the corn on a (wood pellet grill) heated to 350 degrees Fahrenheit (177 degrees Celsius). Cooked for 25 minutes, turning once or twice.
- Then, whisk together the garlic, mayonnaise, cream, red pepper and Chile till smooth.
- Removed the corn from the grill when it is done, set it aside for a few minutes, and then coat it with the mayonnaise.
- Sprinkle the cilantro, cotija cheese and more chili spice. Served with lime wedges on the side.

5.8: Roasted Fennel and Baby Carrots

Preparation Time: 5 minutes

Cooking Time: 30 minutes

Servings: 8

Ingredients:

- Salt, to taste
- 1-pound of (454 g) slender rainbow carrots, Peeled and washed
- 2 tbsp. of extra virgin olive oil
- 2 whole fennel bulbs, finely chopped

Steps:

- Preheat the grill to 500 degrees Fahrenheit (260 degrees Celsius). When cooking, use the wood pellets of your choice. Cook for 15 minutes with the lid closed.
- Toss all of the ingredients on a (sheet tray) with the spices and oil.
- Put on the (grill grate) for around 30 minutes to cook.

5.9: Cinnamon Spiced Root Vegetables

Preparation Time: 15 minutes

Cooking Time: 45 minutes

Servings: 6

Ingredients:

- 1 bunch of red beets, trimmed, peeled
- 1 bunch of golden beets, trimmed, peeled
- 1 large size peeled red onion
- 1 large yam, peeled
- 3 tbsp. of thyme leaves
- 3 tbsp. of olive oil
- 1 butternut squash, peeled
- 1 large size carrot, peeled

- Salt as required
- Ground black pepper as required
- 1 cinnamon stick
- 6 cloves of garlic, peeled
- 1 large parsnips, peeled
- 2 tbsp. of honey

Steps:

- Warm the grill by turning it on, (filling the grill hopper) with (hickory flavored wood pellets), using the (control panel) to turn it on, selecting 'smoke' on the temperature dial, or setting the temperature to 450 degrees F (232 degrees C) and letting it preheat for at least (15) minutes.

- In the meanwhile, chop all of the veggies into (1/2-inch pieces), put them in a large size mixing bowl, put the cinnamon, garlic and thyme, drizzle with oil, and stir to combine.

- Line a large (baking sheet) with foil, layer veggies on top, and (seasons) with pepper and salt.

- Once the grill has reached temperature, opening the cover, set the prepared cookie sheet on the (grill grate), close the grill, and smoked for around 45 minutes, or until the meat is cooked.

- Move the veggies to a serving dish, sprinkle with honey, and immediately serve.

5.10: Baked Crispy Kale Chips

Preparation Time: 5 minutes

Cooking Time: 45 minutes

Servings: 4

Ingredients:

- Olive oil as required
- 2 bunches kale, stems removed
- Pepper and Salt according to your taste

Steps:

- Preheat the grill to 350 degrees Fahrenheit (177 degrees Celsius). When cooking, use the wood pellets of your choice. Cook for 15 minutes with the lid closed.

- Toss all of the ingredients in a dish for coating the (kale with oil).

- Arrange the leaves on a baking pan and equally distribute them across the whole sheet.

- Grill for 30 minutes, just before the kale leaves are (crispy).

5.11: Mayo Cherry Pear Salad

Preparation Time: 5 minutes

Cooking Time: 0 minutes

Servings: 6

Ingredients:

- ¼ cup of mayonnaise

- ¼ cup of (shredded) sharp Cheddar cheese

- 1 (16-ounce / 454-g) can pear halves, drained

- 12 to 18 large iceberg lettuce leaves, dried and rinsed

- 6 cherries, fresh (pitted) or maraschino

Steps:

- Arrange (pear halves) on a platter, cutting side up. Fill the (cavity of each pear) with around 2 tbsp. of mayo.

- Toss the cheese on top of the mayo. A cherry should be placed on top of each one.

- Cover and (chill) the pears for minimum 3 hours.

- Before serving, put 2 to 3 lettuce leaves on a platter and top with the pear slices.

5.12: Moms Smoked Cheesy Mushrooms

Preparation Time: 10 minutes

Cooking Time: 1 hour 15 minutes

Servings: 12

Ingredients:

- ½ cup of parmesan cheese
- 12-16 white mushrooms, large, cleaned and stems removed
- 2 garlic cloves, minced
- Salt and pepper, to taste
- ½ cup of bread crumbs (Italian)
- ¼ -⅓ cup of olive oil
- 2 tbsp. of fresh chopped parsley

Steps:

- Preheat the oven to 375 degrees Fahrenheit (191 degrees Celsius). Trim the (bottom stem) of the mushroom and cut the remaining into tiny pieces.
- In a large size mixing bowl mix salt and pepper, bread crumbs, mushroom stems, garlic, parmesan cheese, parsley and 3 tbsp. of oil. Mix until everything is smooth.
- Arrange the mushrooms in a (disposable pan) and filled them (halfway) with the batter. More oil should be drizzled on top.
- Preheat the grill and put the pan on it. Cook for around 1 hour and 20 minutes, or until the mixture become browned and the mushrooms are soft.
- Take it out the pan from the oven and immediately serve.

5.13: Smoked Vegetables with Chicken Seasoning

Preparation Time: 10 minutes

Cooking Time: 35 minutes

Servings: 15

Ingredients:

- 1 yellow squash, sliced
- 1 ear corn, fresh, husks and silk strands removed
- 1 red onion (cut into wedges)

- 1 red pepper (cut into strips)

- 1 green pepper (cut into strips)

- 1 yellow pepper (cut into strips)

- 2 tbsp. of oil

- 1 cup of mushrooms, halved

- 2 tbsp. of chicken seasoning

Steps:

- (Soak the pecan wood pellets) for an hour in water before using. Cover the (smoker box) with the (wet pellets) that have been removed from the water.

- Close the cover on the (smoker box) and place it underneath the grill. Preheat the grill on high for 10 minutes, or just before the wood chips begin to smoke.

- On the meanwhile, combine the vegetables with the spices and oil before placing them in a (grill basket).

- Cook for 10 minutes, rotating halfway through. Enjoy your meal!

5.14: BBQ rubbed Cabbage Tomato Slaw

Preparation Time: 10 minutes

Cooking Time: 0 minutes

Serving: 12

Ingredients:

- 2 medium size diced sweet onions

- 2 small heads green cabbage, coarsely chopped

- 3 cups of mayonnaise

- 2 ripe tomatoes, diced

- Salt kosher

- Basic barbecue rub, optional

- Freshly ground black pepper

Steps:

• 	Mix together the onions, salt and pepper, cabbage, tomatoes and mayonnaise in a large size mixing bowl. Whisk until well combined. (You may make this (up to six hours ahead of time and keep it refrigerated)

• 	Just before serving pour the salt and mix the slaw.

• 	If required, serve with (basic barbecue rub).

5.15: Smoked Peppery Okra

Preparation Time: 5 minutes

Cooking Time: 30 minutes

Serving: 4

Ingredients:

• 	1 pound of (454 g) whole okra

• 	Nonstick cooking spray or butter, for greasing

• 	2 tbsp. of (extra-virgin) olive oil

• 	2 tsp. of freshly ground black pepper

• 	2 tsp. of seasoned salt

Steps:

• 	Fill your (smoker with wood pellets) and fire it up according to the package recommendations. Prepare the oven to 400 degrees Fahrenheit (204 degrees Celsius) and close the cover. Spray a small (rimmed baking sheet) with cooking spray and wrap it with (aluminum foil).

• 	Place the (okra) in a thin layer on the pan. Pour the olive oil over the top and flip to coat. Add pepper and salt and pepper on both sides.

• 	Set the baking tray on the (grill grate), cover, and smoked for 30 minutes, just before the bacon is slightly browned and crispy. Otherwise, bake for around 30 minutes in the microwave. Immediately serve.

5.16: Buttery Spaghetti Squash

Preparation Time: 15 minutes

Cooking Time: 40 minutes

Serving: 4

Ingredients:

- 1 spaghetti squash
- ½ tsp. of salt
- 2 tbsp. of (extra-virgin) olive oil
- 1 tsp. of (freshly ground) black pepper
- 4 tbsp. of (½ stick) unsalted butter
- 2 tsp. of garlic powder
- 4 tbsp. of (½ stick) unsalted butter
- ½ cup of white wine
- 2 tsp. of (chopped) fresh parsley
- 1 tbsp. of (minced) garlic
- 1 tsp. of red pepper flakes

Steps:

- (Wood pellets) should be used in your smoker, and the maker's instructions should be followed a distinct start-up technique. Heat the oven to 375°F and close the lid.
- Split the squash in (half lengthwise) after removing both ends. Scrape out the seeds and toss them away.
- Pour the olive oil into the (squash flesh) and season with a pinch of garlic powder, and a pinch of salt.
- Close the cover and smoke the (squash cut-side up on the grill grate for around 40 minutes, just until vegetables are soft
- The Sauce
- Mix the white wine, butter, minced garlic, pepper and salt, parsley and red pepper flakes in a medium size saucepan at medium flame and (simmer) for approximately 5 minutes, or until cooked fully.
- Let the sauce hot by reducing the heat to low.
- Take out the squash from the (grill) and set aside to cool (slightly) before shredded with a (fork) and discarding the (skin).

- Toss the (shredded squash) into the (garlic-wine butter sauce) just before serving.

5.17: Simple Zucchini Ratatouille Salad

Preparation Time: 10 minutes

Cooking Time: 25 minutes

Serving: 6

Ingredients:

- 1 whole diced red onion
- 1 whole squash
- 1 whole zucchini
- 1 large size diced tomato
- Pepper and salt, as required
- 1 whole sweet potato
- Vegetable oil, as required

Steps:

- Heat the grill at high temperature for around 10-15 minutes with the (lid) covered. Thinly slice all veggies to a thickness of (1/4 inches).
- Drizzle a little oil over each veggie and top with pepper and salt or Veggie Shake.
- Arrange zucchini, sweet potato, onion, and squash on (grill grate) and cook for 20 minutes, (turning halfway through), or until cooked.
- Put some the tomato slices on the (grill) for the (last) remaining 5 minutes.
- Arrange the veggies in a vertical layer for presentation.

5.18: Brussels sprouts with Chipotle Butter

Preparation Time: 10 minutes

Cooking Time: 45 minutes

Serving: 6

Ingredients:

- ¼ cup of (extra-virgin) olive oil
- 1 tbsp. of packed brown sugar
- 16 to 20 long toothpicks
- 2 tsp. (minced) garlic
- ½ pound (227 g) of bacon (cut in half)
- 1 tbsp. of Cajun seasoning
- 1 pound (454 g) of Brussels sprouts, trimmed and wilted, leaves removed
- ¼ cup of balsamic vinegar
- ¼ cup of (chopped) fresh cilantro

Steps:

- Soaking the (toothpicks) for 15 minutes in water.
- Fill your (smoker) with wood pellets and fire it up according to the package recommendations. Preheat the oven to 300°F (145°C) and cover it.
- Fold a (half piece of bacon around each Brussels sprout) and fix with a toothpick.
- Mix the Cajun spices and brown sugar in a small size mixing bowl. Roll each (wrapped Brussels sprout) in the (sweet rub) to cover it completely.
- Put the sprouts on the (grill grate) on a (parchment paper–lined baking sheet), covered, and (smoke) for around 45 minutes to 1 hour, flipping as required, until uniformly cooked and the bacon is crunchy.
- Combine the olive oil, balsamic vinegar, garlic and cilantro garlic in a small mixing bowl.
- Take out the toothpicks from the (Brussels sprouts) and place them on a platter with the (cilantro-balsamic sauce poured) on top.

5.19: Veggie Seasoned Grilled Vegetables

Preparation Time: 5 minutes

Cooking Time: 15 minutes

Serving: 8

Ingredients:

- 1 veggie tray
- 2 tbsp. of veggie seasoning
- ¼ cup of vegetable oil

Steps:

- Set the (wood pellet grill) to 375 degrees Fahrenheit (191 degrees Celsius).
- Put the veggies in the oil and spread them out on a (baking sheet).
- Season with (vegetable spice) and cook on a hot grill.
- Cook for around 15 minutes on the (grill), or until the vegetables are soft.
- Set aside to cool before serving.

5.20: Instant Potato Wedges

Preparation Time: 5 minutes
Cooking Time: 30 minutes
Serving: 8
Ingredients:

- 1 tbsp. of olive oil
- Pepper and salt, to taste
- 5 potatoes, sliced into planks
- 1 tsp. of onion powder

Steps:

- Preheat the (wood pellet grill) to high temperature.
- While the lid is closed, warm it for 15 minutes.
- Drizzle some oil over the potatoes.
- Season with onion powder and salt and pepper.
- Cook the potatoes for around 15 minutes on the grill.

5.21: Canola oil Smoked Mushrooms

Preparation Time: 10 minutes

Cooking Time: 45 minutes

Serving: 5

Ingredients:

- 1 tbsp. of canola oil
- 4 cups of Portobello, (whole and cleaned)
- 1 tbsp. of onion powder
- 1 tbsp. of salt
- 1 tbsp. of granulated garlic
- 1 tbsp. of pepper

Steps:

- Combine all of the (ingredients) in a large size dish and stir thoroughly.
- Preheat the (wood pellet grill) to 180°F (82°C), then put the mushrooms on the (grill) immediately.
- Cook the mushrooms for around 30 minutes after they've been smoked.
- Raise the heat to high and cooked the mushrooms for a few minutes.
- Finally, enjoy and serve.

5.22: Smoked Beans and Dijon Mustard Salad

Preparation Time: 10 minutes

Cooking Time: 20 minutes

Serving: 6

Ingredients:

- 2 tbsp. of olive oil
- 1 can of Great Northern Beans, drained and rinsed
- 1 pound of (454 g) fresh green beans, trimmed
- 1 can of Red Kidney Beans, drained and rinsed
- 1 shallot (sliced thinly)
- 1 tsp. of Dijon mustard
- 2 tbsp. of red wine vinegar

- Paper and salt, according to your taste

Steps:

- Preheat the (grill) to 500°F (260°C) and cook with appropriate wood pellets. Warm for 15 minutes and closed the lid.

- Pour olive oil over the beans and spread them out on a baking sheet. To taste, (season) with pepper and salt.

- Put it on the (grill) for around 20 minutes to cook. When the beans are done, take them from the pot and set them in a dish. Allow time for cooling.

- Combine the other (ingredients) and shallots in a mixing bowl. If needed, add extra salt and pepper. Mix the beans in the (seasoning) to evenly coat them.

5.23: Thyme spiced Cherry Tomato Skewers

Preparation Time: 10 minutes

Cooking Time: 50 minutes

Serving: 4

Ingredients:

- ¼ cup of olive oil
- 2 tbsp. of chives, (finely chopped)
- 1 tsp. of salt kosher
- 24 cherry tomatoes
- 3 tbsp. of balsamic vinegar
- 1 tbsp. of fresh thyme, (finely chopped)
- 4 cloves of (minced) garlic
- 1 tsp. of ground black pepper
- 1 tsp. of salt kosher

Steps:

- Set the (pellet grill) to 425 degrees Fahrenheit (218 degrees Celsius).

- Combine garlic, olive oil, thyme and balsamic vinegar in a medium-sized mixing bowl. Toss in the tomatoes for coating.

- Allow tomatoes to soak in the marinade for 30 minutes (at room temperature).

- Take the tomatoes out of the (marinade) and (thread) four tomatoes onto each skewer.

- (Season) each skewer with ground pepper and salt kosher on both sides.

- Set on (grill grate) and cook for around 3 minutes on each side, or until browned on both sides.

- Removed (from the grill) and let aside to rest for 5 minutes. Serve with chives as a garnish, and enjoy!

5.24: Smoked Veggies with Mushroom

Preparation Time: 10 minutes

Cooking Time: 30 minutes

Serving: 6

Ingredients:

- 1 medium size yellow squash, (½-inch slices)
- 1 ear fresh corn,
- 2 tbsp. of vegetable oil
- 1 small size red bell pepper, (1-inch strips)
- 1 small size red onion, thin wedges
- 1 cup of pecan wood chips
- Vegetable seasonings
- 1 small size green bell pepper, (1-inch strips)
- 1 cup of mushrooms, halved
- 1 small size yellow bell pepper, (1-inch strips)

Steps:

- Place all of the veggies in a large size mixing bowl and mix well. Season it with pepper and salt, then toss it with all of the veggies.

- Fill the smoker with water and wood chips.

- Set the smoker for ten minutes at 100 degrees Fahrenheit (37 degrees Celsius).

- Place the veggies in a pan on the (electric smoker's middle rack).

- Smoked the vegetable for around thirty minutes, or until it is soft.

- Once everything is ready, present and have fun.

5.25: Cinnamon Smoked Acorn Squash

Preparation Time: 10 minutes
Cooking Time: 2 hours
Serving: 6
Ingredients:
- 3 tbsp. of olive oil
- 3 acorn squashes, halved and seeded
- ¼ cup of brown sugar
- ¼ cup of unsalted butter, unsalted
- 1 tbsp. of chili powder
- 1 tbsp. of ground cinnamon, ground
- 1 tbsp. of ground nutmeg

Steps:
- Rub the cut sides of the squash with (olive oil) and wrap in foil, (poking holes in the foil) to allow smoke and steam to escape.
- Set the oven to 225 degrees Fahrenheit (107 degrees Celsius).
- Arrange the (squash halves cut side down on the grill) and cook for 1 1/2- 2 hours. Take out the steaks (from the grill).
- Leave it to cool while you make the spiced butter. In a pan, melted the butter, then adding the sugar and spices, tossing to incorporate.
- Take out the (squash halves) from the foil.
- Spread 1 tbsp. of the (butter mixture) on each side.
- Finally, enjoy and serve!

5.26: Citrusy Grilled Fingerling Potato Salad

Preparation Time: 10 minutes
Cooking Time: 15 minutes

Serving: 8

Ingredients:

- 1 small jalapeno, sliced
- 2 tsp. of salt
- 1 ½ pound of (680 g) fingerling potatoes
- 10 scallions
- 2 tbsp. of rice vinegar
- ½ cup of olive oil, divided
- 2 tsp. of lemon juice

Steps:

- Warm the grill by turning it on, filling the (hopper with pecan-flavored wood pellets), using the (control panel) to turn it on, selecting 'smoke' on the (temperature dial), or setting the temperature to 450 degrees F (232 degrees C) and letting it warm for at least 5 minutes.

- In the meanwhile, ready the scallions by brushing them with oil.

- Once the grill has reached temperature, remove the lid, set the scallions on the (grill grate), close the grill, and cook for around 3 minutes, or until lightly browned.

- Then move the scallions to a chopping board, put aside for 5 minutes to cool before cutting into slices.

- Spray potatoes with oil, sprinkle black pepper and salt, put on (grill grate), close grill, and (smoke) for 5 minutes, or until potatoes are well cooked.

- Poured oil into a large size mixing bowl, add the lime juice, vinegar and salt and toss to blend.

- Toss in the potatoes and grilled scallion until thoroughly combined, and serve immediately.

5.27: Smoked Cheesy Tomato Dip

Preparation Time: 15 minutes

Cooking Time: 1 hour

Serving: 4

Ingredients:

- 8 ounces (227 g) Colby shredded cheese
- 1 cup of sour cream
- 8 ounces (227 g) smoked shredded mozzarella cheese
- ½ cup of parmesan cheese, grated
- 1 cup of sun-dried tomatoes
- 1 tsp. of (fresh ground) pepper
- 1 and ½ tsp. of salt
- 1 tsp. of (dried) basil
- 1 tsp. of red pepper flakes
- 1 tsp. of (dried) oregano
- 1 clove of garlic (minced)
- French toast, serving
- ½ tsp. of onion powder

Steps:

- Prepare your smoker to 275 degrees Fahrenheit (135 degrees Celsius) and fill it with your favorite wood.
- Combine the salt, pepper, garlic, basil, onion powder, cheeses, tomatoes, oregano and red pepper flakes in a large mixing bowl.
- Pour the solution to a (small metal pan) and smoke it. Smoking time is 1 hour.
- Toss with (toasted French bread) before serving.

5.28: Grilled Mayo Lettuce Salad

Preparation Time: 10 minutes

Cooking Time: 20 minutes

Serving: 6

Ingredients:

- 2 cloves of garlic (minced)
- ¼ cup of (extra virgin) olive oil
- 1 tsp. of Dijon mustard

- Pepper and salt according to your taste
- 1 cup of mayonnaise
- 2 head Romaine lettuce
- Croutons, optional
- ¼ cup of parmesan cheese

Steps:

- Whisk together the mayo, garlic, olive oil and mustard in a small size mixing bowl. Add the salt according to your taste. Combine all (ingredients) and put aside.

- Halve the (Romaine lengthwise), keeping the ends uncut to prevent it (from falling apart).

- Preheat the (grill) to 400 degrees Fahrenheit (204 degrees Celsius). While cooking, use the (wood pellets) of your choice. Warm for 15 minutes with the top closed.

- Rub the cut side of the (Romaine lettuce) with oil and set it on the (grill grate). Cooked for 5 minutes in the oven.

- Once the lettuce is done, cut it and arrange it in a dish. Combine the croutons, salad dressing and parmesan cheese in a mixing bowl.

5.29: Crispy Cayenne spiced Sweet Potato Chips

Preparation Time: 10 minutes

Cooking Time: 40 minutes

Serving: 3

Ingredients:

- 2 sweet potatoes
- 1 tbsp. of cornstarch
- 1 quart warm water
- ¼ cup of (extra-virgin) olive oil
- 1 tbsp. of (packed) brown sugar
- 1 tbsp. of salt
- 1 tsp. of (ground) cinnamon

- ½ tsp. of cayenne pepper
- 1 tsp. of (freshly ground) black pepper

Steps:

- Slice thinly the (sweet potatoes) on a (mandolin). In a large size mixing bowl, combine the potato pieces, warm water and 1 tbsp. of cornstarch. Allow 15 to 20 minutes to (soak).
- Fill your smoker with (wood pellets) and fire it up according to the package recommendations. Set the oven to 375°F (191° C) and closed the lid.
- Peel the (potato slices) and place them in a (single layer) on a perforated pizza pan or an (aluminum foil-lined baking tray). Spray the olive oil on both ends of the potato pieces.
- Combine the cinnamon, salt, black pepper, cayenne paper, brown sugar and the remaining 2 tbsp. of (cornstarch) in a small size dish. Season all sides of the potatoes with this spice mix.
- Put the baking sheet or pan on the (grill grate), shut the lid, and smoked for 35 to 45 minutes, until the chips become crispy, turning after 20 minutes. Keep the (container) sealed.

5.30: Perfectly Smoked Artichoke Hearts

Preparation Time: 10 minutes

Cooking Time: 2 hours

Servings: 6

Ingredients:

- 1/4 cup of (extra virgin) olive oil
- 4 cloves of (minced) garlic
- 2 tbsp. of fresh parsley (finely chopped)
- 12 canned whole artichoke hearts
- 1 tbsp. of fresh lemon juice freshly squeezed
- Lemon for garnish
- Salt according to your taste

Steps:

- Preheat the (Smoke Temperature) to 350°F for about 10 to 15 minutes and cover it.
- Mix the other (ingredients) in a bowl and dump over the (artichokes).
- Grill the (artichokes) for about 2 hours on a (grill rack).
- Serve immediately with a drizzle of lemon halves and (extra virgin) olive oil.

5.31: Finely Smoked Russet Potatoes

Preparation Time: 15 minutes

Cooking Time: 2 hours

Servings: 6

Ingredients:

- 8 (large size) russet potatoes
- Salt kosher and black pepper to taste
- 1/2 cup of garlic-infused olive oil

Steps:

- Set the (Smoke Temperature) to (225°F) for 10 to 15 minutes and close the lid.
- Wash and clean your potatoes, then stab them all over with help of fork.
- Sprinkle with (garlic-infused olive oil) and season all of the potatoes thoroughly with pepper and salt.
- Shut the cover of (pellet smoker) and put the potatoes inside.
- Grill the potatoes for 2 hours.
- Serve immediately with your preferred dressing.

5.32: Simple Smoked Green Cabbage (Pellet)

Preparation Time: 10 minutes

Cooking Time: 45 minutes

Servings: 4

Ingredients:

- 1 (medium head) of green cabbage
- Salt and (ground) white pepper to taste
- 1/2 cup of olive oil

Steps:

- Adjust the Smoke Temperature to 250°F and warm for 10 to 15 minutes and close the lid.
- Clean the cabbage by rinsing it (under) water.
- Slice the (stems) in halve, then each portion into two to three slices.
- Pour olive oil over cabbage and sprinkle (liberally) with white ground pepper and salt.
- Place the (cabbage leaves) on a smoker dish, and cover it.
- Cook the cabbage for 20 minutes (each side) in the smoker.
- Take out the (cabbage) and set it aside to cool for 5 minutes.
- Immediately serve.

5.33: Smoked Corn Cob with Spicy Rub

Preparation Time: 40 minutes

Cooking Time: 1 hour

Servings: 4

Ingredients:

- 1/2 cup of macadamia nut oil
- 1/2 tsp. of garlic powder
- 10 ears of fresh sweet corn on the cob
- 1/2 tsp. of hot paprika flakes
- 1/4 tsp. of ground mustard
- 1/2 tsp. of dried parsley
- Kosher salt and fresh ground black pepper according to your taste

Steps:

- Preheat the (Smoke Temperature) to 350°F for 10 to 15 minutes and close the lid.

- Mix spicy paprika flakes crushed mustard, dry parsley, garlic powder and with (macadamia nut oil).

- Arrange your corn on a (grill rack) and brush it with the (macadamia nut oil) mixture.

- Corn should be smoked for around 80 to 90 minutes.

- Serve immediately.

5.34: Smoked Sweet Pie Pumpkins

Preparation Time: 10 minutes

Cooking Time: 2 hours

Servings: 6

Ingredients:

- Avocado oil to taste

- 4 small pie pumpkins

Steps:

- Pre heat the (Smoke Temperature) to 250°F and warm for 10 to 15 minutes and cover the lid.

- Pumpkins should be cut in half from start to end and drizzled with avocado oil.

- Arrange the pumpkin on the grill.

- Cook the pumpkins for around 2 hours

- Removed the (smoked pumpkins) from the oven and set aside to cool.

- Present with pepper and salt.

5.35: Smoked Vegetable "Potpourri" (Pellet)

Preparation Time: 15 minutes

Cooking Time: 1 hour

183

Servings: 6

Ingredients:

- 1/2 cup of olive oil
- 2 Russet potatoes (sliced)
- 2 large zucchinis (sliced)
- 1 red onion (sliced)
- 2 red bell peppers (sliced)
- Salt and ground black pepper according to your taste

Steps:

- Pre heat the (Smoke Temperature) to 350°F for 10 to 15 minutes and cover the lid.
- Meanwhile, clean and cut all veggies, and then dry with paper towels.
- Add pepper and salt for seasoning, then sprinkle with olive oil.
- Grill your sliced veggies for around 40 to 45 minutes on a barbecue rack or on a barbecue basket.
- Serve immediately.

5.36: Smoked Asparagus with Parsley and Garlic

Preparation Time: 10 minutes

Cooking Time: 1 hour

Servings: 3

Ingredients:

- 1 tbsp. of (finely chopped) parsley
- 1 bunch of fresh asparagus, cleaned
- Salt and (ground) black pepper to taste
- 1/2 cup of olive oil
- 1 tbsp. of (minced) garlic

Steps:

- Preheat the (Smoke Temperature) to 225°F for 10 to 15 minutes and cover the lid.

- Remove the ends of the asparagus and wash it.
- Mix minced garlic, chopped parsley, olive oil, and salt & pepper in a baking dish.
- Sprinkle your asparagus with a combination of salt and pepper and olive oil.
- Wrap the edges of a (heavy-duty foil) over the asparagus.
- Cook for around 55 to 60 minutes, or until the meat is tender (turn every 15 minutes).
- Serve immediately.

Chapter 6: Chicken Recipes

6.1: Zesty Chile Cilantro Lime Chicken Wings

Preparation time: 60 minutes

Cooking time: 20 minutes

Servings: 4

Ingredients:

- 2 lbs. split chicken wings
- 1 tsp ancho chili powder
- 2 tsp (blackened sriracha rub) spice
- 2 tbsp. chopped cilantro, divided
- 1 tsp of cumin

- 1 lime (zest and juice)
- 1 1/2 tbsp. extra virgin olive oil

Steps:

- Combine 1 tbsp. of cilantro, olive oil, lime juice and zest, cumin blackened sriracha, ancho chili powder in a medium mixing bowl.
- Combine chicken wings and cilantro mixture in a resalable gallon bag. Place in the refrigerator for 1 hour to marinate, turning periodically.
- Preheat the pit boss platinum range kc combination to 350 degrees Fahrenheit. Set the grill to medium heat when you're using a charcoal grill or gas.
- Remove the hot wings from the marinate and cook over indirect heat on the grill. 15 to 18 minutes on the grill, flipping and twisting every 3 to 5 minutes.
- Remove the (chicken wings) from the grill and serve warm, garnished with the remaining cilantro.

6.2: Bacon-Wrapped Stuffed Chicken Breasts

Preparation Time: 30 minutes

Cooking Time: 270 minutes

Servings: 4 - 6

Ingredients:

- 5 oz. of frozen spinach, thawed and strained
- 8 bacon pieces
- 1 tbsp. of butter
- 4 boneless, skinless, butterflied chicken breasts
- 2 garlic cloves, minced
- 1 cup shredded Italian cheese mix
- 8 oz. of thinly sliced mushrooms
- 1 tbsp. of olive oil
- 1 tbsp. of (pit boss hickory bacon) seasoning
- 1 yellow onion, diced

Steps:

- Preheat the Pit Boss KC Combo to 375°F on both the grill and the griddle. Set the grill to medium heat if using a gas or charcoal grill. Heat (cast iron skillet) on grill grates for all other grills.

- On a griddle, heat the butter and olive oil, add the (mushrooms) and cook for 3 minutes, turning regularly. Cook for 2 minutes after adding the chopped onion and garlic. Add the spinach and cook for a further minute before transferring the veggies to a heat-safe dish to cool somewhat.

- Season both sides of the chicken breasts with (Hickory) Bacon. Half of the cheese should be sprinkled over each (butterflied chicken breast), followed by the sautéed veggies and the remaining cheese.

- Arrange two bacon pieces on a sheet metal tray. Fold the (chicken breast) halves together gently and put on top of the bacon pieces, then wrap firmly with bacon. To keep it together, tuck the ends of the bacon beneath or use a toothpick. Carry on with the remaining breasts in the same manner.

- Place the chicken breasts directly on the grilled grate with the bacon seam down and cook, rotating once or again, unless the bacon is crunchy and golden brown, approximately 25 to 30 minutes, or unless the temperature reaches 165°F.

- Remove from the grill, set aside for 5 minutes to rest, then remove any toothpicks and serve hot.

6.3: Bossin' Buffalo Chicken Wings

Preparation Time: 10 minutes

Cooking Time: 25 minutes

Servings: 4-6

Ingredients:

- 2 lbs. chicken wings
- ½ cup (pit boss sweet heat rub)
- Bleu cheese dip
- 2/3 cup buffalo sauce
- Celery

Steps:

• Preheat your Pit Boss to 450 degrees Fahrenheit. Set the grill to high heat if using a gas or charcoal grill.

• Generously coat wings with (Pit Boss Sweet Heat Rub) and place on wing rack.

• Cooked for 20 minutes on the grill, turning every 10 minutes.

• Brush with the sauce, then covered and cook for another 5-7 minutes. Note that the amount of time it takes to cook the wings can depend on their size. When done, the interior temperature of the wings should be 165°F.

• Remove the wings from the grill and place them on a baking sheet to cool for approximately 5 minutes.

• Toss the wings with the (Buffalo Sauce) in a large mixing dish. To mix, lightly shake the dish or use a spoon to coat all of the wings.

• Garnish with celery, additional sauce, and (bleu cheese dip) while still hot.

6.4: Cajun Patch Cock Chicken

Preparation time: 30 minutes

Cooking time: 2.5 hours

Servings: 4

Ingredients:

• 4-6 glasses additional virgin olive oil

• 4-5 pounds new or frozen chicken

• 4 tbsp. of Cajun spice lab

• Lucile's bloody Mary mix seasoning (Cajun hot, dry herb) mix

Steps:

• Place the chicken breast, chest down, on a cutting board. Cut down the side of the spine using cooking or chicken scissors and remove.

• To flatten the chicken's breast, flip it over and push down hard. Then, remove the skin from the breast, thighs, and drumsticks with care.

• Olive oil may be rubbed freely beneath and on the surface. Season the chicken on all sides and rub the seasoning into the flesh under the skin. Cover the poultry in aluminum foil and refrigerate for 3 hours to soak up the flavor.

- Recommended (Wood Pellet Smokers and Grills) are used. Set up a Smoke grill for indirect cooking using pecan pellets, hickory, or a combination of the two, and warm to 225 degrees F. Place the probes into the thickest portion of the breast if the device has a Smoked Level chicken probe input, such as a MAK Grills 2 Star. Allow 1.5 hours for the chicken to cook.

- Increase the (pit Smoke Temperature) to 375 ° F after one and a half hours at 225 ° F and roast until the thickest portion of the breast reaches 170 ° F and the thighs reach at least 180 ° F. Before cutting, cover the chicken with a loosely aluminum tent for 15 minutes.

6.5: Teriyaki Smoked Drumstick

Preparation time: 15 minutes (more marinade overnight)

Cooking time: 1.5 hours to 2 hours

Servings: 4

Ingredients:

- Teriyaki marinade and cooking sauce like Yoshida's original gourmet 3 cup

- Garlic in powder form 1 tsp

- Poultry seasoning 3 tsp

- Chicken drumsticks 10

Steps:

- Combine the marinade and cooking sauce in a medium mixing bowl with the chicken spice and garlic powder. To help the marinade penetrate the drumstick, peel off the skin.

- Place the (drumstick) in a marinade pan or a 1-gallon plastic sealable bag, and pour in the marinated ingredients. Refrigerate for at least one night.

- In the morning, rotate the chicken leg. For indirect cooking, set up a smoking barbecue. Put the skin on the drumstick and place it on a chicken thigh and wings racks to soak the baking sheet on the counter while the grill heats up.

- If you don't have a chicken leg and feather rack, tap the drumstick with a paper towel to dry it.

- Use hickory or maple pellets to preheat the smoker grill to 180 degrees F. For 1 hour, marinate the chicken leg.

- Grill the drumstick for another 30-45 minutes, or until the thickest portion of the stick achieves an inner Smoke Temperature of 180 ° F, after raising the whole Smoked Temperature to 350 ° F after 1 hour.

- Before serving, cover the chicken drumsticks with a loose aluminum tent for 15 minutes.

6.6: Smoked Bone In-Turkey Breast:

Preparation time: 20 minutes

Cooking time: 3-4 hours

Servings: 6-8

Ingredients:

- Extra virgin olive oil (6 tbsp.)

- Yang original dry lab or poultry spices (5)

- 1 (8-10 pound) boned turkey breast

Steps:

- Remove the skin and extra fat from the turkey breast. Then, remove the skin from the chest with care and let it alone.

- Olive oil should be used on the chest, beneath the skin, and on the surface. Carefully rub or season underneath the chest cavity, beneath the skin, and on the skin.

- To make it easier to handle, put the turkey breast on a V-rack or straight on a grilled grate with the chest up.

- Preheat the Smoker grill and leave the turkey breast on the countertop at room Smoke Temperature.

- Preheat a Smoker grill for indirectly cooking to 225 degrees Fahrenheit use hickory or pecan pellets. Smoked the (boned turkey breast) on a V rack or the grill for 2 hours at 225°F.

- Increase the (pit Smoke Temperature) to 325 ° F after 2 hours of hickory smoke. Roast until the juices are clear and the thickest portion of the chicken breast achieves an inner Smoke Temp of 170 ° F.

- Place a loose foil tent over the hickory-smoked chicken breast for 20 minutes, then brush the grain.

6.7: Smoked Whole Duck

Preparation Time: 15 minutes

Cooking Time: 2 hours 30 minutes

Servings: 6

Ingredients:

- Whole duck 5 pounds.
- Onion small (1)
- 1 wedged apple
- 1 quartered orange
- 1 tbsp. of finely chopped parsley
- 1 tbsp. of freshly chopped sage
- ½ tsp of onion powder
- 2 tsp of smoked paprika
- Dried Italian spice (1 tsp)
- Dried Greek seasoning (1 tbsp.)
- Pepper 1 tsp
- Sea salt 1 tsp

Steps:

- After removing the giblets, clean the duck from the inside with cool running water.
- Pat dry with paper towels. With the edge of a sharp knife, cut the (duck) skin all over. Make careful you don't pierce the skin.
- Tie the duck thighs together with butcher's thread.
- To make the rub, combine the pepper, Greek spice, onion powder, salt, Italian seasoning, and paprika in a mixing bowl.
- Put the onion, orange and apple in the duck's cavity. Finely chopped parsley and sage should be stuffed into the duck. Apply a thick layer of the rubs mixture on both sides of the duck.
- Switch to smoke mode on your pellet grills and let the head open till the fire starts to burn. Then, warm the grill to 325°F with the cover closed for 10 minutes.

- Place the (duck) on the grill grate. Roasting for 2 to 2 ½ hours, and until the surface of the duck is brown, and the internal temperature of the thigh smoke reaches 160°F.

- Remove the (duck) from the heat and place it on a cooling rack. Slice into proper sizes to serve.

6.8: Chicken Tenders

Preparation Time: 10 minutes

Cooking Time: 8 minutes

Servings: 6

Ingredients:

- Six pieces of chicken tenders
- ¼ tsp garlic granules (not garlic powder)
- ¼ tsp pepper
- 1 tsp of paprika powder
- ½ tsp of kosher salt
- 1 tbsp. of extra virgin olive oil
- 1 tbsp. of juice of a lemon
- 1 tsp seasoning (Italian)
- 1 tbsp. of parsley, chopped

Steps:

- Mix the salt, pepper, garlic, lemon, Italian seasoning, and paprika in a large mixing dish. Toss in the chicken tenders to mix.

- Freeze for 1 hour after covering the bowl. Erase the chicken wings from the marinate and set aside to settle for 1 hour, or until room temperature.

- Using paper towels, pat dry Preheat your grill to 450°F and set it up for direct smoking. Grill the chicken tenders for 8 minutes, 4 minutes per side, on the grill.

- Take the tenders off the grill and set them aside. Serve with fresh chopped parsley as a garnish.

6.9: Thanksgiving Turkey

Preparation Time: 15 minutes

Cooking Time: 4 hours

Servings: 12

Ingredients:

- 2 cups melted butter
- 1 tbsp. of cracked black pepper
- Salt (kosher)
- 2 tbsp. of rosemary freshly chopped
- 2 tbsp. of parsley freshly chopped
- 2 tbsp. of freshly chopped sage
- 2 tsp of dried thyme (minced)
- 1 turkey (18 pounds)

Steps:

- Mix the sage, butter, thyme, 1 tsp black pepper, rosemary, 1 tsp salt, parsley, and garlic in a mixing dish.
- Peel the skin from the (turkey) with your fingertips.
- Rub the butter mixture underneath the bird skin as well as all over the turkey.
- Season the turkey liberally with the herb mixture.
- Heat the griddle to 300°F for 15 minutes with the lid covered.
- Put the (turkey) on the grill and cook for 4 hours, just until the internal temperature of the turkey thigh reaches 160°F.
- Take the turkey off the grill and set it aside for a few minutes to rest.
- Cut into serving sizes.

6.10: Spatchcock Smoked Turkey

Preparation Time: 15 minutes

Cooking Time: 4 hours 30 minutes

Servings: 12

Ingredients:

- 1 (18 pounds) turkey

- 2 tbsp. of parsley finely chopped fresh

- 1 tbsp. of finely chopped fresh rosemary

- 2 tbsp. of thyme finely chopped fresh

- ½ cup butter (melted)

- 1 tsp of garlic powder

- 1 tsp of onion powder

- 1 tsp powdered black pepper

- 2 tsp salt or to taste

- 2 tbsp. of finely chopped scallions

Steps:

- Remove the giblets from the turkey and rinse it thoroughly under cold running water, inside and out.

- Place the turkey breast side down on a work surface. To remove the turkey backbone, slice the turkeys on both sides of the backbone with a poultry shear.

- Turn the turkey over to the reverse side. Now flatten the turkey by pressing it down.

- Mix the parsley, rosemary, scallions, thyme, butter, pepper, salt, garlic, and onion powder in a mixing dish.

- Rub the butter mixture all over the turkey.

- Prepare your grilled to HIGH (450°F) for 15 minutes with the lid closed.

- Cook the turkey for 30 minutes straightly on the grill grate. Cook for an extra 4 hours, or until the inner Smoke Temperature of the widest part of the thigh reaches 165°F. Lower (Preferred Wood Pellet) to 300°F and continue to cook for 4 hours, or until the inner Smoke Temperature of the thickest portion of the thigh reaches 165°F.

- Take the turkey off the griddle and let it aside for a few minutes to rest.

- Cut into bite-size pieces and serve.

6.11: Smoked chicken leg quarters

Preparation Time: 15 minutes

Cooking Time: 2 hours

Servings: 8

Ingredients:

- Eight-piece of chicken leg quarters
- 2 tbsp. of olive oil
- 1 tsp. salt or to taste
- ½ tsp. of chili in powder form
- ½ tsp. of paprika
- ½ tsp. of chopped thyme
- 1 tsp. of dried rosemary
- ½ tsp. of cayenne pepper
- 1 tsp. of garlic powder
- 1 tsp. of onion powder

Steps:

- Merge garlic, chili, cayenne, salt, rosemary, onion powder, paprika and thyme to make the rub.
- Sprinkle oil over the chicken thigh quarters and liberally season with the rub mix.
- Utilizing apple Hard Wood pellets, preheat the skillet to 180°F with the lid closed for 15 minutes.
- Place the chicken on the grill grate in a single layer. One hour of smoking, flipping halfway through.
- Raise the grill's fume temperature to 350 degrees Fahrenheit. Fry for an extra 1 hour, or until the chicken quarters' Smoke Temperature reaches 165°F.
- Remove the chicken from the grill and set it aside to rest for 15 minutes.
- Serve and have fun.

6.12: Chicken Fajitas

Preparation Time: 10 minutes

Cooking Time: 20 minutes

Servings: 4

Ingredients:

- 2 pounds of chicken breast
- 1 big onion (chopped)
- Two celery stalks (chopped)
- One big red bell pepper (chopped)
- One big orange bell pepper (chopped)
- Lemon juice 2 tbsp.
- One green bell pepper (minced)
- 2 tsp of cumin
- 2 tsp of chili powder
- 1 tsp brown sugar
- ½ tsp of paprika powder
- 1 tbsp. of extra virgin olive oil
- Salt
- ½ tsp of powdered black pepper

Steps:

- Stir the cumin, lime juice, salt, black pepper, paprika, and sugar in a large mixing basin. Toss in the chicken breasts to mix. Refrigerate for 1 hour after covering the dish tightly with aluminum foil.

- Erase the chicken from the marinade and set it aside to rest for 1 hour or until it reaches room temperature.

- Set your skillet too high for 15 minutes with the lid closed.

- Pour the oil into a skillet and place it on the grill grate.

- Add the red bell pepper, onion, orange pepper, celery and green bell pepper to the heated oil. Cook until the vegetables are soft.

- Turn off the heat and cover the skillet to keep the vegetables warm.

- Place the chicken breasts on the grill grate in a single layer. Cook for 10 seconds, 6 mins, or until the chicken breasts' internal Smoke Temperature reaches 165°F. Remove the chicken from the fire and set it aside to cool.

- Thinly slice the chicken breast.

- Toss with the tortilla and sautéed vegetables.

6.13: Lemon Garlic Smoked Chicken

Preparation Time: 20 minutes

Cooking Time: 3 Hours 10 Minutes

Servings: 10 servings

Ingredients:

- Whole Chicken (3-lbs., 1.4-kg.)
- The Brine
- Salt – ½ cup
- Brown sugar – 1 cup
- Water – 3 ½ liters
- The Rub
- Minced garlic – ¼ cup
- Garlic powder – 2 (tbsp.)
- Three tbs. of lime juice
- Paprika powder– 2 ½ tbsp.
- 2 (tbsp.) of chili powder.
- ¾ tbsp. of thyme
- Cayenne – 2 tbsp.
- Salt – 1 tbsp.
- 2 tbsp. Of black pepper.
- Five cloves of garlic
- The Filling
- One cup of chopped onion.
- Five sprigs of thyme.

Steps:

- Toss in the salt and brown sugar with the water and stir until well dissolved.
- Soak the poultry in the brine for 24 hours. Then, refrigerate to keep things healthy.

- Take the chicken out of the fridge the following day, wash it, and allow it to dry. Remove from the equation.

- In a mixing bowl, combine the minced garlic, paprika, garlic powder, salt, lemon juice, chili powder, thyme, cayenne, and black pepper.

- Rub the spice mixture all over the chicken, then stuff it with chopped onion, garlic, and thyme.

- Finally, insert the Pellet Smoker into the hopper and plug it on. Turn on the light.

- Preheat the Smoker for indirect heat by selecting the "Smoke" option.

- Preheat the Smoker to 225°F (107°C) and add the entire seasoned chicken to the Smoker.

- Smoked the chicken for about 3 hours, just until the inner Smoke Temperature rises 165 degrees Fahrenheit (74 degrees Celsius).

- When the smoked chicken is done, take it from the (Pellet smoker) and set it aside for approximately 10 minutes.

- Arrange the smoky chicken on a plate and serve.

6.14: Red Pepper Chicken Thighs

Preparation Time: 45 minutes

Cooking Time: 4 hours

Servings: 6

Ingredients:

- Garlic powder 1 tbsp.
- Curry powder 1 tbsp.
- Red pepper flakes 1 tbsp.
- Black pepper 1 tbsp.
- Olive oil 2 tbsp.
- ½ c. of chicken broth
- Oregano 1 tbsp.
- Paprika 1 tbsp.
- Chicken thighs 2 pounds

Steps:

- Arrange the chicken pieces in a single layer on a large flat dish.

- Combine the oregano, pepper, garlic powder, curry powder, olive oil, oregano, paprika, red pepper flakes, and broth in a mixing bowl. To mix, stir everything together well.

- Pour the mixture over the chicken and stir well.

- Marinate the chicken for four hours.

- Fill your Smoker with Recommended Wood Pellet pellets and start your cooker according to the package recommendations. Preheat your Smoker, lid closed, until it reaches 450 degrees.

- Take the chicken thighs out of the bag and set them aside. To dry them, blot them with paper towels. Place them skin-side down on a hot grill and smoke for 10 minutes. Cook for a further ten minutes after flipping.

6.15: Spicy Chicken Thighs

Preparation Time: 45 minutes

Cooking Time: 4 hours

Ingredients:

- Dry barbecue spice 1 tbsp.
- Coriander 1 tbsp.
- Oregano 1 tbsp.
- 1/3 c. of balsamic vinegar
- Mustard 2 tbsp.
- 1/3 c. of olive oil
- Salt
- Pepper
- Two cloves of chopped garlic
- Chicken thighs 6

Steps:

- Arrange the pork chops in a single layer in a shallow dish.

- Combine the dry barbecue seasoning, olive oil, balsamic vinegar, coriander, oregano, pepper, salt, mustard, and garlic in a mixing dish. To mix, stir everything together well.

- Coat the chicken with the mixture.

- Set aside for four hours in the refrigerator.

- Fill your Smoker with Recommended Wood Pellet pellets and start your cooker according to the manufacturer's instructions. Preheat your Smoker to 350 degrees with the lid closed.

- Remove the chicken thighs from the pan and wipe them dry using paper towels.

- Place their skin down on the prepared grill and smoke for 10 minutes. Cook for another ten minutes on the other side.

6.16: Turkey Burgers

Preparation Time: 10 minutes

Cooking Time: 30 minutes

Servings: 6

Ingredients:

- ½ tsp of oregano
- ½ tsp of thyme
- Salt
- Pepper
- A single big egg
- ½ bunch parsley, chopped
- 2-pound turkey minced
- One small red bell pepper, chopped
- One onion, coarsely chopped

Steps:

- In a large mixing dish, combine all of the ingredients.

- Using your hands, thoroughly blend all ingredients.

- Form six patties from the mixture. If the meat starts to cling to your hands, you may drop your hands into the water.

- Fill your Smoker with Recommended Wood Pellet pellets and follow your cooker's starting instructions.

- Preheat your Smoker, lid closed, until it reaches 350 degrees.

- Put them on the grill and cover those with foil for five minutes or until grill marks appear. Cook for another five minutes on the other side of each burger.

- Check to check whether the burgers' internal Smoke Temperature has reached 11. 165 degrees Fahrenheit.

- Top with your favorite burger toppings and serve.

6.17: Turmeric Chicken

Preparation time: 10 minutes

Cooking Time: 35 minutes

Servings: 4

Ingredients:

- 1 tbsp. of turmeric

- Salt

- ½ c. of bacon fat

- Minced garlic four cloves

- Chicken breasts four-piece

Steps:

- In a big shallow dish, place the chicken breasts.

- Combine the turmeric, bacon grease, garlic and salt in a separate dish. To mix, stir everything together well.

- Use a large amount of the mixture to coat each chicken breast.

- Fill your Smoker with Recommended Wood Pellet pellets and start your cooker according to the manufacturer's instructions. Preheat your Smoker to 350 degrees with the lid closed.

- On the grill, smoke the chicken. Do this for approximately 10 minutes. Smoke for another 10 minutes after flipping them.

6.18: Mediterranean Chicken

Preparation Time: 6 minutes

Cooking time: 3 hours

Servings: 6

Ingredients:

- Garnish with lemon slices
- Season with salt and pepper
- ½ c. white wine
- 1 tbsp. of chopped rosemary
- Three garlic cloves minced
- 1 lemon zest
- 1 tbsp. of oregano
- 1 small, chopped onion
- 4 chicken breasts
- ¼ cup olive oil

Steps:

- In a large zip-top bag, place the chicken breasts.
- Combine the onion, pepper, white wine, lemon zest, olive oil, garlic, oregano, rosemary, and salt in a separate bowl. To mix, stir everything together well.
- Using this mixture, coat the chicken.
- Set aside for 2 to 3 hours in the refrigerator.
- Fill your Smoker with Recommended Wood Pellet pellets and start your cooker according to the manufacturer's instructions. Preheat your Smoker to 350 degrees with the lid closed.
- After removing the chicken breasts from the bag, wipe them dry using paper towels. Then, place them on the grill for 15 minutes to smoke.
- Allow for a 10-minute rest period before slicing. Serve with sliced lemon as a garnish.

6.19 Pineapple Turkey Wings

Preparation Time: 15 minutes

Cooking Time: 6 hours

Servings: 6

Ingredients:

- ¼ tsp of garlic powder
- Pepper and salt
- 2-pound turkey wings
- 1 tbsp. brown sugar
- 2 tbsp. chili powder
- ¼ tsp of powdered ginger
- One 11-ounce Can of pineapple, undrained
- One 11-ounce Can of tomato sauce

Steps:

- Arrange the turkey thighs in a wide serving dish. Assemble them in a single layer.
- Combine the garlic powder, ginger, salt, chili powder, pepper and brown sugar in a mixing bowl tomato sauce, pineapple, and sugar. Mix everything up well.
- Drizzle this mixture over the turkey.
- Set aside for 4 - 5 hours in the refrigerator.
- To start your Smoker, add Recommended Wood Pellet pellets and follow the manufacturer's instructions. Next, preheat your Smoker to 350 degrees with the lid closed.
- Remove the turkey wings from the marinade and set them aside. To dry them, use paper towels. Place them on the grill for 5 minutes on each side to smoke. Then, move to the cool side and continue to smoke for another 40 minutes.
- The internal smoke temperature must be 165 degrees Fahrenheit.

6.20: Cheesy Turkey Patties

Preparation Time: 10 minutes

Cooking Time: 15 minutes

Servings: 4

Ingredients:

- Pepper 1 tsp

- ½ cup of avocado
- 1 tsp of chili powder
- Two wheat pita rounds, sliced in half
- ¼ c. of light cream cheese
- 1 tomato
- ¼ c. of shredded cheddar cheese
- 1 tsp. of oregano
- 2 t. chopped green onion
- 1 t. oregano
- 1 lb. minced turkey

Steps:

- In a mixing bowl, combine the salt, pepper, oregano and turkey.
- Using your hands, combine all of the ingredients. Make four patties out of the mixture.
- Fill your Smoker with Recommended Wood Pellet pellets and start your cooker according to the manufacturer's instructions. Preheat your Smoker to 380 degrees Fahrenheit with the lid closed.
- On the grill, smoke the patties. Every side should take around five minutes to prepare.
- Combine the cream cheese, green onion, cheddar cheese, chili powder, and salt while the patties are cooking.
- Cut the pita bread in half and distribute the filling inside the pita.
- Add a turkey patty, avocado, cucumber, tomato to the inside slices.

6.21: Chicken Patties

Preparation time: 5 minutes

Cooking Time: 40 minutes

Servings: 6

Ingredients:

- paprika (two teaspoons)

- 2/3 cup onion, minced
- 2 tbsp. parsley, chopped
- 2 tbsp. of lemon juice
- 1 tbsp. of cilantro, chopped
- 1 tbsp. of red pepper flakes
- ½ tsp cumin
- 2 tbsp. of olive oil
- 2 lbs. of minced chicken

Steps:

- Finely cut the onions once they have been washed. Combine the onions and the other two ingredients in a mixing bowl.

- Mix all of the ingredients with your hands. Continue to mix until all of the ingredients are completely combined. Make six patties out of the mixture. Place them in the refrigerator for 20 minutes.

- Fill your Smoker with Recommended Wood Pellet pellets and start your cooker according to the manufacturer's instructions. Preheat your Smoker, lid closed, until it reaches 350 degrees.

- Start smoking every side of the patties for approximately 10 minutes on the grill.

- Served on buns with your favorite toppings.

6.22: Traeger bbq chicken breasts

Preparation Time: 20 minutes

Cooking Time: 30 minutes

Servings: 4

Ingredients:

- 4 chicken breasts, whole
- ¼ cup of extra virgin olive oil
- 1 tsp. of garlic, freshly squeezed
- 1 tsp. of Worcestershire sauce
- Fin & Feathers Rub Traeger

- Traeger (Sweet & Heat BBQ) Sauce (1/2 cup)
- Traeger 'Spicy BBQ Sauce (1/2 cup)

Steps:

- Whisk together the garlic, olive oil, (Worcestershire sauce), and Traeger Fin & Feather rub in a small bowl. Mixture should be applied on chicken breasts.

- Combine equal amounts Traeger Qu BBQ and Trager Sweet Heat sauce in a separate bowl.

- Temperature was set to 500°F and warm for 15 minutes with the lid covered when ready to cook.

- Place the chicken firmly on the grill grate and cook for 30 minutes, or until the thickest portion of the breast reaches 160°F. Glaze the chicken with the BBQ sauce mixture five minutes before it's done.

- Remove the steak from the grill and set aside for 5 minutes before slicing. Enjoy!

6.23: *Faithfully Italian Herbed Chicken*

Preparation Time: 10 minutes

Cooking Time: 4 hours

Servings: 8-10

Ingredients:

- One whole (5 pounds) spatchcocked chicken
- Onion powder 2 tbsp.
- Garlic powder 3 tbsp.
- Powdered rosemary 1 tbsp.
- Powdered parsley 1 tbsp.
- 1 lemon, zested
- Salt 2 tsp

Steps:

- Fill your Smoker with Recommended Wood Pellet Chips and turn on the smoke.

- Increase the temperature to 200 degrees Fahrenheit.

- If you haven't done so previously, butterfly the chicken.
- Combine the dry spice and lemon zest in a bowl.
- Rub the mixture liberally from both sides of the chicken.
- Place the chicken breast side up in the Smoker and cook for 4 hours.
- Ensure that you continue to add snacks every 30-45 minutes.
- The chicken is done when the inner Smoking Temp of the thickest portion reaches 165 degrees F.
- Remove it from the oven and set it aside for 20 minutes to cool.
- Cut into slices and serve. Enjoy!

6.24: Cilantro-Lime Chicken

Preparation Time: 1 hour
Cooking Time: 4 hours
Servings: 4
Ingredients:
- Salt
- Pepper
- Minced garlic four cloves
- ½ c. of lemon juice
- Honey 1 cup
- Olive oil 2 tbsp.
- ½ c. of chopped cilantro
- Chicken breasts four pieces

Steps:
- In a large zip-top bag, place the chicken breasts.
- Combine the pepper, garlic, honey, salt, lime juice, olive oil and cilantro in a separate bowl. To mix, stir everything together well.
- Use half of the marinade and save the remainder for another time.
- Set aside for 4 - 5 hours in the refrigerator.

- Fill your Smoker with Recommended Wood Pellet pellets and start your cooker according to the manufacturer's instructions. Preheat your Smoker to 350 degrees with the lid closed.

- Take the chicken breasts out of the bag. To dry them, use paper towels. Allow them to smoke for approximately fifteen minutes on the grill.

- About 5 minutes until the chicken is done, baste it with the remaining sauce.

- Marinade.

6.25: Spicy Buffalo Chicken Leg

Preparation time: 5 minutes

Cook timing: 40 Minutes

Serving: 6

Ingredients:

- Chicken legs 12
- Salt ½ tbsp.
- Buffalo seasoning 1 tbsp.
- Buffalo sauce 1 cup

Steps:

- Set the wood pellet grill to 325 degrees Fahrenheit (163 degrees Celsius).
- Place the legs on the prepared grill after sprinkling them with salt and buffalo spice.
- Grill for 40 minutes, turning them twice throughout the cooking process.
- Cook for a further ten min until either the temp reaches 165°F (74°C) by brushing the legs with buffalo sauce.
- Erase the legs from the skillet, spray with additional sauce, and serve while still warm.

6.26: Pepper spiced Cornish Game Hen

Preparation time: 5 minutes

Cooking time: 2 hours

Serving: 4

Ingredients:

- Cornish game hens 4
- Salt 2 tsp
- Freshly powdered black pepper 1 tsp
- Olive oil
- Celery seeds 1 tsp

Steps:

- Fill the grill with (wood pellets) and fire it up according to the manufacturer's instructions. Preheat the oven to 275°F (135° C) with the lid closed.
- Season the game chickens with salt, pepper, and celery seeds all over and beneath the skin with olive oil.
- Put the birds squarely on the grill grate, cover, and smoke for 2 to 3 hours, till a meat thermometer is put into each bird registers 170°F (77°C).
- Cornish game chickens should be served hot.

6.27: Smoked BBQ Chicken Wings

Preparation time: 5 minutes

Cooking time: 35 minutes

Servings: 16

Ingredients:

- Chicken wings 16 pieces
- Olive oil 1 tbsp.
- Chicken Rub 1 tbsp.
- Commercial BBQ sauce of choice 1 cup

Steps:

- Excluding the BBQ sauce, combine all the ingredients in a mixing bowl. The marinade should be massaged into the chicken breasts.
- Marinate for 4 hours in the refrigerator.

- Preheat the grill to 350 degrees Fahrenheit. Pellets made from maple wood should be used. Preheat the grill for 15 minutes with the lid closed.
- Put the wings on the grilled grate and shut the lid for 12 minutes on each side.
- Place the cooked chicken wings in a clean dish.
- Drizzle the BBQ sauce over the chicken and toss to coat.

6.28: Smoked Avocado Cornish Hens

Preparation time: 5 minutes

Cooking time: 40 minutes

Servings: 6

Ingredients:

- Avocado oil 3 tbsp.
- Cornish hens 6
- Rubs of choice 6 tbsp.

Steps:

- Preheat the wood pellet to 275°F (135° C) by lighting it.
- Brush the chickens with oil and then liberally cover them with rub. Place the chickens on the griddle with their chests down, breasts up.
- Allow 30 minutes for smoking. Next, raise the grilled temp to 400°F (204° C) and flip the chickens. Cooked till the (inner temperature) reaches 165 degrees Fahrenheit (74 degrees Celsius).
- Remove the steaks from the grill and set them aside to rest for ten minutes before serving.
- Enjoy!

6.29: Citrus Barbecue Chicken Legs

Preparation time: 10 minutes

Cooking time: 2 hours

Servings: 4

Ingredients:

- Brown sugar 1 tbsp.
- Lemon zest 1 tbsp.
- Chili powder tbsp.
- Cumin in powdered form ½ tsp
- Espresso in powdered form ½ tbsp.
- Salt, according to taste.
- Olive oil 2 tbsp.
- Chicken legs eight pieces
- Barbecue sauce ½ cup

Steps:

- Combine the sugar, lime zest, chili powder, cumin, espresso powder, and salt in a mixing bowl.
- Drizzle oil over the chicken legs. Using a pastry brush, coat the chicken in the sugar mixture.
- Wrap in foil and place in the refrigerator for 5 hours. Preheat the (wood pellet grill) to 180°F (82°C).
- Close the cover and warm it for 15 minutes. 1 hour of smoking chicken legs
- Change the temp to 350 degrees Fahrenheit (176 degrees Celsius).
- Cook the chicken thighs for a further hour on the grill, turning once. Toss the grilled for another 10 minutes after basting the chicken with barbecue sauce.

6.30: Spicy Crispy Chicken

Preparation time: 10 minutes

Cooking time: 5 hours

Serving's time: 6

Ingredients:

- Brown sugar dark ¾ cup
- Espresso beans in powdered form ½ cup
- Cumin powdered 1 tbsp.
- Cinnamon powdered 1 tbsp.

- Garlic powder 1 tbsp.

- Cayenne pepper 1 tbsp.

- Salt and black pepper.

- Whole chicken1 (4-lb/1.81 kg)

Steps:

- Preheat the griddle to 200-225 degrees F (107 degrees C) with the lid covered for 15 minutes.

- Combine spices, brown sugar, salt, powdered espresso, and black pepper in a mixing bowl.

- Rub the spice mixture all over the chicken.

- Put the chicken on the grill for 3-5 hours to cook.

- Remove the chicken from the grill and set it aside for 10 minutes until carving.

- Sliced the chicken into wanted pieces with a sharp blade and serve.

6.31: BBQ Turkey Legs

Preparation time: 10 minutes

Cooking time: 5 hours

Servings: 4

Ingredients:

- Four pieces of turkey leg

To make the brine:

- ½ cup of salt for curing

- 1 tbsp. of black peppercorns, whole

- 1 cup rub for grilling

- ½ cup sugar (brown)

- Bay leaves (two)

- 2 tsp liquid cigarette smoke

- 16 cups of hot water

- 4 quarts ice

- 8 cups chilled water

Steps:

- To make the brine, fill a large stockpot halfway with heated water, add the peppercorns, bay leaves, and liquid smoke, mix in the salt, sugar, and BBQ spice, and bring to a boil.

- Remove the saucepan from the heat and let it cool to room temperature before adding cold water, ice cubes, and chilling the brine in the refrigerator.

- Then put the (turkey legs) in it, fully immerse them, and refrigerate for 24 hours.

- Remove the (turkey legs) from the brine after 24 hours, rinse well, and allow to dry.

- While ready to cook, turn on the grill, load the grilled hopper with hickory-flavored wood pellets, turn on the grill with the control panel, choose 'smoke' on the temp dial, or control the (temperature) to 250 degrees F (121 degrees C) and allow it to warm for at least 15 minutes.

- After the grill has warmed, open the lid, put the (turkey legs) on the grilled grate, close the grill, smoke for 5 hours, or until the inner temperature hits 165 degrees F (74 degrees C).

- Serve right away.

6.32: Yummy Grilled Duck Breast

Preparation time: 5 minutes

Cooking time: 25 minutes

Servings: 4

Ingredients:

- Chicken rub (2 tbsp.)
- Boneless duck breasts 4 (6-oz/170 g)

Steps:

- Preheat the griddle to 275 degrees F (135 degrees C) with the lid covered for 15 minutes.

- Score the duck's skin into a 14-inch diamond pattern with a sharp knife.

- Rub the duck breast evenly with the rub.

- Cook the duck breasts for approximately 10 minutes, flesh side down, on the grill.

- Preheat the griddle to 400 degrees F (204 degrees C).

- Place the breasts skin-side down on a baking sheet and bake for approximately 10 minutes, turning halfway through. Remove the skewers from the grills and place them on a serving platter.

6.33: Honeyed Citrusy Chicken Breast

Preparation time: 10 minutes

Cooking time: 15 minutes

Servings: 4

Ingredients:

- Six skinless and boneless chicken breasts
- ½ cup oil
- 1-3 thyme sprigs
- 1 tsp of crushed black pepper
- Salt 2 tsp
- 2 tsp of honey
- 1 garlic clove, minced
- One lemon, juiced and zested

Steps:

- Combine the thyme, pepper, garlic, salt, lemon zest, honey, and juice in a basin to make the marinade. Mix well until all of the ingredients are dissolved.

- Whisk in the oil.

- Clean the breasts, wipe them dry, and put them in a bag with the marinade and chill for 4 hours.

- Prepare the grill to 400 degrees Fahrenheit (204 degrees Celsius).

- Drain the chicken and smoke it for approximately 15 minutes, or unless the temp reaches 165°F (74°C). Serve and have fun!

6.34: Crispy Beer Chicken

Preparation time: 5 minutes

Cooking time: 1 hour

Servings: 6

Ingredients:

- Beer 1 can
- Chicken 5 pound
- Dry chicken rub ½ cup

Steps:

- With the lid open, heat you're (wood pellet grilled) on smoke for 5 minutes.
- Close the cover and heat the oven to 450 degrees Fahrenheit (232 degrees Celsius).
- Put half of the beer, then cram the can between the chicken's legs to create a tripod.
- Grill the chicken until it reaches an internal temperature of 165°F (74°C).
- Take the steaks off the grill and set them aside for (20 minutes) before serving.
- Enjoy.

6.35: Grilled Tender Chicken

Preparation time: 5 minutes

Cooking time: 1 hour

Servings: 4

Ingredients:

- Chicken rub 1(batch)
- Boneless, skinless chicken breast (450 gram)

Steps:

- Fill the grill with (wood pellets) and fire it up according to the manufacturer's instructions. Preheat the grill to 180°F (82° C) with the lid covered.

- Rub the rub all over the chicken tenders. Then, rub into the meat with your hands.

- Smoke the tenders for 1 hour direct on the grill grate.

- Raise the temperature of the grill to 300°F (149°C) and continue cooking until the tenders achieve an internal temperature of 170°F (77°C).

- Take the tender from the skillet and serve right away.

6.36: Grilled Apple Turkey

Preparation time: 10 minutes

Cook time: 5 hours

Servings: 6

Ingredients:

- One turkey (12 pound/5 kg) with giblets removed

- Olive oil, extra-virgin, for rubbing

- A quarter cup of chicken seasoning

- One stick unsalted butter melted eight tbsp.

- A half-cup of apple juice

- 2 tsp. of sage (dried)

- 2 tsp. of thyme (dried)

Steps:

- Fill the Smoker with (wood pellets) and fire it up according to the manufacturer's instructions. Preheat the oven to 250°F (121°C) with the lid closed.

- Coat the turkeys with oil and sprinkle them inside and out with poultry seasoning, being sure to reach under the skin.

- To use for basting, mix the sage, softened butter, thyme, apple juice in a dish.

- Place the turkey in a roasting pan on the grill, cover, and cook for 5 to 6 hours, basting every hour, or unless a meat thermometer placed in the thickest part of the thigh registers 165°F (74°C).

- Allow 15 to 20 minutes for the bird to rest before cutting.

6.37: Rub Seasoned Turkey

Preparation time: 5 minutes

Cooking time: 2 hours

Servings: 14

Ingredients:

- Turkey 1
- Extra virgin olive oil 2 tbsp.
- Chicken Rub 1

Steps:

- Fill the Smoker with (wood pellets) and fire it up according to the manufacturer's instructions. Preheat the grill to 350°F (177°C) with the lid covered.
- Put the turkey on its breast on a cutting board to remove the backbone. Cut down one edge of the turkey's backbone, then the other, using kitchen shears. Remove the bone.
- Rotate the (turkey) breast-side up and smooth it after the backbone has been removed.
- Rub the turkey on both surfaces with the rub and coat it with olive oil. Work the rubs into the flesh and skin with your hands.
- Place the turkey, breast-side up, firmly on the grill grate and cook until the temperature reached 170°F (77° C).
- Take the (turkey) from the skillet and set it aside for 10 minutes to rest before slicing and serving.

6.38: Cheesy Garlic Chicken Wings

Preparation time: 10 minutes

Cooking time: 20 minutes

Servings: 6

- Chicken wings 5 pounds
- Shredded cheese 1 cup
- Chicken rub ½ cup

- Chopped parsley 3 tbsp.

For the Sauce:

- Chopped garlic 5 tsp.
- Chicken rub 2 tbsp.
- Unsalted butter 1 cup

Steps:

- Warm the grill by turning it on, filling the grill hopper with cherry-flavored wood pellets, using the control panel to turn it on, selecting 'smoke' on the temperature scale, or setting the temp to 450 degrees F (232 degrees C) and letting it preheat for at least 15 minutes.

- Meanwhile, in a large mixing bowl, toss the chicken wings with the chicken rub until thoroughly coated.

- Once the grill has reached temperature, open the lid, put the chicken wings on the grilled grate, close the grill, smoke for 10 minutes on each side, or unless the temperature reaches 165°F (74°C).

- Meanwhile, make the sauce by placing all of the sauce ingredients in a medium saucepan over medium heat, cooking for 10 minutes until smooth, then set aside until needed.

- Transfer the chicken wings to a serving dish, cover with the prepared sauce, and toss to combine, sprinkle with cheese and parsley, and serve.

6.39: Grilled Goose with Juniper berries

Preparation time: 15 minutes

Cooking time: 3 hours

Servings: 12

Ingredients:

- Kosher salt, 1 ½ C.
- 1 cup of brown sugar
- Water at 20 degrees Celsius
- One whole goose (12 lbs.) with giblets removed
- One naval orange, peeled and sliced into six wedges
- One onion, peeled and sliced into eight wedges

- ¼ C. (juniper berries), crushed two bay leaves
- 12 peppercorns, black (to taste, season with salt and freshly powdered black pepper).
- One apple, peeled and sliced into six wedges
- 2-3 sprigs of fresh parsley

Steps:

- Trim any excess skin from your neck. After that, remove the very first two joints from the wings.
- Rinse the geese with (cold running water) and wipe dry with paper towels. Prick the goose with the point of a paring knife all around the skin.
- Mix (kosher salt) and (brown sugar) in water in a big pitcher and three orange slices squeezed into the brine.
- Refrigerate for 24 hours after adding the goose, four onion wedges, bay leaves, juniper berries, and peppercorns to the brine. Preheat the grill to 350 degrees F (176 degrees C) with the lid covered for 15 minutes.
- Remove the geese from the brine and wipe dry thoroughly using paper towels. Season the inside and exterior of the goose with equal amounts of salt and black pepper.
- Place apple wedges, herbs, the leftover orange and onion wedges in the cavity. Bind the thighs together loosely with kitchen threads.
- Arrange the geese on a rack in the bottom of a wide roasting pan.
- Cook the geese for approximately an hour on the grill.
- Eliminate a few of the fats from the pan using a basting bulb and cook for approximately 1 hour.
- Remove any extra fat from the saucepan and simmer for another 1 to 2 hours. Before carving, remove the geese from the grill and put them on a work surface for approximately 20 minutes.
- Split the goose into wanted pieces with a sharp blade and serve.

6.40: Honey Glazed Garlic Chicken Thighs

Preparation time: 10 minutes

Cooking time: 30 minutes

Servings: 4

Ingredients:

- ¼ cup honey
- 2 garlic cloves chopped
- 2 tsp. of soy sauce
- 4 (5-oz.) skinless, boneless chicken thighs
- ¼ tsp. of red pepper flakes, crushed
- 2 tbsp. of extra virgin olive oil
- 2 tsp. of rub de Sucre
- A quarter tsp. of red chili powder
- black pepper, freshly in powder form to taste

Steps:

- Preheat the griddle to 400 degrees F (204 degrees C) with the lid covered for 15 minutes.
- In a small mixing bowl, blend the garlic, honey, soy sauce, and red pepper flakes using a wire whisk.
- Drizzle oil over chicken thighs and liberally sprinkle with sweet rub, chili powder, and black pepper.
- Place the poultry drumsticks on the grill, skin side down, and cook for 15 minutes on each side.
- Brush the thighs with the garlic mixture in the final 4-5 minutes of cooking. Serve right away.

6.41: Grilled Pepper Turkey Breast

Preparation time: 5 minutes

Cooking time: 2 hours

Servings: 4

Ingredients:

- Turkey breast 1.3 kg
- Salt, to taste

- Freshly powdered black pepper, to taste
- Garlic powder 1 tsp.

Steps:

- Fill the Smoker with (wood pellets) and fire it up according to the manufacturer's instructions. Preheat the grill to 180°F (82°C) with the lid covered.

- Sprinkle pepper, garlic powder, salt all over the turkey breast.

- Smoke for 1 hour by placing the chicken firmly on the grill grate.

- Raise the temperature of the grill to 350°F (177°C) and continue cooking until the internal temperature of the turkey reaches 170°F (77°C).

- Take the breast off the grill and serve right away.

6.42: Dried Sage spiced Whole Turkey

Preparation time: 10 minutes

Cooking time: 5 hours

Servings: 6

Ingredients:

- One giblet-free turkey (10 to 12 pound/5.4 kg)
- Olive oil, extra-virgin, for rubbing
- A quarter cup of chicken seasoning
- One stick unsalted butter melted 8 tbsp.
- A quarter-cup of apple juice
- 2 tsp. sage (dried)
- 2 tsp. thyme (dried)

Steps:

- Supply your Smoker with wood pellets and follow the manufacturer's specific start-up procedure. Next, Preheat, with the lid closed to 250°F (121° C).

- Rub the turkey with oil and season with the poultry seasoning inside and out, getting under the skin.

- To use for basting, mix the melted butter, sage, apple juice and thyme in a bowl.

- Put a turkey in the roasting pan over the grill, then close the lid, and grill for 5 to 6 hours, basting every hour until the skin is brown and crispy, or until a meat thermometer inserted in the thickest part of the thigh reads 165°F (74°C).

- Let the bird rest for 15 to 20 minutes before carving.

6.43: Authentic BBQ Chicken

Preparation time: 5 minutes

Cooking time: 2 hours

Servings: 8

Ingredients:

- Boneless chicken breast eight pieces
- Salt 2 tsp.
- Garlic powder 2 tsp.
- Black pepper 2 tsp.
- BBQ Sauce 2 cup.

Steps:

- Fill the grill with (wood pellets) and fire it up according to the manufacturer's instructions. Preheat the oven to 250°F (121° C) with the lid closed.

- In a large pan, season the chicken breasts on both sides with salt, pepper, and garlic powder, carefully massage beneath the skin.

- Put the frying pan on the grill, cover, and cook for 1 hour, 30 min to 2 hours, or unless a meat thermometer inserted into the thickest portion of each breast registers 165°F (74°C). Wrap the poultry with 1 cup of bbq sauce during the final 15 minutes of cooking.

- Toss the chicken bbq sauce and serve warm.

6.44: Espresso Drizzled Barbecue Chicken

Preparation time: 10 minutes

Cooking time: 2 hours

Servings: 4

Ingredients:

- 1 tbsp. of sugar (brown)
- 1 tbsp. zest of lime
- 1 tbsp. Of cayenne pepper
- ½ tsp. of cumin powder
- ½ tbsp. espresso powder
- Season with salt to taste
- 2 tbsp. of extra virgin olive oil
- ½ cup of barbecue sauce eight chicken legs

Steps:

- Mix the lime zest, cumin, chili powder, sugar, powdered espresso, and salt in a mixing bowl. Drizzle some oil over the chicken legs.
- Using a pastry brush, coat the chicken with the sugar mixture. Freeze for 5 hours after covering with foil.
- Preheat the (wood pellet grills) to 180 degrees Fahrenheit (82 degrees Celsius). Close the cover and heat it for 15 minutes.
- Cook the chicken thighs for 1 hour in the Smoker. Change the (temperature to 350) degrees Fahrenheit (176 degrees Celsius).
- Cook the poultry legs for a further hour on the grill, turning once. Coat the poultry with bbq sauce and cook for a further 10 minutes on the grill.

6.45: Cumin spiced Turkey Breast

Preparation time: 15 minutes

Cooking time: 30 minutes

Servings: 6

Ingredients:

For the Brine:

- 2 pound (907 g) deboned turkey breast
- ¼ cup salt
- 1 cup of brown sugar

- 4 cups of cold water

For the BBQ Rub, combine the following ingredients.

- 2 tbsp. of onions (dry)
- Garlic powder (about 2 tsp)
- Paprika (1/4 cup)
- 2 tbsp. black pepper, powdered
- 1 tbsp. of salt
- Brown sugar (2 tbsp.)
- Red chili powder, 2 tbsp.
- Cayenne pepper, 1 tbsp.
- 2 tbsp. of sugar
- 2 tbsp. of cumin powder

Steps:

- Prepare the brine by combining black pepper, sugar, salt in a large mixing basin, then adding water and stirring until the sugar has dissolved.

- Place the (turkey breast) in it, immerse it thoroughly, and refrigerate it for at least 12 hours.

- Meanwhile, make the BBQ rub by combining all of the ingredients in a small dish and stirring until mixed. Set away until needed.

- Remove the (turkey breast) from the brining and sprinkle well with the BBQ rub.

- When ready to cook, turn on the grill, load the grilled (hopper with apple-flavored wood pellets), turn on the grill with the control panel, choose 'smoke' on the temperature scale, or control the temperature to 180 degrees F (82 degrees C) and allow it to warm for at least 15 minutes.

- After the grill has warmed, open the lid, put the turkey breast on the grilling grate, close the grill, lower the smoking temperature to 225°F (107°C), and smoke for 8 hours, or unless the temperature reaches 160°F (71°C).

- When the turkey is done, move it to a work surface, just let rest for ten min, then slice it and serve.

6.46: Nutritious Roasted Turkey

Preparation time: 10 minutes

Cooking time: 3 hours 30 minutes

Servings: 12

Ingredients:

- 4 pound (1.8 kilograms) cleaned turkey
- 2 tbsp. of mixed herbs, chopped
- Rubs for pork and poultry, as required
- ¼ tsp. of black pepper, powdered
- 3 tbsp. of unsalted butter, melted
- 8 tbsp. of unsalted, softened butter
- 2 quarts chicken stock

Steps:

- Remove the giblets from the turkey, wash it inside and out, and then wipe it dry using paper towels before placing it on a baking dish and tucking the turkey wings with butcher's thread.

- Warm the grill by turning it on, filling the (grill hopper with hickory flavored wood pellets), using the control panel to turn it on, selecting 'smoke' on the temperature dial, or setting the temp to 325 degrees F (163 degrees C) and letting it preheat for at least 15 minutes.

- Meanwhile, make herb butter by placing melted butter in a small bowl, adding black pepper and mixed herbs, and whisking until frothy.

- Using the (handle) of a wooden spoon, rub a few of the generated herb butter beneath the turkey's skin to evenly distribute the butter.

- Rub melted butter all over the outside of the turkey, seasoning with pork and chicken rub, then pour the liquid into the roasting pan.

- When the grill is hot, open the lid, put the roasting pan with the turkey on the grill grate, close the grill, smoke for 3 hours and 30 minutes, or unless the temperature reaches 165 degrees F (74 degrees F C) and the top is golden brown.

- When the turkey is done, move it to a cutting board and set it aside for 30 minutes to rest before carving it into pieces and serving.

6.47: Spicy Rich Smoked Chicken

Preparation time: 15 minutes

Cooking time: 55 minutes

Servings: 6

Ingredients:

- 1 beaten egg
- 1/2 cup of milk
- 1 cup flour (all-purpose)
- 1 tbsp. of freshly powdered black pepper
- 2 tbsp. of salt
- 2 tsp. white pepper
- Cayenne pepper, two tbsp.
- 2 tsp. of powdered garlic
- 2 tsp. of powdered onion
- 1 tsp. paprika (smoked)
- A quarter-cup (1 stick) melted unsalted butter
- One entire chicken, chopped into bite-sized portions

Steps:

- Fill the (Smoker with wood pellets) and fire it up according to the manufacturer's instructions. Preheat the oven to 375°F (191° C) with the lid closed.
- Whisk together the beaten egg and milk in a clean bowl and put aside.
- Combine the black pepper, garlic powder, white pepper, salt, cayenne, flour, onion powder, and smoked paprika in a separate medium bowl.
- To make cleaning easier, cover the bottom part of a high heavy metal cookie sheet with aluminum foil.
- Put the softened butter into the pan that has been prepared.
- Immerse the chicken pieces in the egg mixture one at a time, then coat well in the seasoned flour. Place the baking pan in the oven.
- Start smoking the chicken in a pan of butter on the grill for 25 minutes with the lid covered, reducing the heat to 325°F (163° C) and flipping the chicken pieces.

- Smoke for another 30 minutes with the lid closed, or unless a meat thermometer placed in the widest part of each poultry piece registers 165°F (74°C). Serve right away.

6.48: Homemade Mini Turducken

Preparation time: 10 minutes

Cooking time: 2 hours

Servings: 6

Ingredients:
- One boneless turkey breast (16 oz./454 g)
- One boneless duck breast (8 to 10 ounces/ 283 g)
- One chicken breast, skinless (8 oz./227 g)
- Season with salt to taste
- Black pepper, freshly crushed, to taste
- 2 c. Italian salad dressing
- Cajun seasoning, 2 tbsp.
- 1 cup seasoned stuffing mix (prepared)
- 8 bacon slices
- String from a butcher

Steps:
- Butter the duck, turkey, and chicken pieces, cover with plastic wrap, and flatten each one to 12-inch thickness with a hammer.
- Season both sides of the meat with a pinch of salt and pepper.
- Whisk together the Italian dressings and Cajun seasoning in a medium mixing basin. Fourteen of the mixture should be spread on the edge of the flat turkey breast.
- Put the (duck breast) on top of the turkey, spread with a quarter of the dressing's mixture, and cover with the stuffed mixture.
- Spread one-fourth of the dressing's mixture over the duck and put the chicken pieces on top.
- Fill your grill with (wood pellets) and fire it up according to the manufacturer's instructions. Preheat the oven to 275°F (135° C) with the lid closed.

- Wrap the stack tightly, knot with butcher's thread, and spread the leftover dressing mixture all over.

- Wrap bacon pieces around the turducken and fasten with toothpicks, or make bacon weaving.

- In a roasting pan, place the turducken roulade. Transfer the turducken on the grill, cover, and cook for 2 hours, or unless a meat thermometer placed in the turducken registers 165°F (74°C). If required, tent with aluminum foil in the final 30 minutes to prevent over-browning.

- Allow 15 to 20 minutes for the turducken to rest before slicing. Warm the dish before serving.

6.49: Honeyed Chicken Drumsticks

Preparation time: 10 minutes

Cooking time: 2 hours

Servings: 6

Ingredients:

- 1 cup of freshly squeezed orange juice

- ¼ cup of honey

- 2 tbsp. of chili sauce (sweet)

- 2 tbsp. hoisin sauce

- 2 tbsp. freshly grated fresh ginger

- 2 tbsp. minced garlic

- 1 tsp. Of sriracha

- ½ tbsp. of sesame oil

- 6 drumsticks de chicken

Steps:

- Preheat the grill to 225 degrees F (107 degrees C) with the lid covered for fifteen min, using charcoal.

- In a mixing bowl, add all ingredients (excluding the chicken drumsticks) and mix thoroughly.

- In a separate dish, set them aside half of the honey mixture.

- Toss the drumsticks with the remaining sauce in a mixing basin.
- Place the chicken's drumsticks on the grills and cook for approximately 2 hours, basting periodically with the leftover sauce.
- Serve immediately.

6.50: One Pan Chicken Fajitas

Preparation time: 10 minutes

Cooking time: 20 minutes

Servings: 10

Ingredients:

- 2 pounds thinly sliced chicken breast
- 1 big red bell pepper
- 1 big onion
- One large huge orange bell pepper Seasoning mix
- 2 tbsp. of oil
- ½ tsp. of onion powder
- 12 tbsp. of garlic granules
- 1 tbsp. of salt

Steps:

- Set the skillet to 450 degrees Fahrenheit (232 degrees Celsius).
- Combine the spices and oil in a mixing bowl.
- Toss in the chicken pieces and stir well.
- Grease a big baking pan and line it with a nonstick baking sheet.
- Allow 10 minutes for the pan to heat up.
- Preheat the grill and add the peppers, chicken and other veggies.
- Cook for 10 minutes on the grill, or unless the chicken is done.
- Take it off the grill and serve it with tortillas and veggies that are still warm.

6.51: Ranch Dressed Chicken Wings

Preparation time: 5 minutes

Cooking time: 1 hour

Servings: 4

Ingredients:

- Chicken wings, 2 pounds (907 g)
- Extra-virgin olive oil 2 tbsp.
- Ranch dressing mix (two packets)
- ¼ cup of prepared ranch dressing (optional)

Steps:

- Supply your Smoker with wood pellets and follow the manufacturer's specific start-up procedure. Then, Preheat, with the lid closed, to 350°F (177° C).
- Place the chicken wings in a large bowl and toss with the olive oil and ranch dressing mix.
- Arrange the wings directly on the grill, line the grill with aluminum foil for easy cleanup, close the lid, and smoke for 25 minutes.
- Flip and smoke for 20 to 35 minutes more, or until a meat thermometer inserted in the thickest part of the wings reads 165°F
- (74°C) and the wings are crispy. (Note: The wings will likely be done after 45 minutes, but an extra 10 to 15 minutes makes them crispy without drying the meat.)
- Serve warm with ranch dressing (if using).

6.52: Worcestershire Turkey Legs

Preparation time: 10 minutes

Cooking time: 4 hours

Servings: 6

For Turkey:

- Worcestershire sauce 3 tbsp.
- Turkey legs 6
- Canola oil 1 tbsp.

For Rub:

- Chipotle seasoning ¼ cup.

- Brown sugar 1 tbsp.

- Paprika powder 1 tbsp.

For Sauce:

- 1 C. of the white vinegar 1

- Canola oil 1 tbsp.

- Chipotle BBQ sauce 1 tbsp.

Steps:

- Combine the canola oil and Worcestershire sauce in a mixing dish for the turkey.

- Loosen the skin on your legs with your fingertips.

- Apply the oil mixture to the undersides of the legs using your fingertips.

- Combine the ingredients for the rubs in a separate dish.

- Generously apply the spice mixture beneath and around the turkey legs.

- Place the legs in a big sealable bag and place in the refrigerator for 2-4 hours.

- Erase the (turkey legs) from the refrigerator and let them come to room temperature before cooking.

- Preheat the griddle to 220 degrees F (104 degrees C) with the lid covered for 15 minutes.

- In a small saucepan, combine all sauce ingredients and simmer over low heat, constantly stirring, until fully warmed.

- Put the (turkey legs) on the grill and cook for 3 to 4 hours, basting every 45 minutes with the sauce.

- Serve immediately.

6.53: Orange flavored Chicken Slices

Preparation time: 10 minutes

Cooking time: 45 minutes

Servings: 6

Ingredients:

- Backbone removed from a 4-pound (1.8 kg) chicken
- 2 tsp. salt for the marinade
- 3 tbsp. of rosemary leaves, chopped
- A couple of tsp. Mustard Dijon
- One orange, peeled and zested
- ¼ cup extra virgin olive oil
- A quarter cup of orange juice

Steps:

- Start preparing the chicken by rinsing it, patting it dry with paper towels, and placing it in a big baking dish.
- Make the marinade by combining all of the ingredients in a medium bowl and whisking until well mixed.
- Cover the meat with the specified marinade, cover with plastic wrap, and marinate in the refrigerator for at least 2 hours, rotating halfway.
- When ready to cook, turn on the grill, load the grill hopper with flavored wood pellets, turn on the grill with the control panel, choose 'smoke' on the temp scale, or adjust the temp to 350 degrees F (176 degrees C) and wait 5 minutes.
- After the grill has warmed, open the cover, put the chicken skin-side down on the grilled grate, close the grill, and smoke for 45 minutes, or until the temp reaches 165 degrees F (74 degrees C).
- When the chicken is done, move it to a work surface, set it aside for 10 minutes, then cut it into pieces and serve.

6.54: Chile Margarita Seasoned Chicken

Preparation time: 10 minutes

Cooking time: 10 minutes

Servings: 10

Ingredients:

- 2-pound breast of chicken
- 1 sliced onion

- One seeded and sliced red bell pepper
- One sliced and seeded orange-red bell pepper
- 1 tbsp. of salt
- 12 tbsp. of powdered onion
- 12 tbsp. of garlic granules
- 2 tbsp. of Chile Margarita Seasoning (Spiceologist)
- 2 tbsp. of olive oil

Steps:

- Set the oven to 450 degrees Fahrenheit and prepare a cookie sheet.
- Toss the pepper and chicken with the spices and oil in a mixing bowl.
- Cover the baking sheet with the cover and heat for 10 minutes.
- Remove the cover and arrange the vegetables and chickens in a single layer in the pan. Cook for 10 minutes, or unless the chickens are no longer pink, with the lid closed.
- Toss with your preferred toppings and serve with warm tortillas.

6.55: Cayenne spiced Chicken Wings

Preparation time: 5 minutes

Cooking time: 15 minutes

Servings: 4

Ingredients:

- Four chicken wings (fresh)
- Garlic powder as needed
- Salt and pepper, to taste
- As needed, onion powder
- Cayenne pepper, if needed
- paprika (as needed)
- BBQ sauce, to taste

Steps:

- Set the (wood pellet grill) to a low setting.

- Combine all of the seasoning ingredients in a mixing dish, and toss the chicken unless thoroughly covered.

- Set the wing on the grill and cook for 20 minutes or until cooked through.

- Set aside for 5 minutes to cool before tossing with BBQ sauce.

- Toss with salad and orzo before serving. Enjoy.

6.56: Hot Sauce Smoked Chicken Wings

Preparation time: 15 minutes

Cooking time: 30 minutes

Servings: 8

Ingredients:

- Chicken wings, 4 pounds (1.8 kg), patted dry
- 2 tbsp. of extra virgin olive oil
- Season with salt and pepper to taste.
- ½ of minced medium yellow onions
- Five garlic cloves, minced
- ½ c. of bourbon
- Ketchup, 2 cups
- A third of a cup of apple cider vinegar
- 2 tbsp. liquid smoke
- ½ tsp. of kosher salt
- ½ tsp. of black pepper
- A smidgeon of spicy sauce

Steps:

- Drizzle olive oil over the (chicken) in a mixing dish. To taste, season with pepper and salt. Combine the remaining ingredients in a separate dish and put them aside.

- Preheat the griddle to 400 degrees Fahrenheit. (Hickory wood pellets) should be used. Allow 15 minutes for preheating after closing the lid.

- Cook the chicken for Twelve minutes on each side of the grill grate.

- Spread the bourbon sauce all over the chicken wings using a brush.

- Remove the cover and simmer the chicken for another 12 minutes. And serve it.

6.57: Thyme herbed Honey Chicken Breasts

Preparation time: 10 minutes

Cooking time: 40 minutes

Servings: 6

Ingredients:

- 1 garlic clove (chopped)
- 1 tsp. of black pepper, crushed
- 2 tsp. of honey
- Salt 2 tsp.
- 2 thyme sprigs (fresh)
- One zested and juiced lemon
- Extra virgin olive oil ½ cup
- Six chicken breasts (boneless, skinless)

Steps:

- Combine the honey, thyme, salt, juice, garlic, pepper, lemon zest in a dish to make the marinade. Whisk everything together until it's smooth.

- Add the chicken to the marinade and toss it around with your hands to cover it with the sauce. Freeze for 4 hours before serving.

- Set the griddle to 400 degrees Fahrenheit (204 degrees Celsius) when ready to cook. Warm for 10 minutes with the lid closed.

- Remove the chicken from the marinade and discard it.

- Add the (chicken breasts) directly on the grilled grates and cooked for 40 minutes, or until the thickest portion of the (chicken) reaches 165 degrees F (74 degrees C).

- Before serving, drizzle with additional lemon juice.

6.58: Cajun Spiced BBQ Chicken

Preparation time: 5 minutes

Cooking time: 6 hours

Servings: 6

- 2 pound boneless, skinless chicken breasts
- 2 tbsp. of oil seasoning with Cajun spices
- 1 cup of barbecue sauce

Steps:

- Preheat the griddle to 225 degrees F (107 degrees C) with the lid covered for 15 minutes.
- Season the chicken breasts liberally with Cajun spice.
- Add the (chicken breasts) to the grill for 4-6 hours to cook.
- Brush the breasts with Barbecue sauce twice during the final hour of cooking.
- Serve immediately.

6.59: Cheesy Chicken Wings with Parsley

Preparation time: 10 minutes

Cooking time: 20 minutes

Servings: 6

Ingredients:

- Chicken weighing 5 pounds (2.26 kg)
- ½ cup of rub for chicken
- 1 cup grated parmesan cheese
- 3 tbsp. of chopped parsley

To make the sauce:

- 5 tsp. of garlic, chopped
- 2 tbsp. of chicken seasoning

- 1 cup unsalted butter melted

Steps:

- Warm the grill by turning it on, filling the (grilled hopper) with cherry-flavored wood pellets, using the control panel to turn it on, preheat for at least 15 minutes.

- Meanwhile, in a medium pot, toss the chicken wings with the chicken rub until thoroughly coated.

- Once the grill has reached temperature, open the lid, put the chicken wings on the grill grate, close the grill, and smoked for 10 minutes on each side.

- Meanwhile, make the sauce by placing all of the sauce ingredients in a medium saucepan over medium heat, cooking for ten min unless smooth, then set aside until needed.

- Transfer the chicken wings to a serving dish, cover with the prepared sauce, and toss to combine, sprinkle with cheese and parsley, and serve.

6.60: Peppery Chicken Lettuce Wraps

Preparation time: 15 minutes

Cooking time: 20 minutes

Servings: 4

Ingredients:

- 2 tsp. seasoning for poultry
- 1 tsp. of black pepper, freshly powdered
- 1 tsp. of powdered garlic
- 1 to 1 ½ lbs. (680 g) Tenders of chicken
- 4 tbsp. of unsalted butter (12 stick), melted
- ½ cup spicy sauce
- Four flour tortillas (10 inches)
- 1 cup lettuce, shredded
- ½ cup tomato, diced
- ½ cup of celery
- ½ cup of red onion
- ½ cup of shredded Cheddar

- ¼ cup of blue cheese crumbles
- ¼ cup of ranch dressing (prepared)
- Two tbsp. of pickled jalapeno peppers, sliced (optional)

Steps:

- Fill your grill with (wood pellets) and fire it up according to the manufacturer's instructions. Next, preheat the oven to 350°F (177°C) with the lid closed.
- To make an all-purpose rub, combine the chicken flavor, pepper, and garlic powder in a small dish, then sprinkle the chicken wings with it.
- Place the tender firmly on the grill, cover, and smoke for twenty minutes, or unless a thermometer scale inserted into the thickest portion of the flesh registers 170°F (77°C).
- Combine the softened butter and spicy sauce in a separate dish and cover the smoke chicken with it.
- To serve, put the tortillas on a dish and cook them on the grill for less than a minute on each side.
- Add some red onion, lettuce, celery, tomato, Cheddar cheese, blue cheese crumbles, ranch dressing, and jalapenos to each tortilla (if using).
- Distribute the meat among the tortillas and roll them up tightly before serving.

6.61: Chinese style Glazed Duck Legs

Preparation time: 10 minutes

Cooking time: 1 hour 10 minutes

Servings: 8

For Glaze:

- ¼ c. of freshly squeezed orange juice
- A quarter-cup of orange marmalade
- ¼ oz. of mirin
- 2 tbsp. of hoisin sauce
- ½ tsp. of crushed red pepper flakes
- 1 tsp. of salt (kosher)

- ¾ tbsp. of black pepper, freshly in powdered form
- ¾ tsp. of powdered Chinese five-spice
- Duck legs (6 oz.) 8

Steps:

- Preheat the griddle to 235 F with the lid covered for 15 minutes.
- For the forb glaze, combine all ingredients in a medium saucepan over medium heat and bring to a moderate boil, stirring constantly.
- Remove the pan from the heat and put it aside.
- To make the rub, combine black pepper, salt, and five spices powder in a small dish.
- Evenly massage the spice rub onto the duck legs.
- Arrange the duck legs skin side up on the grill and cook for 50 minutes.
- Brush the (duck legs) with glaze and bake for approximately 20 minutes, turning and glazing every 5 minutes.

6.62: Spice-Rubbed Chicken Wings with Sauce

Preparation time: 15 minutes

Cooking time: 40 minutes

Servings: 6

Ingredients:

- 1.3 kg chicken wings with tips removed
- 2 tbsp. of olive oil

To make the rub:

- 1 tsp. of powdered onion
- 1 tsp. of kosher salt
- 1 tsp. of powdered garlic
- Paprika (1 tbsp.)
- 1 tsp. of black pepper, crushed
- 1 tsp. of seeded celery
- Cayenne pepper (1 teaspoon)

- 2 tsp. of sugar (brown)

To make the sauce:

- Four jalapeño crosswise cut
- 8 tbsp. of unsalted butter
- ½ cup of spicy sauce
- ½ cup of carrots leaves

Steps:

- Warm the grill by turning it on, filling the grilled hopper with (hickory flavored wood pellets), using the control panel to turn it on, or setting the temp to 350 degrees F (176 degrees C) and letting it preheat for at least 15 minutes.

- Assemble the chicken wings by removing the tips, cutting each piece of chicken through union into two parts, and placing them in a large mixing basin.

- Make the rub by combining all of the ingredients in a small dish and stirring until well mixed.

- Toss the chicken wings in the prepared rub until well covered.

- However, when the grill is hot, open the lid, put the chicken wings on the grilled grate, close the grill, and smoke for 40 minutes, rotating halfway until golden brown and crisp.

- Meanwhile, make the sauce by melting the butter in a small saucepan over medium-low heat, then adding the jalapeño and cooking for 4 minutes.

- Erase the pan from the heat and whisk in the spicy cilantro sauce until well combined. Transfer the chicken wings to a serving dish, cover with the prepared sauce, toss to coat, and serve.

6.63: Sweet mesquite seasoned Chicken Breasts

Preparation time: 10 minutes

Cooking time: 30 minutes

Servings: 4

Ingredients:

- ¼ cup of olive oil
- 1 tsp. of crushed garlic

- Worcestershire sauce, 1 tbsp.
- 1 tbsp. of sweet mesquite seasoning
- Four breasts of chicken
- 2 tbsp. of normal barbecue sauce
- 2 tbsp. of BBQ sauce (spicy)
- 2 tbsp. of honey bourbon barbecue sauce

Steps:

- Set the griddle to 450 degrees F (232 degrees C) with the lid covered for 15 minutes.
- Combine the garlic, oil, Worcestershire sauce, and mesquite spice in a large mixing bowl.
- Evenly coat the chicken breasts with the spice mixture.
- Cook the chicken breasts for 20-30 minutes on the grill.
- Meanwhile, combine all three BBQ sauces in a mixing dish.
- Brush the breasts with the BBQ sauce mixture in the final 4-5 minutes of cooking.
- Serve immediately.

6.64: Onion and Garlic spiced Chicken

Preparation time: 10 minutes

Cooking time: 3 hours

Servings: 4

Ingredients:

- ½ cup of vinegar
- 8 tbsp. of (1 piece) butter, melting
- ½ cup of Cajun seasoning (distributed)
- 1 tsp. of powdered garlic
- 1 tsp. of powdered onion
- One whole chicken (4 pound/1.8 kg) with giblets removed
- Olive oil, extra-virgin, for rubbing

- 1 (12-ounce/340-gram) beer can
- 1 quart of apple juice
- ½ cup of extra-virgin olive oil

Steps:

- Combine the butter, vinegar, ¼ cups Cajun spice, onion powder, garlic powder in a small bowl.

- Inject the liquid into different places on the bird using a meat-injecting syringe. For example, ½ of the mixture should be inserted into the chicken breasts, as well as the other half should be spread throughout the remainder of the bird.

- Drizzle the chicken with oil and sprinkle with the remaining 14 cups of Cajun spice, being care to massage it in thoroughly.

- Drink half of the beer or toss it, then set the empty drink can on a sturdy surface.

- Put the chicken's cavity on the edge of a can and arrange it so that it sits up on its own. To keep the bird more sturdy, push the legs forward or purchase a cheap, specifically constructed stand to keep the wine can and poultry in place.

- Fill the smokers with (wood pellets) and fire them up according to the manufacturer's instructions. Preheat the oven to 250°F (121° C) with the lid closed.

- Blend the apple juice and olive oil in a fresh 12-ounce (340 g) spray bottle. Before each usage, cover the mop sauce and give it a good shake. 8. Place the chicken on the griddle with care. Close the top and smoke the chicken for 4 hours, unless the golden browned inserted thermometer in the thigh registers' widest part of the thigh registers 165°F (74°C).

- Have a piece of foil on ready to cover the chicken lightly if the skin browns too fast.

- Set aside for five min before slicing the meat.

6.65: Simple Grilled Duck Breast

Preparation time: 5 minutes

Cooking time: 20 minutes

Servings: 4

Ingredients:

- Duck breasts boneless 4

- Chicken rub 2 tbsp.

Steps:

- Preheat the griddle to 275 degrees F (135 degrees C) with the lid covered for 15 minutes.

- Score the duck's skin into a 14-inch diamond pattern with a sharp knife.

- Cover the (duck breast) equally with the rub.

- Cook the duck breasts for approximately 10 minutes, flesh side down, on the grill.

- Set the griddle to 400 degrees F (204 degrees C).

- Place the breasts skin-side down on a baking sheet and bake for approximately 10 minutes, turning halfway through. Remove the skewers from the grills and place them on a serving platter.

6.66: Garlic Buttered Turkey

Preparation time: 5 minutes

Cooking time: 5 hours

Servings: 14

Ingredients:

- One turkey, entire (make sure the turkey is not pre-brined)

- Injectable Garlic Butter, two batches

- 3 tbsp. of extra virgin olive oil

- 1 pound of chicken rub

- 2 tbsp. of unsalted butter

Steps:

- Fill the grill with (wood pellets) and fire it up according to the manufacturer's instructions. Preheat the grill to 180°F (82°C) with the lid covered.

- Inject the garlic buttered injectable all over the bird. Season the turkey with the rub and a little coating of olive oil. Stir the rub into the flesh and skin with your hands.

- Put the turkey straight on the grilling grate and smoke for 3 or 4 hours, brushing it with buttered every hour and cook for 4 hours).

- Raise the temperature of the grill to 375°F (191°C) and continue cooking until the temp of the turkey reaches 170°F (77°C).

- Take the turkeys from the skillet and set them aside for 10 minutes to rest before slicing and serving.

6.67: Sweet and Citrusy Chicken Breast

Preparation time: 10 minutes

Cooking time: 30 minutes

Servings: 4

Ingredients:

- Six skinless and boneless chicken breasts
- ½ cup of oil
- 1-3 sprigs of fresh thyme
- 1 tsp. of black pepper, powdered
- 2 tsp. of kosher salt
- Honey (two tsp.)
- One lime juiced and zested one clove of garlic, chopped
- Slices of lemon

Steps:

- Combine the thyme, lime juice, honey, pepper, salt, garlic in a dish to make the marinade. Mix well until all of the ingredients are dissolved.

- Stir in the oil. Wash the breast and wipe them dry before placing them in a bag with the marinade and chilling for 4 hours.

- Set the grill to 400 degrees Fahrenheit (204 degrees Celsius). Rinse the chicken and smoke it for approximately 15 minutes, or unless the temp hits at 165°F (74°C).

- Serve and enjoy!

6.68: Moms Mayo Chicken Legs

Preparation time: 10 minutes

Cooking time: 1 hour 30 minutes

Servings: 6

Ingredients:

- In the case of brine:
- ¾ cup of light brown sugar
- 1 cup of kosher salt
- Six chicken leg halves 16 C. water
- ½ C. of mayonnaise (for glaze)
- 2 tbsp. of barbecue sauce
- 2 tbsp. of c
- hopped fresh chives
- 1 tbsp. of minced garlic

Steps:

- To make the brine, mix brown sugar and salt in water in a container.
- Freeze the chicken halves in the brine for approximately 4 hours, covered.
- Set the grill to 275 degrees F (135 degrees C) with the lids covered for 15 minutes.
- Wash the chicken halves over cold water after removing them from the brine. Dry the chicken parts
- To make the glaze, put all of the components in a mixing dish and stir until mixed.
- On the barbecue with the (chicken leg quarters). Grill for 1-112 hrs. Serve right away.

6.69: Paprika Chicken with Rosemary

Preparation time: 10 minutes

Cooking time: 2 hours

Servings: 7

Ingredients:

- 4-6 breasts of chicken

- 4 tbsp. of extra virgin olive oil
- 2 tbsp. paprika (smoked)
- ½ tbsp. Of salt
- ¼ tbsp. of pepper
- 2 tbsp. of powdered garlic
- 2 tsp. garlic powder
- 2 tsp. of black pepper
- Cayenne pepper (1 tsp.)
- 1 tsp. of rosemary (optional)

Steps:

- Use your preferred wood Pellets to warm the smokers to 220 degrees Fahrenheit (104 degrees Celsius).

- Cut your chicken breasts into preferred shapes and place them in a greased baking tray.

- In a medium mixing basin, combine spices and whisk thoroughly. Apply the spice mixture to the chicken and place it in the Smoker.

- Smoked for an hour and a half to an hour and a half. Cook for another 30 minutes on the other side.

- When the temp reaches (74 degrees Celsius), remove the pan from the oven. Erase the meat from the grill and wrap it in foil.

- Set aside for 15 minutes to cool. Enjoy!

6.70: Cornish Game Hen with Celery seeds

Preparation time: 5 minutes

Cooking time: 2 hours

Servings: 4

Ingredients:

- Cornish game chickens (four)
- Olive oil, additional, for rubbing
- 1 tsp. of freshly crushed black pepper, two tablespoons salt

- 1 tsp. of seeds de celery

Steps:

- Fill the smokers with (wood pellets) and fire them up according to the manufacturer's instructions. Preheat the oven to 275°F (135° C) with the lid closed.

- Rub the olive oil all over the game chickens, including under the skin, and season with pepper, salt, and celery seeds.

- Put the (birds) directly on the grilling grate, cover, and smoked for 3 hours, or unless thermometer placed into each bird registers 170°F (77°C). Cornish game chickens should be served hot.

6.71: Italian Spicy Duck Roast

Preparation time: 15 minutes

Cooking time: 2 hours 30 minutes

Servings: 6

Ingredients:

- 5 kilos (2.26 kg) duck in its entirety
- 1 big apple
- One tiny onion (quartered) (wedged)
- A single orange (quartered)
- 1 tbsp. of parsley, finely chopped
- 1 tbsp. of sage, freshly chopped
- 12 tsp. onion powder
- 2 tsp. paprika (smoked)
- 1 tsp. of Italian seasoning (dry)
- 1 tbsp. of Greek seasoning (dry)
- 1 tsp. of black pepper to taste
- 1 tsp. of sea salt

Steps:

- Rinse the duck inside and out with cold running water after removing the giblets. Then, using paper towels, pat dry.

- Split the (duck) surface all over with the point of a sharp knife. Make sure you don't cut through the flesh. Butcher's string should be used to tie the (duck legs) together.3. Mix the salt, onion powder, Italian seasoning, pepper, Greek spice, and paprika in a mixing bowl to create a rub.

- Place the onion, orange, and apple in the cavity of the duck. Next, fill the duck with parsley and sage that has been finely cut.

- Rub the duck on both sides liberally with the rub mixture.

- Set your pellet grill to smoke mode and leave the lip open until the fire ignites. Set the grill to 325°F (163° C) for 10 minutes with the lid closed.

- Put the (duck) on the grill grate and close the lid.

- Roast for 2 to 212 hrs.

- Take the duck from the heat and set it aside to cool.

- Cut into serving portions.

6.72: Butter Chicken with Bacon

Preparation time: 10 minutes

Cooking time: 1 hour 30 minutes

Servings: 7

Ingredients:

- Four chicken breasts, boneless and skinless

- Season with salt and pepper

- 12 uncooked bacon slices

- 1 quart of maple syrup

- ½ cup of butter softened

- 1 tsp. of liquid cigarette smoke

Steps:

- Set the Smoker to a temperature of 250 degrees Fahrenheit (121 degrees Celsius). Preheat the oven to 350°F and sprinkle the chicken with salt and pepper.

- Cover the whole surface of the chicken with three bacon pieces and fasten with toothpicks.

- In a moderate mixing bowl, combine maple syrup, butter, and liquid smoke.

- Set aside a third of this combination for later use, dip the chicken breasts into the butter mixture, and coat them thoroughly.

- Set up a dish in your smoking and add the chicken to it.

- Cook for 1 to 12 hours in the Smoker. Brush the chicken with the remaining butter and continue to smoke for another 30 minutes, or unless the temp hits 165°F (74°C). Enjoy!

6.73: Sage Rubbed Spatchcock Turkey

Preparation time: 10 minutes

Cooking time: 1 hour 45 minutes

Servings: 6

Ingredients:

- 1 turkey, entire
- ½ cup of oil
- ¼ cup of rubs for chicken
- 1 tbsp. of powdered onion
- 1 tbsp. of powdered garlic
- 1 tbsp. of sage, rubbed

Steps:

- Preheat the (wood pellet grills) to high temperature.

- Now, put the turkey breast side down on a plate and remove the spine by cutting on each side of the backbone.

- Sprinkle both sides of the turkey before placing it on the prepared grilled or on a pan to collect the drippings.

- Cook for 30 minutes on high, then lower to 325°F (163° C) and cook for another 45 minutes, or unless hit at 165°F (74°C).

- Erase the steak from the skillet and set it aside to rest for 20 mins before cutting and serving. Enjoy.

6.74: Honeyed Sherry Marinated Turkey Breast

Preparation time: 10 minutes

Cooking time: 4 hours

Servings: 6

Ingredients;

- 12 cups. honey
- 14°C sherry (dry)
- One tablespoon of melted butter
- 2 tbsp. of freshly squeezed lime juice
- Season with salt to taste
- Turkey breast skinless (3-312 pound)

Steps:

- Heat sherry, honey and margarine in a small saucepan over low heat, constantly stirring, unless the batter is smooth.

- Take the pan off the heat and add the lemon zest and salt. Allow cooling before serving. Fill a sealable bag with the turkey breast and honey mix.

- Close the bag and shake it thoroughly to coat everything evenly. Refrigerate for a minimum of 6 hours and up to 10 hours.

- Set the griddle to 250 degrees F (121 degrees C) with the lid covered for 15 minutes.

- Put the turkey breast on the skillet and cook for 2 to 4 hours, depending on how done you want it.

- Remove the turkey breast from the grill and set it aside for 15-twenty minutes before slicing. Slice the (turkey breast) into required pieces with a sharp blade and serve.

Chapter 7: Desserts recipes

(Image by: Tim Pierce)

7.1: Smoked Carolina Pulled Pork Sandwiches

Preparation time: 0 minutes

Cooking time: 8 hours

Servings: 6 - 8 adult-sized humans

Ingredients:

- One boned Boston buttocks (6 - 7 pounds)
- 1 cup of vinegar

- Poultry rub and pork
- 1 quart of beer
- 2 tbsp. freshly squeezed lemon juice
- 1 tbsp. of Worcestershire
- 1 tsp. of crushed red pepper

For buns:

- 2 cups of apple cider vinegar
- ½ cup of ketchup
- ¼ cup of brown sugar
- 5 tsp. of salt
- 2 - 4 tsp. of red pepper flakes
- 1 tsp. of finely crushed black pepper
- 1 tsp. of freshly crushed white pepper (freshly ground)
- ½ cabbages (large, cored, shredded)

Steps:

- Rub the rub all over the pork butt and make sure it's evenly distributed.
- Refrigerate your seasoned butt for 8 hours after wrapping it in plastic.
- To create the mop sauce, combine the lime juice, Worcestershire sauce, apple cider vinegar, beer, and red pepper flakes in a nonreactive dish. After that, put it away.
- On the BBQ
- Arranged your Smoke grill to cook in the indirect mode.
- Set your Smoker grill to 180 degrees Fahrenheit with the lid closed for 15 minutes.
- Remove the plastic wrap from the pork butt and place it directly on the grill grates. Smoke your pork for three hours, mopping with the mopping sauce after each hour.
- Increase the temperature of the head to 250 degrees Fahrenheit, and then maintain it there.
- Roast your pork unless the inner temp hits 160°F (10°C). This should take around 3 hours longer. Continue mopping each hour on the hour with the mop sauce.

- Cover your pork butt with foil and continue to cook till the inner Smoke Temperature reaches 204 degrees Fahrenheit.

- Cover the pork in foil, then wrap it in thick bath towels and place it in an insulated refrigerator for one hour at most.

- To create the vinegar sauce, combine the water, apple cider vinegar, ketchup, brown sugar, red pepper flakes, salt, white pepper, and black pepper in a large mixing bowl. Stir everything together until the sugar and salt crystals are completely dissolved.

- Check for seasoning and adjust with additional sugar or red pepper as needed. Then let it aside for an hour to allow the flavors to combine properly.

- To create the Carolina coleslaw, combine cabbage, 1 cup vinegar sauce, and 14 chopped red onions, as well as some shredded carrots in a mixing bowl.

- To make the pulled pork, cut the pork into small pieces, removing the bone and any gristle or fat. Next, shred the pork and place the pieces in a reusable roasting pan to pull it apart.

- Use the liquids in the foil, as well as part of your vinegar sauce, to keep the meat moist.

- Place the meat on the buns and top with coleslaw. Have a fantastic dinner!

7.2: Fajita Sandwiches

Preparation time: 25 minutes

Cooking time: 15 minutes

Servings: 4 - 6 adult-sized humans

Ingredients:

- Skirt steak, 2 pounds (trimmed)

- 4 limes (squeezed)

- A quarter cup of soy sauce

- Tequila (2 tbsp.) (optional)

- 2 tbsp. of Worcestershire seasoning

- 2 garlic cloves (minced)

- 1 and a half tsp. of cumin (crushed)

- A quarter tsp. of chili powder

255

- 1 tsp. of kosher salt
- 1 tbsp. of vegetable oil + ½ cup
- 1 tsp. of freshly crushed black pepper (freshly powdered)
- 3 cayenne peppers
- 1 big onion (red or white)
- 6 ciabatta rolls (grilled or toasted)
- A third of a cup of cilantro leaves
- Serving suggestions include guacamole, Pico de gallo, guacamole, sour cream, pickled sliced jalapenos, grated cheese, and spicy sauce.

Steps:

- Cut your steak into four even pieces, and then put them in a reseal able plastic baggie. Set that aside as you prepare the marinade.
- Grab a jar that is nice and airtight. Add in your lime juice from the four limes, your tequila, soy sauce, and Worcestershire sauce if you are using it.
- Also, add in your cumin, rub, salt, garlic, and ½ cup of vegetable oil. Shake it all up as vigorously as you can, and then pour all of that over your meat.
- Massage the bag as well as you can so that the meat is properly coated.
- Then seal the bag and keep it in your fridge for 4 to 8 hours. Do not go any longer than 8 hours, or the texture of the meat will get weird.
- On the Grill
- Grab a cast iron skillet and set it on one side of your Smoker grill.
- Preheat your Smoker grill on high, with the lid open. Once the fire gets which should take 4 to 5 minutes, tops — close the lid for 10 to 15 minutes.
- Drain the marinade from the steak, and then pat your steak dry with some paper towels so that your meat can sear better.
- Season the marinated meat with freshly ground black pepper.
- Toss the rest of your oil (the tablespoon) onto your skillet.
- Now, place your steak on the grill grate.
- Toss half of your bell peppers and your onions onto the skillet, which should be hot by now.
- Grill your steaks, making sure you turn them once, cooking each side for 2 to 3 minutes, or until it is done the way you like it.

- Stir your vegetables a bit to give them a nice char, for 10 to 12 minutes.

- Move the steaks to a large platter and tent them with some aluminum foil. As the steaks rest, sauté the rest of your veggies in the skillet and then toast your ciabatta rolls on the grill if you want. Make sure the cut sides of your ciabatta rolls are down.

- Slice the steak as thinly as you can, going against the grain, and then arrange them on one side of the platter.

- You can now pile the onions and peppers on the other side. You could also some of the sliced steak and veggies right of the skillet.

- Garnish with some cilantro.

- Wrap up your ciabatta rolls with a cloth napkin, and serve them in a basket, as well as your veggies and meat and the condiments to accompany them.

7.3. Baked S'mores Donut

Preparation time: 10 minutes

Cooking time: 35 minutes

Servings: 8 - 12 adult-sized humans

Ingredients:

For the doughnuts, follow these instructions:

- 1 cup flour (all-purpose) Cooking spray

- A quarter tsp. of baking soda

- 1/3 cup of sugar

- A third of a cup of buttermilk

- 2 tbsp. of unsalted melted butter

- A single egg

- ½ tsp. of extract de vanilla

- 4 bars of chocolate (whatever kind you want)

- For the Glaze, cut 24 marshmallows in half.

- A quarter-cup of whole milk

- 1 tsp. of extract de vanilla

- 2 cup confectioners' suction.'

Steps:

- Using frying spray, coat the doughnut pans.

- Whisk together the flour, sugar, and baking soda in a large mixing basin.

- In a separate dish, mix the egg, buttermilk, and vanilla extract, butter

- Using a spoon, stir the drying components together properly.

- Fill the oiled donuts pans halfway with batter.

- On the Barbie

- Arranged your Smoker grill to cook indirectly.

- Warm the Smoker grill to 350 degrees Fahrenheit for 10 to 15 minutes.

- Bake for 25 minutes, or until your donuts are lovely and puffy and a toothpick inserted to inspect them comes out clean. After that, let it cool in the pan.

- In a saucepan, combine the milk and vanilla and cook over low heat until warm.

- Sift the confectioner's sugar into the milk and vanilla mixture until everything is well mixed.

- Erase the Glaze from the heat and place it in a basin of warm water to cool.

- Dip your wonderful doughnuts into the Glaze straight away, then put your rack over a little foil and place the donut on the rack to chill for 5 minutes.

- Place your split marshmallows and even some chocolate between the halves of the donuts.

- Grilled these sandwiches for 4-5 minutes on each side. You want the marshmallows and chocolate to melt.

- Remove them from the grill, plate them, and enjoy!

7.4: Baked Cherry Cheesecake Galette

Preparation time: 10 minutes

Cooking time: 20 minutes

Servings: 6 - 8 adult-sized humans

Ingredients:

To make the cherry filling, combine the following ingredients in a mixing bowl.

- Cherries, 1 pound (thawed, drained)
- ¼ cup of sugar
- Cornstarch, 1 teaspoon
- 1 tsp. of coriander, chopped
- A grain of salt
- 1 tbsp. Zest of orange
- ½ tbsp. of lemon zest

To make the cream cheese filling, combine the following ingredients in a mixing bowl.

- Cream cheese, 8 oz. (softened)
- 1 tsp. of vanilla extract
- ¼ cup of sugar
- A single egg

For the Galette, combine the following ingredients.

- 1 pie crust (refrigerated)
- Washes of eggs
- Ice cream (vanilla) to serve with granulated sugar

Steps:

- Combine the orange juice, coriander, cherries, lemon zest, half of the sugar, starch, and a sprinkle of salt in a medium mixing bowl.

- In a separate dish, whisk together your vanilla, egg and cream cheese.

- Prepare them as soon as possible.

- Put the pie dough on a baking sheet and spread it out like a rolling pin. Get it to a diameter of approximately 1 inch.

- In the center of the pie crust, spread out the cream cheese filling. Make sure to leave a one-inch margin around the edge. After that, put your cherry mixture on top of the cream cheese.

- Fold the corners of the pie crust into small pieces and place them over the filling.

- Brush the pie dough's edges with (egg wash) and then sprinkle with granulated sugar.

- On the Barbie

- Established your Smoker grill to cook indirectly.

- Set your Smoker grill for 15 minutes at 350 Fahrenheit with the lid closed.

- Place your sheet pan on the grilling grate and bake for 15 minutes. The crust should become a beautiful golden brown, and the cheesecake filling should be fully set.

- Serve the Galette with ice cream while it's still warm. Then sit back and relax.

7.5: *Grilled Fruit with Cream*

Preparation Time: 15 minutes

Cooking Time: 10 minutes

Servings: 4 - 6

Ingredients:

- Halved Nectarine 1

- 2 peaches, halved

- A quarter cup of blueberries

- ½ cup of berries (raspberries)

- Honey, 2 tbsp.

- 1 orange, including the peel

- 2 quarts cream

- ½ cup of balsamic vinaigrette

Steps:

- Set the skillet to 400 degrees Fahrenheit with the lid covered.

- Grill for 4 minutes on each side the apricots. Peaches, nectarines.

- Turn the burner to medium heat and place a pan on top of it. 2 tbsp. of honey, 2 tbsp. of vinegar, 2 tbsp. Orange peel Cook until the sauce has thickened to a medium consistency.

- Meanwhile, combine and cream and honey in a mixing dish. Whip until the mixture achieves a soft consistency.

- Arrange the fruit on a dish for serving. Lastly, top with berries. Finally, drizzle the balsamic reduction over the top.

- Enjoy with a dollop of sour cream!

7.6: *Apple Pie on the Grill*

Preparation Time: 20 minutes

Cooking Time: 30 minutes

Servings: 4 - 6

Ingredients

- Sugar ¼ cup
- 4 diced apples
- Cornstarch, 1 tbsp.
- 1 tsp. 0f powdered cinnamon
- 1 refrigerated pie crust softens according to the directions: on the package
- ½ cup of (peach) preservatives

Steps:

- Set the skillet to 375 degrees Fahrenheit with the lid covered.
- Combine the sugar, apples, cinnamon, and cornstarch in a mixing basin. Remove from the equation.
- In a pie pan, place the pie crust. Put the apples on top of the preserves. Lightly fold the crust.
- To avoid brill/baking the pie immediately on (Preferred Wood Pellet), put a pan on the griddle (upside-down).
- The cooking time is 30-40 minutes. Set away to rest after completed.
- Serve and have fun!

1.7. *Grilled Layered Cake*

Preparation Time: 10 minutes

Cooking Time: 14 minutes

Servings: 6

Ingredients:

- 2 pounds of cake

- Whipped cream (three cups)

- ¼ cup of butter, melted

- blueberries, 1 cup

- 1 cup raspberry berries

- 1 cup strawberries, sliced

Steps:

- Close the cover and set the grill to high.
- Approximately 10 slices per cake loaf (3/4 inch) Butter both sides of the bread.
- Cook for 7 minutes each side on the grill. Remove from the equation.
- Begin stacking your cake after it has fully cooled. Put the cake first, then the berries, and finally the cream.
- Serve with berries as a garnish.

7.8: Coconut Chocolate Simple Brownies

Preparation Time: 15 minutes

Cooking Time: 25 minutes

Servings: 4 - 6

Ingredients:

- Eggs 4

- Cane Sugar 1 cup

- Coconut oil ¾ cup

- 4 oz. of chocolate, chopped

- ½ tsp. of Sea salt

- Cocoa powder, unsweetened ¼ cup

- Flour ½ cup

- Chocolate chips 4 oz.

- Vanilla 1 tsp.

Steps:

- Set the skillet to 350 degrees Fahrenheit with the lid covered.

- Grease a 9x9 baking pan and line it with parchment paper.

- Stir the cocoa powder, salt, and flour in a mixing dish. Set aside after stirring. Warm the chopped chocolate and coconut oil in the microwave or a double boiler. Allow it to cool for a few minutes.

- Combine the eggs, vanilla and sugar in a mixing bowl. To mix the ingredients, whisk them together.

- Add chocolate chips to the flour mixture. Fill a pan halfway with the mixture.

- Put the grate on top of the pan. Preheat oven to 350°F and cook for 20 minutes. Bake for an additional 5 to 10 minutes if you want drier brownies.

- Allow them to cool completely before cutting.

- Serve the brownies cut into squares.

7.9: *Seasonal Fruit on the Grill*

Preparation Time: 5 minutes

Cooking Time: 5 minutes

Servings: 2 - 4

Ingredients:

- Peaches apricots, two plums

- Sugar, 3tbsp.

- As desired (Gelato)

- Honey ¼ cup

Steps:

- Set the skillet to 450 degrees Fahrenheit with the lid covered.

- Remove the pits from each fruit before slicing it in half. Apply honey on the brush. Add some sugar to the top.

- Grill the meat on the grates unless grill marks appear. Remove from the equation.

- Serve with a spoonful of gelato for each person. Enjoy!

7.10: Cinnamon Sugar Pumpkin Seeds

Preparation Time: 30 minutes

Cooking Time: 30 minutes.

Servings: 8-12

Ingredients:

- Powdered sugar 3 tbsp.
- Pumpkin seeds
- Cinnamon 1 tsp.
- 2 tbsp. of softened butter

Steps:

- Fill your smoker with (Recommended Wood Pellet pellets) and fire it up according to the manufacturer's instructions. Preheat your smoker to 350 degrees with the lid closed.

- Toss the seeds in the butter after cleaning them. Combine the cinnamon and sugar in a mixing bowl. Place them on a baking tray and smoke them for 25 minutes on the grill. And serve it.

7.11: Blackberry Pie

Preparation Time: 30 minutes.

Cooking Time: 40 minutes.

Servings: 8

Ingredients:

- Grease with butter
- ½ cup of all-purpose flour
- Blackberries, 2 quarts
- 2 c. of sugar (distributed)
- 1 package of piecrusts (kept in the fridge)
- 1 melted butter stick
- 1 tbsp. of margarine

- Ice cream with vanilla flavor

Steps:

- Fill your smoker with (Recommended Wood Pellet pellets) and fire it up according to the manufacturer's instructions. Preheat your smoker to 375 degrees with the lid closed.

- Using butter, coat a cast-iron skillet.

- Unwrap a pie crust and place it in the skillet's lower part and up the sides. Poke gaps in the crust with a fork.

- Place the (skillet) on the grill and cook for 5 minutes, or unless the surface is golden brown. Turn on the grill.

- Combine 12 cups flour, sugar and melted butter in a mixing bowl. Toss in the (blackberries) and combine everything.

- Toss the berry mixture into the skillet. After that, the whole milk should be poured over the top. Finally, half of the chopped butter goes on top.

- The 2nd pie crust should be unrolled and placed on top of the skillet. To make it appear like a lattice, cut it into pieces and weave them on top. Sprinkle the remaining chopped butter over the top. Return the skillet to the grill and sprinkle the remaining sugar over the top.

- Reduce the heat to low and smoked for 15 to 20 minutes, just until the meat is brown and bubbling. For the last few minutes of cooking, you may also want to cover it with foil to prevent it from burning. Serve the heated pie with vanilla ice cream on the side.

7.12: *S'mores Dip*

Preparation Time: 30 minutes.

Cooking Time: 20 minutes.

Servings: 6-8

Ingredients:

- Chocolate chips 12oz.

- ¼ c. of whole milk

- 2 tbsp. of softened salted butter

- Marshmallows 16 oz.

- Graham crackers
- Wedges of apples

Steps:

- Fill your smokers with (Recommended Wood Pellet pellets) and fire it up according to the manufacturer's instructions. Preheat your smoker to 450 degrees with the lid closed.

- Put a cast-iron pan on your grill and pour in the milk and melted butter.

- Mix everything over a minute.

- Once it's warmed up, sprinkle the chocolate chips on top, ensuring they're in a single layer. Next, put the marshmallow on top of the chocolate, standing them on end and coating it.

- Cover and set aside for five or six minutes to smoke. The marshmallow should be gently toasted before serving.

- Remove the saucepan from the (Recommended Wood Pellet) and serves with blue cheese dressing and apple wedges and Graham crackers are a kind of biscuit.

7.13: Ice Cream Bread

Preparation Time: 30 minutes.

Cooking Time: 1 hour.

Servings: 12-16

Ingredients:

- 1 ½ quart butter (full-fat) softened pecan ice cream
- 1 tsp. of salt
- Semi-sweet chocolate chips (two cups)
- 1 cup sugar
- 1 heated butter stick
- Grease with butter
- A quarter cup of self-rising flour

Steps:

- Fill your smoker with Recommended Wood Pellet pellets and fire it up according to the manufacturer's instructions. Preheat your smoker to 350 degrees with the lid closed.

- With only a hand blender set to medium, combine the sugar, salt, flour, and ice cream for two minutes.

- While the blender has still been working, add the chocolate chips and continue to beat until everything is well combined.

- Using cooking spray, coat a Baking pan or tube pan. If you use a solid-bottomed pan, the middle will take too much time to cook. As a result, a tube or Bundt pan is ideal.

- Pour the batter into the pan that has been prepared.

- Place the cakes on the fire, cover them, and let them smoke for 50 to an hour. If you use a toothpick, this should look clean.

- Remove the pan from the grill and set it aside. Cool the bread for 10 minutes. Then, removed the bread from the pan with care and brushed it with melted butter.

7.14: Bacon Chocolate Chip Cookies

Preparation Time: 30 minutes.

Cooking Time: 30 minutes.

Servings: 12

Ingredients:

- 8 cooked and chopped bacon slices
- 2 ½ tablespoons apple cider vinegar
- 1 tsp. of vanilla
- Semi-sweet chocolate chips (two cups)
- Two eggs, room temperature
- 1 ½ tsp. of baking soda
- 1 c. of sugar, granulated
- ½ tsp. salt
- 2 ¾ cup flour (all-purpose)
- 1 c. brown sugar (light)

- 11/2 stick butter, softened

Steps:

- Combine the flour, baking soda, and salt in a mixing bowl.

- Combine the butter and sugar in a mixing bowl. Reduce the pace. Combine the vinegar, eggs, and vanilla extract in a mixing bowl.

- Slowly pour in the flour mix, bacon bits, and chocolate chips while still on low.

- Fill your smoker with Recommended Wood Pellet pellets and fire it up according to the manufacturer's instructions. Preheat your smoker to 375 degrees with the lid closed.

- Place a parchment paper on a baking tray and put a tsp of cookie dough onto it. Allow them to cook for about 12 minutes on the grill, cover, or unless they are golden. Enjoy.

7.15: Chocolate Chip Cookies

Preparation Time: 30 minutes.

Cooking Time: 30 minutes.

Servings: 12

Ingredients:

- ½ cup walnuts, chopped and vanilla 1 tsp

- Choco chips (two cups)

- 1 tbsp. baking powder

- 2 ½ c. of all-purpose flour

- ½ tsp. of salt

- ½ stick butter, melted

- A pair of eggs

- A cup of brown sugar

- ½ cup of sugar

Steps:

- Fill your smoker with Recommended Wood Pellet pellets and fire it up according to the package recommendations. Preheat your smoker to 350 degrees with the lid closed.

- Combine the salt, flour, baking soda in a bowl and mix.

- Sugar, brown sugar, and margarine are combined in a mixing bowl. Stir in the eggs and vanilla until all are well combined.

- While continuing to beat, gradually add in the flour. Add the walnuts and chocolate chips after all of the flour has been mixed. Fold the egg whites into the batter with a spoon.

- Place a piece of aluminum foil on top of the grill. Drop a dollop of dough onto the aluminum baking sheet and bake for 17 minutes.

7.16: Apple Cobbler

Preparation Time: 30 minutes.

Cooking Time: 1 hour. 50 minutes.

Servings: 8

Ingredients:

- 8 apples, Granny Smith

- 1 tbsp. sugar

- 1 tsp. of cinnamon

- A pinch of salt

- ½ cup of brown sugar

- A pair of eggs

- 2 tbsp. of baking soda

- 2 c. of all-purpose flour

- ½ cup of sweetener

Steps:

- Apples should be peeled and quartered before being placed in a dish. Combine the cinnamon and one cup of sugar in a mixing bowl. Stir well to coat, then put aside for one hour.

- Fill your smoker with Recommended Wood Pellet pellets and fire it up according to the manufacturer's instructions. Preheat your smoker to 350 degrees with the lid closed.

- Combine the sugar, flour, baking powder, salt, eggs, and brown sugar in a large mixing basin. Mix until crumbs form.

- In a Dutch oven, place the apples. Drizzle the melted butter on top of the crumble mixture.

- Preheat the grill to medium-high and cook for 50 minutes.

7.17: Pineapple Cake

Preparation Time: 30 minutes.

Cooking Time: 1 hour. 20 minutes.

Servings: 8

Ingredients:

- 1 cup sugar

- A tsp. of baking soda

- A cup of buttermilk

- ½ tsp. of salt

- 1 maraschino cherry jar

- ¾ cup granulated sugar 1 piece butter, divided

- Pineapple pieces are available.

- ½ cup flour

Steps:

- Fill your smoker with (Recommended Wood Pellet pellets) and fire it up according to the manufacturer's instructions. Preheat your smoker to 350 degrees with the lid closed.

- Heat one-half-piece butter in a moderate cast iron pan. Make sure the whole skillet is coated. In a cast-iron skillet, sprinkle brown sugar.

- Place the pineapple slices on the upper part of brown sugar. Place a cherry in the center of each pineapple ring.

- Combine the baking powder, salt, flour, and sugar in a mixing bowl. In a large mixing bowl, whisk together the egg, one-half piece softened butter and buttermilk. To mix the ingredients, whisk them together.

- Cooking for an hour on the grill with the cake.

- Remove the steak from the grill and put it aside for 10 minutes. Transfer to a serving dish.

7.18: Caramel Bananas

Preparation Time: 15 minutes.

Cooking Time: 15 minutes.

Servings: 4

Ingredients:

- Chopped pecans 1/3 cup
- Condensed milk sweetened ½ cup
- Bananas 4
- Brown sugar ½ cup.
- Corn syrup 2 tbsp.
- ½ c. of melted butter

Steps:

- Fill your smoker with pellets and fire it up according to the manufacturer's instructions.
- Set your smoker to 350 degrees with the lid closed.
- Bring the butter, corn syrup, milk, and brown sugar to a boil in a large pot. Simmer the mixture over low heat for five minutes. Stir the mixture regularly.
- Place the bananas on the grill with their skins on and cook for five minutes. Cook for another five minutes on the other side. The peels will be black and prone to splitting.
- Place on a plate to serve. Remove the ends of the banana and cut the skin in half. Remove the skin from the bananas and top with caramel.
- Pecans should be sprinkled on top.

7.19: Vanilla Flavored Marshmallow Apples

Preparation time: 15 minutes

Cooking time: 1 to 1½ hours

Servings: 6

Ingredients:

- 6 crisps of honey or Fuji apples, crunchy and delicious
- 6 tbsp. of unsalted butter (3/4 stick) at room temperature
- ¼ cup of firmly stuffed dark brown sugar
- ¼ cup of dried currants
- ¼ cup of powdered almonds, gingersnap crumbs, graham cracker crumbs.
- ½ tsp. of powdered cinnamon
- ¼ tsp. of freshly grated nutmeg
- 1 tsp. of pure vanilla extract
- 6 cinnamon sticks
- Effective vanilla ice cream

Steps:

- Preheat your smoker to 275°F (135°C) according to the manufacturer's instructions.

- Slice the apples, but don't cut all the way through; the aim is to create a hole for filling.

- In a medium-sized mixing basin, cream together brown sugar and butter until creamy. Combine the vanilla, currant, cookie crumbs, cinnamon, and nutmeg in a mixing bowl. Evenly distribute the filling among the apples. Put a marshmallow half on top of each apple and put a cinnamon stick straight through the filling.

- Place the apples on the smoker rack on grill rings or place them directly on the rack. Smoke the apples for 1 to 112 hours, just unless the sides are tender but not collapsing. If the marshmallows begin to brown too quickly, cover the apples loosely with aluminum foil. If preferred, serve the smoked apples with ice cream on the side.

7.20: Vanilla Flavored Cheesecake

Preparation time: 15 minutes

Cooking time: 1½ to 2 hours

Servings: 8 to 10

Ingredients:

For the crust, use vegetable oil to grease the pan.

- 12 ounces of (340 g) (about 36) gingersnaps
- A third of a cup of light brown sugar
- 1 stick unsalted butter, melted 8 tbsp.

The Stuffing:

- 4 packets of (8 oz./227 g each) room temperature cream cheese
- 1 cup of light golden sugar, tightly packed
- 2 tsp. of vanilla extract (pure)
- 1 tbsp. of fresh lime juice
- ¼ stick (2 tbsp.) softened unsalted butter
- A dozen big eggs
- Sauce with burnt sugar (optional)

Steps:

- Preheat your grill to medium-high 400°F (204°C) for indirect cooking. Set your oven to 400 degrees Fahrenheit (204 degrees Celsius). Wrap a piece of plastic wrap over the outside of the springs from the pan and lightly grease it.

- In a food processor, split the cookies into pieces and crush with the (brown sugar) to a fine powder. You'll need about 134 cups of crumbs. To make a crumbly dough, add the softened butter and pulse the machine in short bursts.

- Spread the mixture equally over the bottom of the spring form pan and halfway up the edges. 5 - 10 minutes on an indirect grill or in the oven until the crust is gently browned. Allow cooling in the pan on a wire rack.

- Clean the bowl of the food processor. Process till smooth the brown sugar lime juice, vanilla, cream cheese, lemon zest, and butter.

- Process the eggs one at a time, till soft after each addition.

- Fill the crust with the contents. To remove any air bubbles, carefully pour the pan on the counter a few times.

- Preheat your smoker to 225°F (107°C) to 250°F (121°C) according to the manufacturer's recommendations. Then, assemble the wood according to the manufacturer's instructions.

- Put the cake in the smoker to cook. Smoke for 112 to 2 hours, just until the topping is bronzed with smokes and the filling is set.

- Gently probe the edge of the pan to see whether the filling is done; it should jiggle, not ripple. Alternatively, pierce the middle of the cake with a thin metal stick; this will come out clean.

- Allow the cheesecake to cool completely in its pan on a wire rack. The cheesecake may be prepared up to 8 hours ahead of time and kept refrigerated until ready to serve.

- Cut around the interior of the spring form pan with a thin knife. Remove the ring by unclasping it. (The cheesecake will be served from the bottom of the pan.) Before serving, let the cheesecake reheat slightly at room temperature.

- Pour part of the sauce over the cake and the remainder into a pitcher if serving with the sauce. Slice into wedges and serve with the rest of the sauce.

7.21: Smoked-Honey Crisp with Bacon

Preparation time: 15 minutes

Cooking time: ¾ to 1 hour

Servings: 8

Ingredients:

- The Stuffing:
- 2 artisanal bacon strips, sliced crosswise into 14-inch slivers, like Nueske's
- 3 pound (1.4 kilograms) Honeycrisp or Gala apples, crisp and delicious
- 1/3 cup of light or dark brown sugar, packed, or to taste
- 11/2 tbsp. of flour (all-purpose)
- 1 tsp. of lemon zest, finely grated
- 1 tsp. of cinnamon powder
- 1 tsp. of salt
- Bourbon (3 tbsp.)
- The Finishing Touch:
- 8 tbsp. of unsalted butter (1 stick), cut into 12-inch chunks and put in
- The freezer until it's bone-chillingly cold
- ½ cup of gingersnap cookies (crushed) or granola
- ½ cup flour (all-purpose)

- ½ cup sugar, granulated
- ½ cup brown sugar (light or dark)
- 1 tsp. of salt
- Vanilla ice cream (regular) for serving (optional)

Steps:

- Preheat your grill to 400 °F for indirect grilling.
- Cook the bacon in a 10" cast-iron pan on medium heat, stirring regularly, till crisp & golden brown, for about 4 minutes. Place the bacon in a large mixing dish.
- Pour out the bacon fat and save it aside for later use. Don't wash the skillet.
- Cut the apples into 1-inch pieces after peeling and coring them. Put them in with the bacon. Stir in the flour, lemon zest, sugar, salt and cinnamon in a mixing bowl. Pour in the bourbon and mix well.
- Check the sweetness of the mixture and add sugar if needed. Fill the skillet halfway with the filling.
- In a food processor, combine the butter, flour, white & brown sugars, cookie crumbs and salt.
- Using the processor in small intervals, grind to the coarse mixture. Do not over process the mixture; it should be loose and crumbly, like sand. Over the apples, strew the topping.
- Remove the crisp from the heat and place it on the smoker rack or grill. Cover the grill and add some wood to coals.
- Smoke-roast the crisp for 45 minutes to 1 hour, or until the topping gets browned and bubbly, the apples become soft (and easily pierced with a stick), and the filling becomes thick.
- Serve the crisps immediately after they have been removed from the smoker or grill.

7.22: Chocolate Pudding with Smoked Ice Cream

Preparation time: 15 minutes

Cooking time: 60 minutes

Servings: 8

Ingredients:

- 1 loaf (454 g/1 pounds) cut into 1-inch chunks brioche (about 8 cups)
- 3 cups of heavy cream (whipped)
- 2 quarts of whole milk
- ½ pound sugar
- 1 tsp. of salt
- 8 ounces 1 vanilla bean (227 g) coarsely sliced bittersweet chocolate
- Four big eggs
- 2 big yolks of eggs
- 1 tsp. of pure vanilla extract (or 1 ½ tsp. of the vanilla bean isn't used)
- For buttering the skillet, use butter.
- Serving ice cream with a smoky flavor (optional)

Steps:

- Preheat your smoker to 225°F (107°C) to 250°F (121°C) according to the manufacturer's recommendations. Then, assemble the wood according to the manufacturer's instructions.
- Place the brioche cubes on an aluminum foil pan in a thin layer in the smoker.
- Smoke for 30 to 45 minutes, stirring periodically to ensure that the cubes smoke evenly.
- Meanwhile, prepare the custard: In a heavy pot, combine the milk, cream, sugar, and salt. If used, split the vanilla bean lengthwise and scoop the tiny black seeds into the cream.
- Finally, toss in the vanilla bean half. Over medium heat, bring to a boil, constantly stirring till the sugar dissolves. Turn off the heat in the pan.
- Discard the vanilla bean half after rinsing, drying, and reusing them.
- Most of the chocolate should be melted by now.
- In a large heat-proof dish, whisk together the egg, vanilla extract, egg yolks, and if using, until smooth. Stir in the hot cream mixture gradually.
- Slowly drizzle it in to avoid curdling the eggs. Next, fold in the smoked bread cubes until they have absorbed the majority of the custard.
- Melt the butter in the skillet and add the pudding mixture. Sprinkle the remaining chopped chocolate on top and use a fork to push the pieces into the bread pudding.

- Raise the temperature of your smoker to 325 degrees Fahrenheit (163 degrees Celsius). Of course, some smokers won't go that high; if that's the case, raise the temperature to 275°F (135°C).
- Smoke the bread pudding for 40 to 60 minutes at the higher temperature, 1 to 112 hours at the lower temperature, or until puffed and browned on top and the custard is set.
- Immediately served the bread pudding

7.23: Caramelized Egg Bake

Preparation time: 10 minutes

Cooking time: 1 to 1¼ hours

Servings: 6

Ingredients:

The Caramel Sauce:

- ¼ cup of water 1 cup sugar
- ½ cup of sugar for the flan
- 3 eggs (big)
- 2 big yolks of eggs
- 1 tsp. of salt 114 cups whole milk
- ½ gallon half-and-half
- 1 vanilla bean, smoked split,
- Vanilla extract 1 tsp.

Steps:

- In a large pot, combine the sugar and water. Cover with a lid and cook for 2 minutes over high heat.
- Open the lid from the pan and turn the heat down to medium. Swirl the pan to
brown the sugar uniformly, but don't stir it, and keep an eye on it, so it doesn't burn or turn bitter. (If it does, you'll have to start from scratch.) Cook for 4 to 6 minutes, or until the syrup is rich golden brown and caramelized.
- Erase the remove from heat as soon as possible. Make sure you don't touch the hot sugar with your hands.

- Slowly transfer the caramel into the ramekins, turning them to cover the bottoms and sides evenly.

- Allow the caramel to cool completely before using. Then, put the ramekins on a baking sheet with a rim.

- In a large heat-proof dish, whisk together the whole eggs, sugar, yolks, and salt.

- In a heavy saucepan, simmer the half-and-half milk and vanilla bean, if using, over moderate flame till very hot but not boiling.

- Whisk in 12 cups of the hot milk mixture at a time into the egg mixture.

- Remove the vanilla bean and drain it into a large heat-proof glass measuring cup. If you're using vanilla extract, add it now. Allow the custard to cool somewhat before pouring it into the ramekins that have been caramelized.

- Preheat your smoker to 225°F (107°C) to 250°F (121°C) according to the manufacturer's recommendations.

- Put the sheet pan with the ramekins in the smoke and smoker for 1 to 114 hours, or until the custard is set. Then, poke one of the ramekins to see if it's done.

- The flan is done when it jiggles (no ripples). The interior temperature should be 180°F (82°C) as measured by an instant-read thermometer.

- Allow the flans to chill in the fridge on a wire rack before refrigerating for at least 4 hours or up to overnight before serving.

- Scrape the tip of a sharp knife along the inner edge of each flan to unmold it. Next, place a plate on top of the ramekin, invert it, and shake it until the flan comes free. Any remaining caramel in the ramekin should be spooned around the flan.

7.24: Yummy Sweet Banana Bowl

Preparation time: 10 minutes

Cooking time: 15 minutes

Servings: 6 to 8

Ingredients:

- 1/2-pound sugar

- 1 can sweet evaporated milk (14 oz. / 397 g)

- 2 quarts of whole milk

- 4 distinct eggs
- Vanilla wafers in a box ½ (12-ounce / 340-g)
- Sifted 3 tbsp. all-purpose flour
- 4 finely sliced ripe bananas
- 1 tsp. of tartar sauce

Steps:

- Mix the sugars and both kinds of milk in a small saucepan. Stir until all of the sugar has dissolved. Reduce the heat to a low setting.
- Toss in the flour and egg yolks into the pan. Stir constantly until the mixture thickens. Allow the mixture to cool in the pan after removing it from the heat.
- Layer half of the chilled custard, halfway of the vanilla wafers, and half of the bananas in a big, transparent oven tray bowl or another serving dish. Carry on with the layering.
- Sprinkle crushed vanilla wafers on top. If wanted, a meringue may be placed on top of the pudding. Remove the dish and set it away.
- Turn the oven on to broil.
- In a large mixing bowl, pour the saved egg whites. To make stiff peaks, whisk the egg whites with the cream of tartar using a handheld electric mixer until firm peaks form.
- Place this meringue on top of the pudding. Cook for 2 to 3 minutes, or until the meringue browns, on a lower rack under the broiler. Take the pudding out of the oven and serve.

7.25: Caramelized Apple Crunch

Preparation time: 10 minutes

Cooking time: 40 to 45 minutes

Servings: 6

Ingredients:

- 4 cups apples, ideally Granny Smith, sliced, cored, and peeled
- A third of a cup of all-purpose flour
- 1 cup of sugar

- 1 tsp. of cinnamon powder
- A quarter tsp. of salt
- 8 tbsp. of unsalted butter (1 stick) at room temperature, cut into pieces,
- Plus a little extra for the baking dish
- Ice cream (Vanilla).

Steps:

- Heat the oven degrees Fahrenheit (177 degrees Celsius). Grease a 9-inch baking sheet lightly. In a baking dish, arrange the apple slices.
- Stir to combine sugar, cinnamon, and salt in the mixing bowl. To mix, pulse a few times. Pulse in the butter until the mixture looks like coarse crumbs.
- Crumble the crumbs on top of the apples.
- Bake the apples for 40 to 45 minutes, or until they are soft. If desired, serve warm with ice cream.

7.26: Smoked Peaches with Vanilla Ice-cream

Preparation time: 10 minutes

Cooking time: 10 minutes

Servings: 4

Ingredients:

- Georgia peaches 4
- (1 stick) unsalted melted butter 8 tbsp.
- 1 cup of (dark brown sugar).
- Dark rum 2 tbsp.
- Apricot preserves 10 ounces.
- Ice cream Vanilla

Steps:

- Preheat, the smoker to 325 degrees Fahrenheit (163 degrees Celsius).
- Remove the pits from the apricots and cut them into quarters. Using skewers, attach the quarters to the skewers. On a large aluminum pan, arrange the skewers.

- Mix the rum, brown sugar, butter, and preserves in a medium saucepan over medium heat. Stir everything together well.

- Cover the peaches with the preserve mixture, put in the smokers, and cook for 4 minutes on each side or until tender. If desired, serve the peaches with vanilla ice cream.

7.27: *Chocolaty Bacon Cookies*

Preparation time: 15 minutes

Cooking time: 15 minutes

Servings: 2

Ingredients:

- 2 ¾ cup flour (all-purpose)
- A total of 1 ½ tsp. baking soda
- A quarter tsp. of salt
- ½ tbsp. of unsalted butter, softened
- 1 cup brown sugar (light)
- 1 cup sugar (granulated)
- 2 room-temperature eggs
- Apple cider vinegar (2 ½ tsp.)
- 1 tsp. of extract de vanilla
- 2 cups chocolate chips (semi-sweet)
- 8 cooked and crumbled bacon slices

Steps:

- In a large mixing dish, whisk together the salt, baking soda, flour.

- Softened butter and sugars in a different large mixing dish with an immersion blender on medium speed. Reduce the mixer's speed to low and add the vinegar, eggs, and vanilla extract.

- Slowly add the dry ingredients, bacon bits chocolate chips while the mixer is still on low.

- Fill your smokers with (wood pellets) and fire them up according to the manufacturer's instructions. Preheat the oven to 375°F (191°C) with the lid closed.

- Preheat oven to 350°F and line a big cookie sheet.
- Place rounded tbsp. Of cookie batter on the grill grate and place on the prepared baking sheet. Close the cover and smoke for 10 to 12 minutes, or until the edges of the cookies have browned.

7.28: Buttery Chocolate with Graham Crackers

Preparation time: 5 minutes

Cooking time: 6 to 8 minutes

Servings: 4 to 6

Ingredients:

- ¼ cup milk
- 2 tsp. of salted butter, melted
- ½ fluid ounces (340 g) chocolate chips, semi-sweet
- 16 oz. of marshmallows that have been jet-puffed
- For serving, use apple wedges and graham crackers.

Steps:

- Fill your smokers with (wood pellets) and fire them up according to the manufacturer's instructions. Preheat the oven to 450°F (232°C) with the lid closed.
- Melt the butter in a cast-iron pan over a hot grill grate, pour in the milk and stir for approximately 1 minute.
- As soon as the mixture begins to heat, sprinkle the chocolate chips on top in an equal layer, then stand the marshmallows up to cover the chocolate completely.
- Start smoking for 5 to 7 minutes, just until the marshmallow is gently toasted, with the lid closed.
- Pull the pan from the heat and serve with graham cracker and apple wedges for the dip.

7.29: Blackberry Pie with Vanilla Ice-cream

Preparation time: 10 minutes

Cooking time: 10 minutes

Servings: 4 to 6

Ingredients:

- For greasing, use nonstick cooking spray or butter.
- 1 carton (2 sheets) piecrusts that have been refrigerated
- 8 tbsp. of unsalted butter (1 stick) melted plus 8 tsp. of (1 stick)
- Sliced into chunks
- ½ cup flour (all-purpose)
- 2 cups sugar (distributed)
- Blackberries, 2 quarts
- ½ cup of milk
- For serving, vanilla ice cream

Steps:

- Fill the smokers with (wood pellets) and fire them up according to the manufacturer's instructions. Preheat the oven to 375°F (191°C) with the lid closed.
- Using a frying spray, cover a cast-iron skillet.
- Fold up 1 frozen pie crust and put it in the skillet's bottom and up the sides. Poke holes in the crust with a fork in various places.
- Place the skillet on the grill grate, cover, and smoke for 5 minutes, or until the bottom is gently browned. Remove the steaks from the skillet and put them aside.
- In a large mixing dish, combine the melted butter, flour, and 1 ½ cups of sugar.
- Toss the blackberries in the flour-sugar mixture until evenly distributed.
- Evenly distributed the berry mixture in the pan and cover with milk. Half of the chopped butter pieces should be strewn around the mixture at random.
- Roll up the leftover pie crust and put it on top of the pan, or cut the dough into equal pieces and weave a lattice out of it. Sprinkle the remaining butter bits over the surface of the crust.
- Return the pan to the smoker and sprinkle the remaining 1/2 cup of sugar on the topping of the crust.
- Cover and cook for 20 minutes, or unless the top is bubbling and brown. To avoid the crust from burning, put aluminum foil over the edges towards the end of the cooking process.
- Serve the pie with vanilla ice cream while it's still warm.

7.30: Cheese Frosted Carrot Cake

Preparation time: 20 minutes

Cooking time: 1 hour

Servings: 4 to 6

Ingredients:

- peeled and grated carrots
- 4 room-temperature eggs
- 1 cup of extra virgin olive oil
- ½ cup of milk
- 1 tsp. of extract de vanilla
- 2 lbs. of sugar
- 2 cups cake flour or self-rising flour
- 2 tsp. of soda bicarbonate
- 1 tsp. of kosher salt
- 1 cup pecans, finely chopped
- For greasing, use nonstick cooking spray or butter.
- 8 fluid ounces (227 g) crème fraiche
- 1 cup of confectionaries sugars
- 8 tbsp. of unsalted butter (1 stick) at room temperature
- 1 tsp. of extract de vanilla
- A quarter tsp. of salt
- ¼ cup of milk
- Cake

Steps:

- Fill the smokers with (wood pellets) and fire them up according to the manufacturer's instructions. Preheat the oven to 350°F (177°C) with the lid closed.
- Mix the shredded carrots, oil, eggs, milk, and vanilla in a blender or food processor and pulse till the carrots are finely chopped.
- Mix the sugar, baking soda, flour, and salt in a big mixing basin.

284

- Stir the carrot mixture into the flour mixture until it is completely combined. Fold in the pecans that have been chopped. 5. Using cooking spray, coat a 9-by-13-inch baking sheet.

- Place the batter in the prepared pan on the grill grate. Close the cover and smoke for 1 hour, or unless a toothpick placed in the middle comes out clean.

- Take the cake from the skillet and set it aside to cool fully.

- The Topping

- Whisk the cream cheese, butter, vanilla, confectioners' sugar, and salt with an electric mixer on low speed, adding two tbsp. to ¼ cup milk to thin the frosting as required.

- To serve, frost the chilled cake and cut it into slices.

7.31: Citrusy Butter Bars

Preparation time: 15 minutes

Cooking time: 1 hour

Servings: 8 to 12

Ingredients:

- A third of a cup of lemon juice
- A ½ cup of sugar
- Two eggs
- 3 yolks of eggs
- 1 12 tsp cornstarch
- 4 tbsp. of butter (unsalted)
- ¼ cup of extra virgin olive oil
- ½ tbsp. of lemon zest
- ¼ cup of granulated sugar 114 cup flour
- A third of a cup of confectioner's sugar
- ¼ tsp of fine sea salt
- 1 tsp. of lemon zest
- 10 tbsp. of unsalted butter, cubed

Steps:

- Preheat the grill to 180°F and shut the cover for 15 minutes when ready to cook2. Stir together eggs, sugars, lemon juice, and yolks, cornstarch, and fine sea salt in a small mixing dish.

- Place on the grill on a baking tray or cake pan. Smoke for 30 minutes, whisking midway through the process. Remove the steaks from the grill and put them aside.

- Pour the contents of the bowl into a small pot. Place on the stovetop over medium heat until it boils. Cook for 60 seconds after the water has reached a boil.

- Remove from the heat and pour into a dish using a mesh strainer.

- Combine the olive oil, butter, and lemon zest in a mixing bowl.

- In a food processor, combine the granulated sugar, flour confectioners' sugar, lemon zest, and salt to form the crust. Pulse in the butter until it becomes a crumbly dough.

- Preheat the grill to 350°F for 15 minutes with the lid covered when ready to cook.

- Bake for 30 to 35 minutes, or until the crust is very faintly golden brown.

- Remove the crust from the grill and spread the lemon filling on top. Return to the grill and bake for another 15 to 20 minutes, or until the filling is barely set.

- Allow it cool to room temperature before refrigerating until completely cold before cutting into bars. Just before serving, dust with confectioners' flaky sea salt and sugars. Enjoy!

7.32: Chocolate Pie with Fudge Sauce

Preparation time: 15 minutes

Cooking time: 1 hour

Servings: 8 to 12

Ingredients:

- ½ cup of chocolate chips (semi-sweet)
- Butter 1cup
- Brown sugar 1
- Sugar 1 cup
- 4 eggs, whole

- 2 tsp. of extract de vanilla
- 2 cups of flour (all-purpose)
- 1/2 cup of unsweetened cocoa powder
- 1 tsp. bicarbonate of soda
- 1 tsp. of kosher salt
- 1 cup chocolate chips (semi-sweet)
- A third of a cup of white chocolate chips
- A quarter cup of nuts (optional)
- Guinness beer, 2 tbsp.
- Hot Fudge sauce 8 oz.

Steps:

- Brush a 10-inch (25-cm) pie dish inside and out with non - stick cooking spray.

- Set the grill to 350°F (177°C) and shut the cover for 15 minutes when ready to cook.

- In the oven, melt 12 cups (100 g) of semi-sweet Choco chips. Combine the brown sugar, butter, and granulated sugar in a mixing bowl.

- Add the eggs one at a time, mixing after each one, and the vanilla extract. Melt the chocolate chips and add them in.4. Sift together the flour, cocoa powder, baking soda, and salt on a big piece of wax paper. Lift the paper's corners and gently pour the butter mixture into them.

- Mix only unless the necessary elements are combined. Combine the remaining almonds, semi-sweet chocolate chips, white chocolate chips in a large mixing bowl. Place the dough in the pie pan that has been prepared.

- Put the brownie pie on the grill and cook for 45 to 50 minutes, or until the center is set. Halfway through cooking, rotate the pan. Cover the surface with a piece of aluminum foil if the top or edges start to brown.

- Melt the fudge sauce in the microwave in an oven measuring cup. Pour in the Guinness and mix well.

- Allow the brownie pie to rest for 20 minutes once it is finished. Then, cut into wedges and serve with fudge sauce on the side. Enjoy.

7.33: Grilled Sweet Cheddar Muffins

Preparation time: 10 minutes

Cooking time: 12 to 15 minutes

Servings: 3

Ingredients:

- 1 butter cake of mix packet
- 8 tbsp. of butter
- Jiffy Corn Muffin Mix (one box)
- 1 cupcake flour or self-rising flour
- 3 ½ cup Cheddar cheese, shredded
- 2 beaten eggs, room temperature
- 2 ¼ oz. buttermilk
- ¼ cup of packed brown sugar, greased with nonstick frying spray or butter

Steps:

- Fill the smokers with (wood pellets) and fire it up according to the manufacturer's instructions. Preheat the oven to 375°F (191°C) with the lid closed.
- Stir the corn muffin mix, cake mix, and flour in a large mixing basin.
- Cut the 11/2 sticks of melted butter into small pieces and mix them in with the dry ingredients. Mix in the cheese well.
- Whisk together the eggs and buttermilk in a medium mixing bowl, then pour to the dry ingredients and whisk until thoroughly combined.
- Grease three ½ -cup mini muffin tins and spoon 1/4 cup of mixture into each cup.
- Place the pans on the grill, cover the lid, and smoke for 15 - 20 minutes, and the muffins are gently browned, keeping an eye on them.
- Make the topping although the muffins are baking: In a small mixing bowl, combine the leftover 1 stick of butter and the (brown) sugar until thoroughly mixed.
- Take the muffins from the grill and set them aside. Serve warm with a dollop of sweet butter on top.

7.34: Smoked S'mores Cake Bars

Preparation Time: 480 minutes

Cooking Time: 240 minutes

Servings: 8

Ingredients:

- 1 melted piece of butter
- 2 cups of chocolate chunks
- 1 egg
- 2 cups of graham cracker crumbs
- 1 ½ cup of tiny marshmallows
- 7 oz. marshmallow crème
- 1 yellow cake mix package

Steps:

- Set the Pit Boss pellet grill to 250° F by turning it on SMOKE mode and letting it run with the cover open for 10 minutes. If you're going to use a gas or coal grill, make sure it's set to low, indirect heat.

- Use aluminum foil to line a 9x13" metal pan.

- In a big mixing bowl, stir the cake mix, butter, egg, and graham cracker crumbs using a hand mixer. 2 cups of graham cracker mixture should be set aside, then spread the leftover (graham cracker) mixture into the prepared baking dish. Dollop the marshmallow crème over the chocolate chips, then put the chocolate chips on top. Sprinkle with tiny marshmallows after spreading into a uniform layer. Top with the graham cracker mixture that was set aside.

- Place on the grill for 45 to 50 minutes to smoke. Before cutting into bars, let it cool fully.

7.35: Chocolate Peanut Butter Cookies

Preparation Time: 30 minutes

Cooking Time: 12 mins.

Servings: 4

Ingredients:

- ½ tsp. of baking soda
- ½ cup of brown sugar
- ½ cup + 1 tbsp. of unsalted butter
- 1/3 cup of dark and unsweetened cocoa powder
- 2 eggs, whisked
- 1/3 cup of tiny chocolate chips
- 1 ½ cup of all-purpose flour
- ¼ tsp sea salt
- ½ cup of granulated sugar
- 1 tsp. of vanilla extract
- 2 cups (butter of peanuts) split

Steps:

- Preheat the Pit Boss Griddle to medium-low temperature. Preheat the cast-iron skillet if using a charcoal grill or gas.

- Now whisk together the baking soda, flour, cocoa powder and salt. Set aside.

- Set a metal saucepan on the skillet, then add ½ cup of butter to melt. Whisk in the vanilla extract and sugars and cook for 2 minutes. Remove the pan from the griddle, and transfer contents to a large mixing bowl.

- Slowly pour the beaten eggs into the sugar mixture, constantly whisking to temper the eggs.

- Combine the dry and wet ingredients. Mix a single cup of chocolate chips and peanut butter chips. Refrigerate this mixture for about 15 - 30 minutes.

- Remove the dough from the refrigerator, then add a cup of peanut butter chips.

- Portion dough into 16 to 18 cookie balls.

- Melt 1 tablespoon of butter on the griddle, then transfer the cookie balls to the skillet. Press down gently on the cookies, then cook for 10 to 12 minutes, flipping halfway.

- Transfer cookies to a cooling rack for 5 minutes before enjoying.

7.36: Bananas Foster

Preparation Time: 10 minutes

Cooking Time: 10 minutes

Servings: 4

Ingredients

- Banana nectar 1/3 cup
- Quartered 4 bananas
- Brown sugar ¾ cup
- Butter ¼ cup
- Cinnamon, powdered ½ tsp
- Dark rum 1/3 cup
- Ice cream of vanilla

Steps:

- Preheat the Pit Boss Skillet to a moderate flame. Heating a cast iron skillet if using a charcoal grill or gas
- Put a big skillet on the grill and melt the butter in it. Next, stir in the caramelized sugar and cinnamon until the sugar is completely dissolved.
- Mix in the bananas and banana nectar. To coat, stir well.
- Pour the rum after the bananas have softened and become brown. Stir in the sauce, then light it with a stick light. Stir the sauce for two min once the flames have died down.
- Spoon the heated sauce over the ice cream and distribute the banana between 4 scoops/bowls of vanilla ice cream. Serve right away.

7.37: Bourbon Bacon Brownies

Preparation Time: 15 minutes

Cooking Time: 60 minutes

Servings: 16

Ingredients

- Caramel sauce

- 2 cups of all-purpose flour
- ¼ cup of bourbon
- 1 cup of brown sugar
- 1 cup of canola oil
- 2 tbsp. of instant coffee
- 1.5 cup chocolate powder
- 1 tbsp. of honey sea salt
- 6 big eggs
- 1 cup of powdered sugar
- 6 slices raw bacon
- 3 cups of white sugar
- ½ tsp. of pit boss smoked-honey sea salt
- 4 tbsp. of water

Steps:

- Get your Pit Boss up and running. The temperature was set to 400°F after it's started.

- Combine the powdered sugar, cocoa, white sugar, instant coffee, and flour in a large mixing dish.

- Stir the oil, eggs, and water into the flour mixture until just mixed.

- Coat a 9 x 13-inch baking pan with cooking spray.

- Drizzle half of the dough in the pan with caramel.

- Pour the remaining batter on top, sprinkle with caramel, and then top with candied bacon.

- Cook the brownies for 1 hour in the smoker, or unless a wooden skewer in the middle comes out clean.

- Remove the meat from the grill and let it cool completely before slicing.

7.38: Crème Brule French toast

Preparation Time: 30 minutes
Cooking Time: 45 minutes

Servings: 6-8

Ingredients

- 1 cup of brown sugar
- 1/2 stick unsalted butter, heated
- 1 tbsp. of cinnamon, crushed
- 1 loaf eggy bread, such as challah, brioche, or Pullman bread, sliced
- 1 tbsp. of (pit boss hickory) honey sea salt flavoring
- 1 tsp. of vanilla essence
- 4 cups of milk

Steps:

- Mix the brown sugar, vanilla, and butter, maple syrup, and (Pit Boss Honey Sea Salt) cinnamon in a mixing dish. In the lower of a 9x13 saucepan baking pan, spread this mixture.

- In a separate large mixing bowl, whisk together all the (eggs and mil). Remove from the equation. Place the bread on top of the sugar mixture in the pan, then pour the milk mixture over it.

- Set your Pit Boss grill to 350°F and cook the bread for 35-40 minutes, or until soft, and the sugar mixture is boiling. Serve right away.

7.39: Smoked blackberry Popsicle with mascarpone and cookie Crunch

Preparation Time: 15 minutes

Cooking Time: 25 minutes

Serving: 6

Ingredients

- Blackberries, 6 oz.
- ½ cup sugar
- Salt pinch
- Lemon juice
- 8 oz. of mascarpone cheese

- 2 tbsp. heavy cream

- A quarter tsp. of cardamom powder

- Nella Wafers (1/2 cup)

- ¼ cup of softened butter

- 1 tbsp. of nonfat dry milk powder

- 2 tbsp. of granulated sugar

Steps:

- Once you're ready to cook, set the oven to 180 degrees Fahrenheit and cook for 15 min with the lid covered. Use Super Smoke if it's available for the best flavor.

- Arrange the blackberries out on a perforated sheet tray and place them immediately on the grill grate. Smoke for 15-20 minutes.

- Remove it from the grill and set it aside to cool. In a blender pitcher, combine the lemon juice, sugar, and a sprinkle of salt. Pulse a few times to break up the berries if you prefer it chunky or puree all the way and strain off the solids for a silky texture. Set aside alone.

- In a medium mixing bowl, mix the cream, mascarpone, cardamom, and salt.

- Scoop 1 tbsp. Of each mixture into a Popsicle shape at a time until the form is full. Attach the stick to the popsicles and place it in the freezer. Freeze for the night.

- To make the cookie crunch, combine the wafers, butter sugar, and milk powder in a food processor bowl. To make a coarse crumble, pulse the ingredients together. Spread the mixture out on a parchment-lined baking sheet.

- Raise the temperature to 350 degrees Fahrenheit.

- Place the sheet tray directly on the grilled grate and cook for 10-15 minutes. Allow it cool to room temperature before breaking up with your fingers.

- When the popsicles have frozen, remove them from the mold and dip them in the cookie crumbs.

7.40: Smoked Mexican hot chocolate

Preparation Time: 15 minutes

Cooking Time: 35 minutes

Serving: 2

Ingredients

- Cayenne pepper 1/8 tsp.
- Powdered cinnamon ½ tsp.
- Smoked paprika ½ tsp.
- Heavy cream 330/500 cup
- 4 cup milk
- Sugar ¼ cup
- Cocoa powder ¼ cup
- Salt 1/8 tsp.
- Chocolate, Bittersweet 1 ¾
- Vanilla essence ½ tsp.

Steps:

- Set the grill to 180° F and heat for 15 minutes with the lid covered when ready to cook.
- In a heat-proof pan, smoke the cayenne pepper for around 30 minutes. Next, add the paprika and cinnamon to the grill and smoke for an additional 5 minutes.
- In a medium saucepan, scald the cream, milk, and sugar. After a few minutes, whisk in the cocoa and salt.
- Once the mixture has warmed, add the vanilla essence, bittersweet chocolate, smoked spices.
- Combine all ingredients in a mixing bowl and serve with marshmallows or whipped cream.

7.41: Smoked Whipped Cream

Preparation Time: 7 hours

Cooking Time: 40 minutes

Serving: 4

Ingredients:

- Heavy cream 3 cup
- Sour cream ½ cup

- Powdered sugar 6 tbsp.
- Vanilla essence ½ tbsp.

Steps:

- When you're ready to cook, preheat the oven to 180°F and cook for 15 min with

the lid covered.

- Place heavy cream in an oven-safe dish or pan. Iron castings should not be used.
- Place the cream on the Traeger grill and cook on the smoke setting for 20 minutes. Cook for 40 minutes to improve the flavor of the smoke.
- Erase the Traeger's cream and set it aside at room temperature for 1 hour. It should be refrigerated for at least six hours.
- Combine all of the ingredients in a mixing dish and stir to combine. Only whisk the milk until stiff peaks appear.
- Garnish with your favorite sweets or fruits. Enjoy!

7.42: Smoked deviled eggs

Preparation Time: 15 minutes;

Cooking Time: 30 minutes

Serving: 4

Ingredients:

- 7 cooked and peeled hard-boiled eggs
- Mayonnaise, 3 tbsp.
- 3 tsp. chives, chopped
- 1 tsp. of apple cider vinegar
- 1 tsp. brown mustard
- Dash hot sauce
- Pepper and salt to taste
- 2 tbsp. of crumbled cooked bacon
- As paprika is required.

Steps:

- Set the Traeger to 180° F and preheat for 15 minutes with the lid covered when ready to cook. Use Super Smoke if it's available for the best flavor.

- Set the cooked and peeled eggs directly on the grill and smoke for 30 minutes.

- Erase the eggs from the grill and set them aside to cool. Slice the eggs lengthwise and scoop the yolks into a top bag with a gallon zip.

- Stir the chives, vinegar, mayonnaise, mustard, spicy sauce, salt, and pepper in a container. Close the bag and knead all the ingredients until completely smooth, using your fingers.

- Squeeze the yolk mixture into the corner of the bag and cut off a little piece of the corner. Put the (yolk mixture) into the hard-boiled egg whites. Paprika over the deviled eggs and top with crumbled bacon. Freeze until ready to serve. Enjoy!

7.43: Smoked banana pudding

Preparation Time: 15 minutes

Cooking Time: 30 minutes

Serving: 4

Ingredients:

- 4 eggs, whole
- a half cup of sugar
- 3 tbsp. of flour (all-purpose)
- 2 cup milk ½ tsp. salt
- 4 Whole Banana
- ½ tsp. of vanilla extract
- 2 tbsp. margarine
- 20 Nilla wafers
- 1/2 cup whisky

Steps:

- To make the pudding, separate the yolk from the 3 eggs and combine them with the entire egg. Whisk until smooth.

- In a saucepan, whisk together half flour, a cup of sugar, milk, and salt. Bring to a moderate boil, then reduce the heat and continue to cook.

- While mixing the eggs, scoop a little amount of the warm milk mixture and gently drop it into the eggs. Add the remaining milk to the pan with the beaten egg mixture after the eggs have warmed. Over medium heat, cook until thick (about 8-10 minutes). Remove the pudding from the heat and stir in the vanilla extract.

- Set the Traeger to high and preheat for 15 minutes with the lid covered when ready to cook.

- Preheat a medium cast iron pan on the grill. Once the pan is heated, add the butter and bananas and sauté until the bananas are gently browned. Make sure not to overwork them, or they'll get mushy and fall apart.

- Once the bananas are browned, sprinkle with brown sugar and stir to dissolve the sugar. When the sugar has melted, and the whiskey has been added, remove the cast iron from the heat. Return the pan to the grill and decrease the liquid until the pan is filled with syrup and bananas. This should just take a few minutes.

- To assemble, place a few tbsp. of pudding in the bottom of a mason jar, top with banana mixture, and a few Nilla wafers. Rep the layering procedure until the pot is full.

- Garnish with a dollop of whipped cream and serve. Enjoy!

7.44: Smoked sweet & spicy Cashews

Preparation Time: 15 minutes

Cooking Time: 1 hour;

Serving: 6

Ingredients:

- Sambal oelek, 3 tbsp.

- Traeger Smoked Simple Syrup, 1 Tbsp.

- ¼ tsp. of cayenne powder

- 1 whole lemon zest

- ½ tsp. of fresh rosemary

- 1 tsp. of red pepper flakes

- ¼ tsp. of cayenne powder

Steps:

- When you're ready to cook, preheat the oven to 225°F and cook for 15 min with the lid covered. Use Super Smoke if it's available for the best flavor.

- In a small cup, combine the lemon juice, rosemary, sambal, simple syrup, red pepper flakes, and cayenne pepper. Cover with a toss and pour the mixture over the cashews.

- Spread the cashews out on a sheet tray and place them immediately on the barbecue grill. Fry the nuts for 1 hour, stirring occasionally. Remove off the grill and set aside to cool. Enjoy!

7.45: Baked Hasselback Apples

Preparation Time: 20 minutes

Cooking Time: 55 minutes

Serving: 4

Ingredients:

- 3 apples, honey crisp or pink lady
- 5 tbsp. of butter (distributed)
- 5 tbsp. brown sugar, split
- ¾ tsp. of cinnamon powder, divided
- 2 tbsp. flour
- 2 tbsp. of rolled oats
- A pinch of salt
- Carmel sauce

Steps:

- Cut the apples in half vertically through the stem and divide them into 1/4-inch slices that stop just before the rim, leaving the pieces intact.

- Once ready to cook, preheat the skillet to 400 degrees F and preheat for 15 minutes with the lid closed.

- Warm 2 tbsp. Of butter and combine with 1/2 tsp cinnamon and 2 tbsp. Brown sugar in a mixing bowl.

- Place the apples cut side down in a baking dish and spray the top with the melted butter.

- Wrap the baking dish in foil and place it immediately on the barbecue grill. With the apples, bake for 30 minutes.

- Remove the grill from the pan, unwrap the foil, and set aside for 10 minutes to cool.

- Combine the remaining butter, sugar, flour, cinnamon, oats, and a sprinkle of salt in a small bowl. Top each apple with the oat mixture by pushing it between the layers.

- Return the baking sheet to the skillet and cook for an additional 15 minutes, or until the oat topping is gently browned.

- Erase from the grill and set aside to cool for 5 minutes before serving.

- For servings, top each apple with a scoop of ice cream and, if preferred, caramel sauce. Enjoy!

7.46: Smoked Margarita

Preparation Time: 10 minutes

Cooking Time: 10 minutes

Serving: 1

Ingredients:

- 12 lime slices, slit in the middle

- 1 cup turbinado sugar

- ½ cup of fresh lime juice strained from grilled limes

- 1 ½ cup of Cointreau

- 3 cup silver tequila

- ½ cup of (Traeger Bloody Mary Cocktail salt)

- Lime wedge, for garnish

- ¾ cup of (Traeger Smoked Basic Syrup), plus more to taste

Steps:

- Set the Traeger to 500°F and preheat for 15 minutes with the lid covered when ready to cook.

- Reduce the limes and dip them in turbinado sugar before placing them fleshy side down on the preheated grill.

- Grill for 5 minutes or until you get a little char. Remove the limes from the grill and squeeze them.

- Combine tequila, lime juice Cointreau, and Traeger Smoked Simple Syrup in a pitcher. To combine the ingredients, stir them together.

- In a low-sided dish, pour (Traeger Bloody Mary Cocktail salt just wide enough to match the glass) rim.

- Run the lime around each rim of the glass, soak the rim in the salt, and pour ice into the glass.

- Drizzle in the (Margarita mixture) and top with a lime slice.

- Enjoy!

7.47: Traeger Paloma Cocktail

Preparation Time: 5 minutes;

Cooking Time: 25 minutes

Serving: 3

Ingredients:

- Required Traeger's Smoke Simple Syrup · 2 grapefruit, divided

- 5 cinnamon sticks

- 1 ½ oz. tequila repos ado

- ½ oz. lime juice

- ½ oz. Traeger Smoked Simple Syrup

- Garnish with grilled lime

- Garnish with the cinnamon stick

Steps:

- Preheat the Traeger to 350°F when ready to cook, and preheat for 15 minutes with the lid closed.

- Fried Grapefruit Juice: 2 grapefruits, cut in half Add a cinnamon stick in the middle of each grapefruit half and drizzle with (Traeger's Smoke Simple Syrup). Set it on the grill and cook for 20 minutes, or until the edges start to brown and the grill marks appear. Erase from the sun and let it cool.

• After the grapefruits have cooled, squeeze and strain the juice. 10 to 12 oz. of juice may be made.

• In a mixing glass, combine the lime juice, tequila, Traeger's Smoke Simple Syrup, and 2 oz. of grilled grapefruit juice.

• Shake and add ice to the mix. Strain over ice in an old-fashioned glass.

• Garnish with a grilled lime slice and a cinnamon stick, if desired. Enjoy!

7.48: Smoke and Bubz Cocktail

Preparation Time: 5 minutes

Cooking Time: 45 minutes

Serving: 1

Ingredients:

• POM Juice 8 oz.

• Pomegranate seeds 1 cup

• Sparkling white wine 3 oz.

• For garnish lemon twist

Steps:

• Preheat the Traeger to 180°F when ready to cook, and preheat for 15 minutes with the lid closed. Utilize Super Smoke if it's available for the best flavor.

• Pomegranate Juice with Smoke: Combine POM juice and a cup of pomegranate seeds on a shallow sheet pan. On the Traeger, smoke for 45 minutes. Erase the grill, strain, and discard the seeds, then set aside to cool.

• Add 1-1/2 ounces of smoked pomegranate juice to the lip of a champagne flute.

• Garnish with a splash of sparkling white wine, a few fresh pomegranate seeds, and a touch of lemon. Enjoy!

7.49: Traeger's gin & tonic

Preparation Time: 10 minutes

Cooking Time: 45 minutes

Serving: 3

Ingredients:

- A quarter cup of berries
- 1 sliced orange
- 1 ½ oz. of gin
- 1 bunch fresh mint for garnish
- ½ cup of tonic water

Steps:

- Preheat the Traeger's to 180° F and preheat for 15 minutes with the lid covered when ready to cook. Use Super Smoke if it's available for the best flavor.
- Smoke Berries spread the blended fresh berries on a sheet pan and place them immediately on the grill. Remove the meat from the grill for 30 min before smoking.
- Preheat the grill to 450 degrees F and preheat for 15 min with the handle closed for orange slices.
- Toss the orange pieces with granulated sugar and grill them right away. Cook for about 5 minutes, rotating once, or unless grill marks appear on the slices.
- Pour the gin into a glass, add the ice and berries, then top with tonic water. Finish with a bunch of fresh mints and a grilled orange wheel. Enjoy!

7.50: Smoked barnburner cocktail

Preparation Time: 5 minutes

Cooking Time: 45 minutes

Serving: 1

Ingredients

- 1 container raspberries (fresh)
- Smoked raspberry syrup, 3/4 oz.
- 1 ½ oz. tequila repos ado
- Lime juice, ½ fluid ounce
- lemon juice, ½ fluid ounce

- 1 lime wheel, grilled (for garnish)

Steps:

- Burn the (Smoked Traeger's grill) once you're able to cook.

- Put the fresh raspberries on a grill mat and smoke on the Traeger for 30 minutes. After the raspberries have been smoked, place them in a shallow sheet pan with 1: 1 simple syrup.

- Put the sheet pan on the grill rack and smoked for 45 minutes.

- Remove off the grill and set aside to cool. Refrigerate when ready to use.

- Stir all of the components in a mixing glass with ice. Shake well and pour over clean ice. Garnish with smoked raspberries and a caramelized raspberry.

7.51: Smoked Pineapple hotel

Preparation Time: 4 hours

Cooking Time: 30 minutes

Serving: 1

Ingredients:

- 1 pineapple, whole and diced
- ¼ cup of sugar
- White rum, ½ fluid ounce
- Lime juice, ¾ fluid oz.
- Pineapple Syrup, ¾ Fluid Ounce
- Apricot brandy (1/2 fluid ounce)
- 1 tsp of angostura bitters

Steps:

- For the syrup, preheat the grill to 180°F and preheat for 15 min with the lid covered when ready to cook.

- Discard the ends and slice the (pineapple) on both sides. Slice the pineapple into 3/4-inch thick pieces. It's not a bad idea to leave it on. Don't even consider the skin. Place the pineapple pieces on the grill and smoke for about 15 minutes on each side.

- In a saucepan over medium heat, while the (pineapple) is smoking, combine the water and sugar and constantly whisk until the sugar has dissolved. Place the syrup in a big tub and set it aside.

- When the pineapple is done cooking, cut each piece into 8 or so wedges and add the wedges to the cup with the simple syrup, toss to coat, and cover.

- Macerate the mixture in the refrigerator for at least four hours, stirring occasionally.

- Strain the syrup into a clean dish using a fine-mesh strainer, then push down on the (pineapple) with a spoon to extract as much liquid as possible. The syrup may be stored in a container and kept in the refrigerator for up to four days.

- To make the cocktail, follow these steps: Add rum, pineapple syrup, apricot brandy, lime juice and bitters to a cocktail shaker or mixing glass. Next, fill the ice cube trays with water and shake them until they're cold.

- Served with a lime wheel as a garnish. Enjoy

7.52: Smoked Sangria Recipe

Preparation Time: 20 minutes

Cooking Time: 45 minutes

Serving: 6

Ingredients:

- A quarter cup of Grand Marnier
- Traeger Smoked Simple Syrup, ¼ cup
- 1 cup fresh cranberries
- 1 apple, whole and diced
- 2 limes, whole and sliced
- Cinnamon stick (four)
- 1 red wine bottle
- As Soda water was required.

Steps:

- When you're ready to cook, preheat the oven to 180°F and cook for 15 min with the lid covered.

- Stir the Grand Marnier and Traeger's Simple Syrup in a mixing bowl and cranberries in a shallow dish and cook them right away.

- Smoke for 30-45 minutes or until the liquid produces the appropriate amount of smoke. Then, remove it off the grill and place it in the refrigerator to cool.

- Pour the red wine into a large pitcher once the mixture has cooled. Add sliced apples, limes, cinnamon sticks, and ice to the pitcher. Add more soda water if necessary. Enjoy!

7.53: Smoky mountain bramble Cocktail

Preparation Time: 20 minutes

Cooking Time: 20 minutes;

Serving: 3

Ingredients

- Blackberries, 8 oz.

- 1 cup of water

- 1 cup of sugar

- Vodka (1 ½ fluid ounces)

- Alpine Preserve, ¾ Fluid Ounce

- Lemon juice (about ¾ fluid ounce)

- Smoked blackberry syrup (1/2 fluid ounce)

Steps:

- Once you're ready to cook, preheat the oven to 180°F and cook for 15 min with the lid covered. Use Super Smoke if it's available for the best flavor.

- To make Smoke Blackberry Simple Syrup, place the blackberries on a grill mat and smoke for 15-20 minutes. Mix the sugar and water in a small saucepan and warm over medium heat until thoroughly combined.

- Remove from the heat and macerate 2/3 of the (blackberries) in the plain syrup. Strain through a fine-mesh strainer and keep for up to 14 days.

- To make your cocktail, muddle 4-5 blackberries in a cocktail shaker: Mix the vodka, ginger, alpine preserves, and smoked blackberry syrup. Double-pressure glass into an old-style glass.

- Sprinkle with smoked blackberries and a lime twist. Enjoy!

Chapter 8: Rubs and Sauce

8.1: Choran Sauce

Preparation Time: 10 minutes.

Cooking Time: 30 minutes.

Servings: 4

Ingredients:

- 1 cup sauce of béarnaise
- ¼ cup of coulis de tomato
- 2 tbsp. of Red wine vinegar,

Steps:

- Put all ingredients in a blender and mix unless smooth.
- Serve the smoothie in a glass

8.2: Hot Sauce with Cilantro

Preparation Time: 10 Minutes
Cooking Time: 30 Minutes
Servings: 4
Ingredients:

- ½ tsp. of coriander
- ½ tsp. of cumin seeds
- A quarter tsp. of black pepper
- Two cardamom pods (green)
- Two cloves of garlic
- 1 tsp. of salt
- Parsley, 1 oz.
- 2 tbsp. of extra virgin olive oil

Steps:

- Put all ingredients in a high-speed blender and mix until smooth.
- Serve the smoothie in a glass.

8.3: Chimichurri Sauce

Preparation Time: 10 Minutes
Cooking Time: 30 Minutes
Servings: 4
Ingredients:

- Parsley 1 cup
- Two cloves of garlic

- ¼ cup of olive oil
- ¼ cup of olive oil
- 1 tbsp. leaves of oregano
- ¼ cup of red wine vinegar
- ½ tbsp. of red pepper flakes

Steps:
- Put all ingredients in a high-speed blender and blend unless smoothie
- Put the smoothie in a glass and serve it

8.4: Basil Pesto Sauce

Preparation Time: 10 Minutes
Cooking Time: 30 Minutes
Servings: 4
Ingredients:
- Two garlic cloves
- Basil leaves, 2 oz.
- 1 oz. of parmesan cheese
- 1 tbsp. of pine nuts
- ½ cup of extra virgin olive oil

Steps:
- Put all the ingredients in a high-speed blender and blend until smoothie
- Put the (smoothie) in a glass and served it

8.5: Vegan Pesto

Preparation Time: 10 Minutes
Cooking Time: 30 Minutes
Servings: 4

Ingredients:

- ½ cup of mint leaves
- Cilantro leaves 1 cup
- Basil leaves 1 cup
- Parsley leaves 1 cup
- ½ c. of walnuts
- 1 tsp. of miso
- 1 tsp. of lime juice
- ¼ cup of extra virgin olive oil

Steps:

- Put all the ingredients in a high-speed blender and blend until smooth
- Put (smoothie) in a glass and served it

8.6: Fennel and Almonds Sauce

Preparation Time: 10 Minutes
Cooking Time: 30 Minutes
Servings: 4
Ingredients:

- Bulb of fennel 1 cup
- Extra virgin olive oil 1 cup
- Almonds 1 cup
- Fennel fronds 1 cup

Steps:

- Put all the ingredients in a high-speed blender and blend it until smoothie
- Put the smoothie in a glass and served it

8.7: Honey Dipping Sauce

Preparation Time: 10 Minutes

Cooking Time: 30 Minutes

Servings: 4

Ingredients:

- Melted unsalted butter 5 tbsp.
- Paste of kimchi 8 tbsp.
- Honey 2 tbsp.
- Sesame seeds 1 tsp.

Steps:

- Put all the ingredients in a high-speed blender and blend it until smoothie
- Served the smoothie in a glass.

8.8: Ginger Dipping Sauce

Preparation Time: 10 Minutes

Cooking Time: 30 Minutes

Servings: 4

Ingredients:

- Ponzi sauce 6 tbsp.
- Ginger 2 tsp.
- Two tablespoons scallions 2 tbsp.
- 2 tsp mirin 2 tsp.
- 1 tsp sesame oil 1 tsp.
- Salt according to taste.

Steps:

- Put all the ingredients in a high-speed blender and blend it until smoothie
- Put the smoothie in a glass and served it.

8.9: Thai Dipping Sauce

Preparation Time: 10 Minutes

Cooking Time: 30 Minutes

Servings: 4

Ingredients:

- Sauce of garlic 6 tsp.
- Fish sauce 2 tbsp.
- Lemon juice 2 tbsp.
- Brown sugar 1 tbsp.
- Flakes of chili 1 tsp.

Steps:

- Put all the ingredients in a high-speed blender and blend it unless smoothie.
- Put the smoothie in a glass and served it.

8.10: Coconut Dipping Sauce

Preparation Time: 10 Minutes

Cooking Time: 30 Minutes

Servings: 4

Ingredients:

- Coconut milk 4 tbsp.
- Curry paste of curry 1 tbsp.
- Soya sauce 2 tsp.
- Lemon juice 2 tbsp.
- Fish sauce 1 tsp.
- Honey 1 tsp.

Steps:

- Put all the ingredients in a high-speed blender and blend it until smoothie
- Put the smoothie in a glass and served it

8.11: Black Bean Dipping Sauce

Preparation Time: 10 Minutes

Cooking Time: 30 Minutes

Servings: 4

Ingredients:

- Peanut butter 2 tbsp.
- Black bean paste 2 tbsp.
- Maple syrup 1 tbsp.
- Olive oil 2 tbsp.

Steps:

- Put all the ingredients in a high-speed blender and blend it unless smoothie.
- Put the smoothie in a glass and served it.

8.12: Maple Syrup Dipping Sauce

Preparation Time: 10 Minutes

Cooking Time: 30 Minutes

Servings: 4

Ingredients:

- Maple syrup 2 tbsp.
- Peanut butter 2 tbsp.
- Extra virgin olive oil 2 tbsp.
- Korean black bean paste 2 tbsp.

Steps:

- Put all the ingredients in a high-speed blender and blend it until smoothie
- Put the smoothie in a glass and served it

8.13: Soy Dipping Sauce

Preparation Time: 10 Minutes

Cooking Time: 30 Minutes

Servings: 4

Ingredients:

- Sugar ¼ cup
- Soy sauce ¼ cup
- Vinegar rice ¼ cup
- Scallions ½ cups
- Cilantro ½ cup

Steps:

- Put all the ingredients in a high-speed blender and blend it until smoothie
- Put the smoothie in a glass and served it well

8.14: Avocado Salsa

Preparation Time: 10 Minutes

Cooking Time: 30 Minutes

Servings: 4

Ingredients:

- Onion 1
- Avocados 2
- Jalapeno 1
- Cloves of garlic 2
- Red wine vinegar ¼ cup
- Lime juice 1 tbsp.
- Parsley leaves ¼ cup.

Steps:

- Put all the ingredients in a high-speed blender and blend until smoothie
- Put the smoothie in a glass and serve it well.

8.15: Barbeque Sauce

Preparation Time: 10 Minutes

Cooking Time: 30 Minutes

Servings: 4

Ingredients:

- Molasses 1 tsp.
- Ketchup ¼ cup.
- Brown sugar 1 tbsp.
- Hot sauce 1 tsp.
- Mustard 1 tsp.
- Powder of onion.

Steps:

- Put all the ingredients in a high-speed blender and blend until smoothie.
- Put all smoothies in a glass and serve it.

Chapter 9: Appetizers and Snacks, Cocktail Recipes

9.1: Homemade Smoked Cheese

Preparation time: 5 minutes

Cooking time: 1½ hours

Servings: 4

Ingredients:

• 1 (2-pound / 907-g) medium Cheddar cheese cube, diced lengthwise, or your preferred cheese

Steps:

• Fill the smoker with (wood pellets) and fire it up according to the package recommendations. Set the grill to 90°F (32°C) with the lid covered.

• Put the cheddar immediately on the grilled grate and smoke for 2 hours and 30 minutes, monitoring to ensure it doesn't melt. Try turning the cheese if it starts to melt. If it doesn't work, take it off the grilled and place it in the refrigerator for approximately an hour before returning it to the cooled smoker.

• Erase the cheese from the pan and put it in a zip-top bag to chill overnight.

• Shred the cheddar and use it to make Smokey mac and cheese, slice it, and distribute it with crackers.

9.2: *Smoked Artisanal Bacon and Crab Meat*

Preparation time: 10 minutes

Cooking time: 40 minutes

Servings: 6 to 8

Ingredients:

• 12 big jalapeno peppers

• 8 oz. of (227 g) room temperature cream cheese

• 1 lemon's finely shredded zest

• 8 ounces (227 g) of crab flesh, rinsed, picked over, and finely sliced or diced

• 1 tsp. of Old Bay seasoning, or to taste

• 12 pieces of artisanal bacon, sliced crosswise in half

• For sprinkling sweet or smoked paprika

Steps:

• Set the smoker to 350°F (177°C) according to the manufacturer's instructions. Assemble the wood according to the manufacturer's instructions.

• Cut each jalapeno in half horizontally, keeping the root in Place after slicing through it.

• Use a grapefruit spatula or a melons baller to scrape away the seed and veins. Arrange the jalapeno halves cut side up on a wire rack.

- In a stirring dish, pour the cream cheese. With such a wooden spoon, whisk in the lime juice and Old Bay flavor until soft peaks form. Curl the crab in gently.

- Fill each jalapeno half with a heaping spoonful of crab mixture.

- Fold a piece of bacon around each jalapeno halfway (leaving the contents exposed at either end).

- Place the popper in a thin layer on the cutting board and attach the bacon with a toothpick.

- In the grill, place the wire rack. Smoke the poppers for 30 to 40 minutes, or until the bacon and stuffing are brown, and the peppers are soft. Arrange the poppers on a serving dish. Allow cooling for a few minutes before serving.

9.3: Bell Pepper Tomato Soup

Preparation time: 15 minutes

Cooking time: 1 hour

Servings: 4

Ingredients:

- 4 beautiful red ripe tomatoes, sliced in half widthwise (approximately 2 pounds / 907 g)

- ½ green or yellow bell peppers sliced into 2 sections

- ½ red bell peppers stemmed, seeded, and sliced in half

- 1 small sweet onion

- 1 clove of garlic peeled

- 3 tbsp. of extra virgin olive oil (plus a little more for sprinkling)

- 2 tbsp. of red wine vinegar or sherry vinegar from Spain

- ½ cup of water, plus more if necessary

- To taste, coarse salt (sea salt or kosher salt) and freshly powdered black pepper

- 1 tbsp. of fresh chives or scallion greens, chopped

Steps:

- In an aluminum foil pan, arrange the cucumber, tomatoes, peppers, and onions cut side up. Garlic should be included now.

- Follow the manufacturer's directions to establish the smoker for cold smoking. Assemble the wood according to the package recommendations.

- In the smokers, put the veggies. 60 minutes, or as required, till bronzed with smoke. The veggies should be left uncooked.

- Remove the veggies from the liquids and cut them into 1-inch pieces. Mix to a coarse or smooth purée in a food processor (your choice).

- Pour in the saved liquids, vinegar, oil, and approximately ½ cup of water to create a pourable soup.

- Season with salt and pepper to taste and a few more drops of vinegar if the veggies are too sweet. Alternatively, combine the veggies, juices, vinegar, and water-oil, in a blender and puree until desired consistency is achieved. Season to taste with pepper, salt, and additional vinegar if desired. The gazpacho may be prepared up to this point in advance, wrapped, and refrigerated, but it should be tasted and re-seasoned before serving. Into serving dishes, ladle the gazpacho. Sprinkle a little more olive oil over the top and scatter the chopped chives on top.

9.4: Chicken Tortilla Chips

Preparation time: 10 minutes

Cooking time: 15 minutes

Servings: 6 to 8

Ingredients:

- A total of Eight cups of tortilla chips

- 2 cups of smoked brisket or chicken, shredded

- 1 can (15 ounces / 425 g) black beans, strained thoroughly in a strainer, washed, and drained again (ideally organic and low-sodium).

- 12 ounces (340 g) approximately 3 cups finely shredded mixed cheeses

- 1/3 cup of drained pickled jalapeno slices or

- 4 fresh jalapeno peppers, stems and thinly cut horizontally

- 4 scallions, trimmed and thinly cut crosswise white and green portions

- 2–4 tbsp. of spicy sauce (I like Cholula) or barbecue sauce

- ¼ cup of fresh cilantro, roughly chopped (optional)

Steps:

• Preheat the smokers to 275°F (135°C), as directed by the manufacturer. Put the hardwood according to the instructions provided by the manufacturer.

• Put another of the tortillas loosely in the grill pan. Sprinkle one-third of the shredded brisket, cheese, bean, jalapenos, and scallions over the shredded brisket, bean, cheese, jalapenos, and scallions on top of the shredded brisket, jalapenos, cheese scallions and bean.

• Pour in the red sauce and shake vigorously. After that, make a second and third stacking of these components.

• Grill the nachos in the smoker pan for 12 to 15 minutes, just until the cheese has melted and is boiling.

• If preferred, garnish with cilantro and dig in. Yes, you eat the nachos right out of the pan, so be careful not to burn your fingertips on the rim.

• Smoked Nachos on the Grill

• For indirect cooking, set the skillet to medium-high 400°F (204°C). Place the nacho dish on the grates away from the fire and sprinkle the wood chips on the embers if the cheddar is melted and bubbling, 5 minutes on an indirect grill.

9.5: Coriander Spiced Chicken Wings

Preparation time: 15 minutes

Cooking time: ½ to 2 hours

Servings: 4 to 6

Ingredients:

• Chicken wings 3 pounds

• Chopped fresh cilantro ½ cup

• Coarse salt (sea or kosher) 2 tsp.

• Black peppercorns cracked 2 tsp.

• Coriander in powdered form 2 tsp.

• Asian (dark) sesame oil 2tbsp.

• Butter 6 tbsp.

• Vegetable oil, for greasing

- jalapeño peppers 4
- 6 tbsp. of sriracha 6 tbsp.
- Chopped dry-roasted peanuts ¼ cup

Steps:

- In a large mixing dish, combine the chicken wings. Stir in ¼ cup cilantro, pepper, salt, and coriander, if using, until well combined.

- Add the sesame oil and mix well. Freeze the bowl and marinate for 15 to 60 mins

- Meanwhile, prepare your smoker to 375°F (191°C) according to the manufacturer's recommendations. Assemble the wood according to the manufacturer's instructions.

- Brush the drumettes with oil and place them on the smoker rack. At temperatures lower, such as 250oF (121oC), you'll need 112 to 2 hours to smoke the wings until they're sizzling, browning with smoked, and cooked through.

- Don't overcook the food. The portions closest to the fire may cook quicker in certain smokers; if this is the situation, move the pieces to cook evenly. Please make a small incision in the thickest section of a couple of the wings to see whether they're done. There should be no remnants of red in the flesh near the bone.

- Place the wings on a heat-resistant plate.

- Melt butter in a cast-iron pan over high heat just before serving. 3 minutes after adding the jalapenos, heat until they crackle and begin to brown. Bring to a boil, stirring in the sriracha. Pour the sauce over the chicken.

- Toss the chickens with the remaining 1/4 cup cilantro and serve immediately with lots of napkins.

9.6: Citrusy Tomato Corn Bowl

Preparation time: 10 minutes

Cooking time: 20 minutes

Servings: 6 to 8

Ingredients:

- 4 delicious ripe red tomatoes, sliced in half widthwise (approximately 2 pounds / 907 g)

- 4 jalapeno peppers, stemmed and sliced lengthwise in half

- 2 delicious corn ears, shucked
- 1 peeled and quartered tiny sweet onion
- ½ cup of fresh cilantro, chopped
- 2 to 3 limes,
- 1/4 cups fresh lime juice, or to taste
- To taste Salt (Coarse)
- To serve, tortilla chips

Steps:

- Set your smoker to 225°F (107°C) according to the manufacturer's recommendations. Assemble the wood according to the manufacturer's instructions.

- Place the tomatoes, jalapenos, onion and corn in the smoker, cut side up. Smoky the veggies for 15 to 20 minutes, or until they have a smoke taste.

- Transfer the veggies to a serving dish and set them aside to cool.

- Set the corn flat on a chopping board and use a chef's knife to slice the kernels from the cob in wide strokes. Place the corn kernels in a large mixing basin.

- Using your hands or a food processor, tomatoes coarsely chop, jalapenos, and onion.

- Toss in the lime juice, cilantro, and salt to taste with the corn. The salsa should have a lot of seasoning. Place the salsa in a serving dish and set it aside.

- Serve with a side of chips.

9.7: Grilled Brie cheese with Baguette slices

Preparation time: 5 minutes

Cooking time: 10 minutes

Servings: 4

Ingredients:

- 8 ounces (227 g) of camembert or tiny Brie cheese
- Tomato jam, pepper jelly or apricot jam, 3 tsp.
- 1 big jalapeno pepper, stems and crosswise thinly sliced
- For serving, use grill or toast baguette slices or your favorite crackers.

Steps:

- Set your grill to medium-high 400°F (204°C) for smoke-roasting.

- Place the plank horizontally over the flame and grilled it until toasted on both sides, 1 to 2 minutes each side, if charring it (this step is optional but adds many flavors). Remove from the oven and set aside to cool.

- Put the cheese in the plank's middle. Using the back of a spoon, spread pepper jelly over the top. The jalapeno slices should be shingled on top in a beautiful design.

- Toss the wood chips or pieces on the embers and put the plank on the skillet away from the flame. Smoke-roast the cheese for 6 to 10 minutes, or until the edges are tender and starting to bulge.

- Serve the cheese on the plank with a basket of grilled baguette pieces or your favorite crackers, fresh off the grill.

9.8: Garden Gimlet Cocktail

Preparation Time: 5 minutes

Cooking Time: 45 minutes

Serving: 1

Ingredients

- 1 cup honey
- 2 zested lemons
- For garnish, use 2 rosemary sprigs
- 2 slices cucumber
- 1 cup of water
- ¾ oz. of lime juice
- 1 ½ oz. vodka

Steps:

- Preheat the Traeger to 180°F when ready to cook, and preheat for 15 minutes with the lid closed. Use Super Smoke if it's available for the best flavor.

- To make smoked lemon and rosemary honey syrup, dilute 1 cup of honey with ¼ cup of water in a shallow pan. 2 rosemary sprigs.

- Preheat the grill and smoke the pan for 45 mins. Remove from the heat, let cool, and strain.

- Add the cucumber, lime juice, 1-ounce smoked lemon and rosemary honey syrup in a mixing glass.

- Apply ice, shake, and double strain after muddling in a coupe glass.

- Garnish with a sprig of rosemary. Enjoy!

9.9: Plum and Thyme Fizz Cocktail

Preparation Time: 15 minutes

Cooking Time: 1 hour

Serving: 1

Ingredients

- Fresh Plums 3

- Thyme sprigs 1

- Traeger smoked simple syrup 1 cup

- Vodka 1 oz.

- Lemon juice ¾ oz.

Steps:

- Preheat the grill to 180° F and preheat for 15 minutes with the lid covered when ready to cook.

- Halve three plums and remove the pit. Place the plum halves on the grill grate and let them smoke for minutes.

- To make the Plum and Thyme Simple Syrup, combine all of the ingredients in a small mixing bowl. Remove the plum from the grill after 25 minutes and cut into quarters. 1 cup Traeger Smoked Simple Syrup, plums, and thyme sprigs Smoke the concoction for 45 minutes. Remove the steaks from the grill and set them aside to cool.

- To make the cocktail, combine 0.75 oz. Fresh lemon juice, 2 oz. Vodka, and 1 oz. Smoked plum and thyme syrup in a mixing glass. Shake and add ice as needed.

- Garnish with a bit of thyme and a slice of smoked plum, then top with club soda. Pour over a clean ice cube tray. Cherish!

9.10: Smoke and Bubz Cocktail

Preparation Time: 5 minutes

Cooking Time: 45 minutes

Serving: 1

Ingredients

- POM Juice 8 oz.
- Pomegranate seeds 1 cup
- Sparkling white wine 3 oz.
- For garnish 1 lemon twist
- Pomegranate seeds 1 tsp.

Steps:

- Preheat the Traeger to 180°F when ready to cook, and preheat for 15 minutes with the lid closed. Use Super Smoked if it's available for the best flavor.
- Pomegranate Juice with Smoke: Combine POM juice and a cup of pomegranate seeds on a shallow sheet pan. On the Traeger, they smoked for 45 minutes. Removed the grill, strain, and discard the seeds, then set aside to cool.
- Add 1-1/2 oz. of smoked pomegranate juice to the lip of a champagne flute.
- Garnish with a splash of sparkling white wine, a few fresh pomegranate seeds, and a touch of lemon. Enjoy!

9.11: Traeger gin & tonic

Preparation Time: 10 minutes

Cooking Time: 45 minutes

Serving: 3

Ingredients

- A quarter cup of berries
- 1 sliced orange
- 1 ½ oz. of gin
- Granulated sugar 2 tsp.

- Mint, for garnish
- Tonic water ½ cup

Steps:

- Preheat the Traeger to 180° F and preheat for 15 minutes with the lid covered when ready to cook. Use Super Smoke if it's available for the best flavor.

- For the Smoke Berries, spread the mixed fresh berries on a sheet pan and place them immediately on the grill. Remove the meat from the skillet for 30 minutes before smoking.

- Preheat the grill to 450 degrees F and preheat for fifteen min with the lid covered for orange slices.

- Toss the orange slices with granulated sugar and grill them right away. Cook for about 5 minutes, rotating once, or till grill marks appear on the slices.

- Pour the gin into a glass, add the ice and berries, then top with tonic water. Finish with a sprig of fresh mint and a grilled orange wheel. Enjoy!

9.12: Smoked barnburner cocktail

Preparation Time: 5 minutes

Cooking Time: 45 minutes

Serving: 1

Ingredients:

- One container of raspberries (fresh)
- Smoked raspberry syrup, ¾ oz.
- 1 ½ oz. tequila repos ado
- Lime juice, ½ fluid oz.
- Lemon juice, ½ fluid oz.
- 1 lime wheel, grilled (for garnish)

Steps:

- Light the (Smoke Traeger grill) once you're ready to cook.

- Place the fresh raspberries on a grill mat and smoke on the Traeger for 30 minutes. After the raspberries have been smoked, place them in a shallow sheet pan with 1: 1 simple syrup.

- Place the sheet pan on the grill rack and cook for 45 minutes. Remove off the grill and set aside to cool. Refrigerate when ready to use.

- Put all of the ingredients in a mixing glass with ice. Shake well and pour over clean ice. On the grill, garnish with smoked raspberries and a candied lime wheel. Enjoy

9.13: Smoked Kentucky Mule

Preparation Time: 5 minutes

Cooking Time: 1 minute

Serving: 1

Ingredients

- High west whiskey 2 oz.
- Lemon juice ½ oz.
- Traeger (smoked simple) syrup ½ oz.
- 4 Fluid Ounce ginger beer 4 oz.
- Mint leaves as required.
- For garnish, use a lime wedge.

Steps:

- Fill an 8-ounce glass halfway with ice and add the lime juice, bourbon and Traeger (Smoked Simple) Syrup. To combine the ingredients, stir them together.

- Finish up with a ginger beer. Stir it again, then garnish with a lime slice and mint. Enjoy!

9.14: Smoked hot toddy

Preparation Time: 10 minutes

Cooking Time: 30 minutes

Serving: 1

Ingredients:

- Lemonade, 8 fluid ounces
- 1 bag of mint tea

- 1 bag of peach tea
- 1 bag of green tea
- 1 lemon wedge
- Whiskey 4 fluid oz.
- Cinnamon 1 stick

Steps:

- When ready to cook, increase the temperature to high and preheat for 15 minutes with the lid covered.

- Put lemonade into a shallow baking dish and place immediately on the grill. Cook for 20-30 minutes, or until the temperature reaches 200 degrees Fahrenheit.

- Put the lemonade into a bottle after removing it from the grill. Steep tea bags in hot lemonade for 2-4 minutes. Remove the tea bags and put in the whiskey.

- Garnish with sliced lemon and a cinnamon stick, if desired. Enjoy!

9.15: Smoked Pineapple hotel National Cocktail

Preparation Time: 4 hours

Cooking Time: 30 minutes

Serving: 1

Ingredients:

- Water ¼ cup
- Sugar ¼ cup
- Pineapple, 1 diced
- White rum (1 ½ fluid ounces)
- Lime juice, 3/4 fluid oz.
- Pineapple Syrup, 3/4 Fluid Ounce
- Apricot brandy (1/2 fluid ounce)
- 1 tsp. of angostura bitters

Steps:

- And for syrup, preheat the grill to 180°F and preheat for 15 min with the lid covered when ready to cook.

- Discard the ends and slice the pineapple on both sides. Slice the pineapple into ¾ -inch thick pieces.

- Don't even consider the skin. Place the pineapple pieces on the grill and smoke for about 15 minutes on each side.

- In a saucepan over low heat, while the (pineapple) is smoking, combine the water and sugar and constantly whisk until the sugar has dissolved. Place the syrup in a big bottle and set it aside.

- When the pineapple is done cooking, cut each piece into 8 or so wedges and add the wedges to the cup with the simple syrup, toss to coat, and cover.

- Macerate the mixture in the refrigerator for at least four hours (or up to 24 hours), stirring occasionally.

- Strain the syrup into a clean dish using a fine-mesh strainer, then push down on the pineapple with a spoon to extract as much liquid as possible. The syrup may be stored in a container and kept in the refrigerator for up to four days.

- To make the cocktail, follow these steps: Combine rum, pineapple syrup, apricot brandy, lime juice, & bitters to a cocktail shaker. Fill the ice cube trays with water and shake them until they're cold.

- Strain into a frozen cocktail bottle. Serve with a lime wheel as a garnish. Enjoy

9.16: Smoked Sangria recipe

Preparation Time: 20 minutes

Cooking Time: 45 minutes

Serving: 6

Ingredients:

- A quarter cup of Grand Marnier
- Traeger smoked simple syrup, ¼ cup
- 1 cup of fresh cranberries
- 1 apple, whole and sliced
- 2 limes, whole and sliced
- Cinnamon stick (four)
- 1 red wine bottle
- As Soda water was required.

Steps:

- When you're ready to cook, preheat the oven to 180°F and cook for 15 minutes with the lid covered.

- Combine the Grand Marnier and Traeger Simple Syrup in a mixing bowl. And cranberries in a shallow dish and cook them right away.

- Smoke for 30-45 minutes or until the liquid produces the appropriate amount of smoke. Remove off the grill and Place in the refrigerator to cool.

- Pour the red wine into a large pitcher once the mixture has cooled. Add sliced apples, limes, cinnamon sticks, and ice to the pitcher.

- Add more soda water if necessary. Enjoy

9.17: Smoky Mountain Bramble Cocktail

Preparation Time: 20 minutes

Cooking Time: 20 minutes

Serving: 3

Ingredients:

- Blackberries 8 oz.
- Water 1 cup
- Sugar 1 cup
- Blackberries 5
- Vodka 1 ½ oz.
- Alpine Preserve ¾ oz.
- Lemon juice ¾ oz.
- Smoked Blackberry Syrup ½ oz.

Steps:

- When you're ready to cook, preheat the oven to 180°F and cook for 15 min with the lid covered. Use Super Smoke if it's available for the best flavor.

- To make Smoked Blackberry Simple Syrup, place the blackberries on a grill mat and smoke for 15-20 minutes. Mix the water and sugar in a small saucepan and warm over medium heat until thoroughly combined.

330

- Remove from the heat and macerate 2/3 of the blackberries in the plain syrup. Strain through a fine-mesh strainer and keep for up to 14 days.

- To make your cocktail, muddle 4-5 blackberries in a cocktail shaker: Mix the vodka, alpine preserves, ginger, and smoked blackberry syrup. Double-pressure glass into an old-style glass.

- Garnish with smoked blackberries and a lemon twist. Enjoy

9.18: Bourbon, Coke & Cherry Smash

Preparation Time: 5 minutes

Cooking time: 10 minutes

Servings: 2

Ingredients:

- Smoked cherries from Traeger
- 4 tbsp. of bourbon
- 4 tbsp. of bourbon
- 2 tbsp. sugar, mashed
- Bourbon, 4 oz.
- Bitters, 8 dashes
- For serving, use 4 whole lime wedges
- Coke 16 ounce

Steps:

- Set the Traeger to 425°F and preheat for 15 minutes with the lid closed when you're ready to cook. As the grill warms up, put a cast iron or grill-safe nonstick pan on it.

- Combine the cherries, bourbon, sugar and bourbon in a mixing bowl.

- Roast for 10 minutes in a hot Traeger pan, or till cherries have darkened in color and are somewhat tender. Allow cooling fully after removing from the grill.

- To make the drink, muddle a few (smoked cherries) with bitters and a lime slice in a cocktail shaker. Pour in the ice, bourbon, and Coke. Serve with a slice of lime as a garnish. Enjoy.

9.19: Grilled Watermelon Punch

Preparation Time: 5 minutes

Cooking time: 15 minutes

Servings: 4

Ingredients:

- Watermelon small seedless 2
- Olive oil 3/8 cup
- Pepper and Salt
- Traeger Smoked Simple Syrup ¼ cup
- Lemon, juiced 4
- For garnish, use a lime wedge
- Soda water

Steps:

- When you're ready to cook, fire up the Traeger according to the manufacturer's directions. Preheat the grill to 450 degrees F and cook for 10 to 15 minutes with the lid closed.

- Drizzle olive oil over watermelon slices and sprinkle with salt. Cook for ten min, or until grill marks appear, immediately on the grill grate.

- Erase off the grill and chill in the refrigerator. Except for two slices of watermelon, which should be saved for garnish, every watermelon should be skinned.

- In a blender, combine the trimmed watermelon, Traeger Smoked Simple Syrup, lime juice. Puree until completely smooth.

- Fill a pitcher halfway with watermelon juice and ice. Fill halfway with soda water and mix well.

- Garnish with a lemon slice and a watermelon slice in a Collins glass. Enjoy!

9.20: Traeger Grilled Tiki Cocktail

Preparation Time: 10 minutes

Cooking time: 15 minutes

Servings: 2

Ingredients:

- Lemons 4
- Sugar 1 cup
- Fresh pineapple 1
- Palm sugar 1 cup
- Peach 2
- Spiced rum 4 oz.
- Ounce brandy 2 oz.
- Peach liquor 2 oz.

Steps:

- To create the Lemon Syrup, begin by combining all of the ingredients in a large mixing bowl. 4 lemons, peeled and placed in a dish with 1 cup of sugar. Allow 30 minutes for the lemon oil from the peel to begin to dissolve the sugar.

- Set the temperature to High and warm for 15 minutes with the lid covered when ready to cook. If possible, raise the temperature to 500°F for best results.

- Peeled lemons should be cut in half and placed face down on the grill. Cook for approximately 8 minutes, or until the lemons have developed a little sear. Remove the lemons from the grill and set them aside to cool.

- Remove the grilled lemon juice once the lemons have cooled. Toss the lemon peel and sugar mixture with the lemon juice. Stir until all of the remaining sugar has dissolved. Remove the lemon peels and keep the grilled lemon syrup refrigerated until ready to use.

- To make the grilled fruit, combine all of the ingredients in a large mixing bowl. Remove the pineapple's outer peel and crown. Using a knife, cut the pineapple into parallel slices. Sprinkle palm sugar over pineapple slices. Cook pineapple slices for 8 minutes on each side directly on the grill grate. Remove from the oven and set aside to cool for 5-10 minutes.

- Peaches should be cut in half and the pit removed. Lightly dust with palm sugar. Place peaches cut side down on the grill grate and heat until grill marks appear, approximately 5 minutes depending on peach ripeness.

- To make the cocktail, follow these steps: In a big pitcher, put 4 huge scoops of ice. Combine the brandy, rum, peach liquor, 4 ounces grilled fruit and lemon syrup in a mixing glass. To fully combine the ingredients, stir them together. Allow 15 minutes for the mixture to dilute.

• Garnish with grilled pineapple chunks, caramelized peaches, a lime twist, and mint leaves in four glasses over ice. Enjoy!

9.21: Traegerade Cocktail

Preparation time: 5 minutes

Cooking time: 10 minutes

Servings: 2

Ingredients:

• Lemons grilled

• 2 sliced lemons

• Traeger Smoked Simple Syrup, 2 tbsp.

• Bourbon, 3 oz.

• Lemon juice, 2 oz.

• Traeger smoked simple syrup, 2 oz.

• 2 For garnish, sprig fresh mint.

Steps:

• Set the Traeger to 500°F and heat for 15 minutes with the lid covered when you're ready to cook.

• To make the grilled lemons, combine all of the ingredients in a large mixing bowl. Place lemon slices on the grill after brushing them with Traeger Smoked Simple Syrup. Cook until caramelized marks form on the surface. Remove the steaks from the grill and put them aside.

• Combine the bourbon, lemon juice, and Traeger Smoked Simple Syrup lemon juice in a mixing glass.

• Shake well and pour into a tall glass filled with clean ice.

• Serve with and mint and lemon as garnish. Enjoy!

9.22: Smoked hibiscus sparkler

Preparation Time: 10 minutes

Cooking Time: 30 minutes

Servings: 4

Ingredients:

- Water ½ cup
- Sugar ½ cup
- Dried hibiscus flowers 2 tbsp.
- For garnish, use ginger
- Wine 1 bottle

Steps:

- Once you're ready to cook, preheat the Traeger to 180°F and cook for 15 minutes with the lid closed.
- Pour half a cup of water into a small baking dish and place it on the grill grate. Start smoking the water for 30 minutes or until the desired smoke flavor is achieved.
- Stir the water, sugar, and hibiscus blossoms in a small saucepan. Over medium heat, bring to a moderate simmer and cook until the sugars have dissolved.
- Erase the hibiscus flowers and set the simple syrup aside to cool in a small container.
- Pour 12 oz. Smokey hibiscus simple syrup into the bottom of a champagne glass and top with sparkling wine. Enjoy! Garnish with a few pieces of crystallized ginger.

9.23: Smoked Ice Mojito Slurpee

Preparation time: 10 minutes

Cooking time: 30 minutes

Servings: 2

Ingredients:

- 1 cup rum (white)
- ½ cup lime juice, freshly squeezed

- ¼ cup smoked simple syrup from Traeger
- ½ mint leaves, fresh
- 4 fresh mint sprigs for garnish
- 4 lime wedges to serve as a garnish

Steps:

- When preparing to cook, preheat the Traeger to 180°F with the lid covered for 15 minutes. If super smoke is available, use it for the best taste.
- Put 3 cups of water into a metal high-sided pan to make smoked ice. Place the pan on the grill and let it smoke for 30 minutes.
- Remove the smoked water from the grill and pour it into ice cream scoop trays. Place in the freezer until completely frozen.
- In a blender, combine the rum, mint, lime juice; Traeger smoked simple syrup and smoked ice.
- Pour into glasses after the mixture has reached a slushy consistency.
- Serve with a lime wedge and a mint sprig as garnish. Enjoy!

9.24: Smoked barnburner cocktail

Preparation time: 5 minutes

Cooking time: 45 minutes

Ingredients:

- Raspberry syrup that has been smoked
- 16 oz. raspberries, fresh
- ½ cup smoked simple syrup from Traeger
- 1 ½ oz. raspberry smoked syrup
- 3 oz. tequila repos ado
- Lime juice, 1 oz.
- Lemon juice, 1 oz.
- 2 lime wheels toasted for garnish

Steps:

- When preparing to cook, preheat the Traeger to 180°F with the lid covered for 15 minutes. If super smoke is available, use it for the best taste.

- Put fresh raspberries on a griddle mat and smoke for 30 minutes to make smoked raspberry syrup. After the raspberries have been smoked, set aside a couple for garnish and combine the rest with Traeger smoked simple syrup in a shallow sheet pan.

- Cook for 45 minutes using a baking sheet on the grill grate. Remove off the grill and set aside to cool. Remove particles by straining through a fine mesh screen. Refrigerate the syrup until you're ready to use it. Approximately 1/2 cup smoked raspberry syrup.

- In a mixing glass, combine 3/4 oz. of tequila, lime juice, smoked raspberry syrup, and lemon juice with ice. Shake well and pour on ice cubes. Smoke raspberries & a toasted lime wheel serve as garnish. Enjoy!

9.25: *Smoked Mulled Wine*

Preparation time: 10 minutes

Cooking time: 1 hour

Servings: 10

Ingredients

- Red wine 2 bottle
- Whiskey ½ cup
- Honey ½ cup
- White rum ½ cup
- Stick of cinnamon
- Star anise 2
- The whole of cloves 4
- Orange peel 1

Steps:

- Set the Traeger to 180°F and preheat for 15 minutes with the lid covered when you're ready to cook. If super smoke is available, use it for the best taste.

- Stir wine, whiskey, cloves, honey, rum, wine, cinnamon stick, star anise, and orange peel in a shallow baking dish. Stir until everything is thoroughly mixed.

- Place the dish on the grilled grate and smoke for one hour, or unless the mixture is warm.

- Remove the cups from the grill and discard the mulling spices. Natural anise, cinnamon sticks, orange zest, or a mix of the three may be used as a garnish. Enjoy!

9.26: Strawberry Cocktail Syrup

Preparation Time: 10 minutes

Cooking Time: 20 minutes

Servings: 6

Ingredients

- Light brown sugar 2 cups

- Water 2 cups.

- Strawberries 3 pounds.

Steps:

- Bring the sugar and water to a boil in a medium saucepan, stirring continuously until the sugar is dissolved. Cut the strawberries' ends off and put them in a glass dish.

- Allow the heated syrup to cool before pouring it over the fruit. Refrigerate for at least 24 hours after covering. Strain, save the strawberries for future use, and use them immediately or keep them in the refrigerator for up to 6 months.

6.27: Pellet Grill & Chill Shrimp Cocktail

Preparation Time: 10 minutes

Cooking Time: 30 mins.

Servings: 6

Ingredients:

- 1 pound U-20 shrimp, raw

- 1 tsp. of powdered onion

- 1 tsp. of powdered garlic

- 1 tbsp. of extra virgin olive oil

- 1 tsp. of kosher salt

Steps:

- Preheat the pellet grill to 350 degrees Fahrenheit before you start cooking.

- Place the shrimp in a medium dish and thoroughly rinse them.

- Place them on paper towels to air dry.

- Return the (shrimp) to the dish and stir in all of the dry ingredients and the olive oil.

- Toss the (shrimp) in the dish with a fork until they are equally covered.

- Place the shrimp immediately on the grill surface that has been preheated.

- Cooking for 10 minutes with the lid closed on the grill.

- Take the (shrimp) from the grill and place them on a baking sheet to cool.

- When serving with cocktail sauce, chill for one hour.

9.28: Smoked Cold Brew Coffee

Preparation time: 15 minutes

Cooking time: 2 hours

Servings: 8

Ingredients:

- Sugar

- Crushed coffee 12 oz.

- Milk or Heavy cream

Steps:

- Fill a plastic container halfway with coffee grinds and gently put 3-1/2 cups of water over the top. Add the remaining grinds and drop another 3-1/2 cup of water in a circular motion over the top.

- Using the back of a spoon, press the grinds into the water. Refrigerate for 18 to 24 hours after covering and transferring to the refrigerator.

- Erase from the refrigerator and strain through a fine-mesh strainer or a double layer of cheesecloth into a clean container.

- When preparing to cook, preheat the Traeger to 180°F with the lid covered for 15 minutes. Fill a small baking dish halfway with cold brew and put it immediately on the grilled grate. Smoke for 1 to 2 hours, depending on how much smoke you want. If super smoke is available, use it for the best taste.

• Remove off the grill and chill in an ice bath. Enjoy! Drink straight up, with cream or sugar, or in your favorite coffee recipe.

9.29: Game Day Micheladas

Preparation time: 5 minutes

Cooking time: 0 minutes

Servings: 4

Ingredients:

• 2 tbsp. Cajun spice

• 2 tbsp. salt (kosher)

• 2 limette, sliced into keile

• Clamato, 6 oz.

• 6 oz. smoked bloody Mary mix from Traeger

• Modelo 12 oz.

Steps:

• In a small bowl, combine the Cajun spice and kosher salt.

• Dip the glass bottle into the Cajun salt mixture after running the lime wedge over the rim.

• In a pint glass, combine Traeger smoked bloody Mary Clamato mix over ice.

• Garnish with a lime wedge and a dash of Modelo. Enjoy!

9.30: Smoky Mountain Bramble Cocktail

Preparation time: 20 minutes

Cooking time: 15 minutes

Servings: 4

Ingredients:

• Simple syrup made with smoked blackberries

- Blackberries, 16 oz.

- 2 cup sugar mixture

- 10 smoked blackberries

- 3 oz. of vodka

- 1 ½ ounce preserve liqueur from the Alps

- 1 ½ ounce from the lime juice

- 1 oz. blackberry smoked syrup

Steps:

- Set the Traeger to 180°F and preheat for 15 minutes with the lid covered when you're ready to cook. If super smoke is available, use it for the best taste.

- Put blackberries on a grilling mat and smoke for 15 to 20 minutes to create smoked blackberry simple syrup. In a small saucepan, mix 1 cup water and sugar and cook over medium heat until sugar is dissolved. Remove from the fire and macerate 2/3 of the berries in the simple syrup.

- Squeeze through a (fine mesh strainer) and keep for up to 14 days in an airtight container.

- To prepare the drink, in a cocktail shaker, muddle 4 to 5 smoked blackberries. Combine the vodka, preserve liqueur, lemon, and smoked blackberry syrup in a mixing glass. Shake vigorously with ice. Pour into an old-fashioned glass with a double strain.

- Serve with a smoking blackberry and a lemon twist as a garnish. Enjoy!

9.31: Smoked Pomegranate Lemonade Cocktail

Preparation time: 5 minutes

Cooking time: 45 minutes

Servings: 4

Ingredients:

- Ice cubes made from pomegranates

- 32 ounces of pomegranate juice

- pomegranate seeds, 2 cups

- 3 oz. of vodka

- Lemonade, 8 oz.

- Serve with a lemon wheel.

- Decorate with fresh mint

Steps:

- When preparing to cook, preheat the Traeger to 225°F with the lid covered for 15 minutes. If super smoke is available, use it for the best taste.

- Put one small container of pom juice) and (1 cup of pomegranate seeds) onto a shallow sheet pan for the smoked pomegranate ice cubes. Smoke for 45 minutes on the Traeger. Remove the grill from the heat and set it aside to cool.

- Fill ice mold with smoked pom juice and place them in the freezer.

- Put the (frozen pomegranate cubes) in a mason jar when ready to serve. Over the ice cubes, pour the vodka and lemonade.

- Serve with a fresh mint and lemon wheel as garnish. Enjoy!

9.32: A Smoking Classic Cocktail

Preparation time: 5 minutes

Cooking time: 1 hour

Servings: 2

Ingredients:

- Angostura (orange) bitters 2 bottle

- Sugar cubes 10

- Champagne 8 oz.

- Lemon twist

Steps:

- When preparing to cook, preheat the Traeger to 180°F with the lid covered for 15 minutes. If super smoke is available, use it for the best taste.

- To make the smoked orange bitters, mix 1 bottle of Angostura orange bitters, a splash of water, and 4 sugar cubes in a small pan.

- Smoked for 60 minutes using a skillet on the grill grate. Return the smoked bitters to the bottle after cooling.

- In each champagne flute, place a sugar cube and soak it in the smoked bitters.

- In a flute glass, combine champagne and a lemon twist. Enjoy!

9.33: Grilled Hawaiian Sour

Preparation time: 15 minutes

Cooking time: 15 minutes

Servings: 2

Ingredients:

- 2 pineapples, cut and trimmed
- Palm sugar (1/2 cup)
- Bourbon, 3 oz.
- 2 oz. pineapple juice (grilled)
- 2 oz. smoked simple syrup from Traeger
- Lemon juice, 10 oz.
- 2 pineapple chunks grilled for garnish
- 2 pineapple leaves, to be used as a garnish

Steps:

- Once ready to cook, preheat the Traeger to 350°F and cook for 15 minutes with the lid covered.
- Sprinkle pineapple slices with palm sugar for the grilled pineapple juice. Cook for 8 minutes on each side, immediately on the grill grate.
- Remove off the grill and set aside to cool. A few pieces should be set aside for garnish. To extract juice, run the remaining pineapple chunks through a centrifugal juicer.
- To prepare the drink, fill a cocktail strainer halfway with ice and add the bourbon, simple syrup, grilled pineapple juice and lemon juice. Shake the bottle vigorously. In a cold coupe glass, strain twice. Serve with grilled pineapple chunks and a pineapple leaf as a garnish.

9.34: Grilled Applejack O'lantern Cocktail

Preparation time: 10 minutes

Cooking time: 30 minutes

Servings: 2

Ingredients:

- Dogfish head pumpkin ale 12 oz.
- Oranges 2 diced
- 1 oz. smoky simple syrup from Traeger
- Apple brandy, 2 oz.
- Lemon juice, 1 oz.
- Orange juice, 1 oz.

Steps:

- When preparing to cook, preheat the Traeger to 500°F with the lid covered for 15 minutes.
- Place the oranges wheel firmly on the grill grate and cook for 20-30 mins, or until the fruit starts to caramelize. Remove off the grill and set aside to cool.
- In a chilly Collins glass, combine all of the ingredients. Serve with a half-grilled oranges wheel sprinkled with three cloves as a garnish. Enjoy!

9.35: Grilled Grapefruit Buck Cocktail

Preparation time: 10 minutes

Cooking time: 10 minutes

Servings: 4

Ingredients:

- Grapefruit juice grilled
- 4 halved grapefruit
- a half-cup of turbinado sugar
- 12 oz. of vodka
- 1 ½ ounce lemon juice (freshly squeezed) from 1 lemon
- 3 oz. of simple smoked syrup from Traeger
- 8 sprigs mint leaves, fresh
- Ginger beer, 12 oz.

- 2 grapefruit slices, cut into 1/2-inch circles as a garnish

Steps:

- When preparing to cook, preheat the Traeger to 500°F with the lid covered for 15 minutes.

- Place the sliced grapefruit on a hot Traeger and coat all sides with turbinado sugar. Grill for 3 minutes on each side or until grill marks appear. Remove the steaks from the grill and put them aside until they are cool enough to handle.

- To extract juice from grilled grapefruit, squeeze it and drain it

- In a pitcher, combine the vodka, lemon juice, grapefruit juice, Traeger smoked simple syrup, and 1 sprig of mint leaves. Stir briskly with a cocktail spoon.

- Mix vigorously for 30 seconds after adding a handful of ice.

- Cover with ginger beer and pour into 6 rocks glasses loaded with ice.

- Serve with a toasted grapefruit slice and a sprig of mint as a garnish. Enjoy!

9.36: Grilled Jungle Juice

Preparation time: 15 minutes

Cooking time: 20 minutes

Servings: 8

Ingredients:

- 1 pineapple, cut
- 3 oranges, cut
- Limes sliced 5
- Fresh strawberries, pound
- a quarter cup of granulated sugar
- 1 pineapple juice bottle
- Cranberry juice, 1 oz.
- Sparkling water, 1 oz.
- 1 Tito's vodka glass
- 1 tequila glass (silver)

- 1 white rum glass
- 1 triple sec glass

Steps:

- Preheat the oven to 350°F and warm for 15 minutes when ready to cook.
- Shake off any extra sugar before tossing the citrus segments with it.
- Cook the pineapple spears, citrus slices, and strawberry directly on the grill grate for 10-20 minutes, or until grill marks appear.
- Remove the (fruit slices) one by one until they complete cooking to avoid overcooking. Allow cooling before serving.
- Add the cooled grilled fruit, followed by all the liquids. Stir everything together well. Enjoy!

9.37: Grilled Peach Mint Julep

Preparation time: 15 minutes

Cooking time: 45 minutes

Servings: 2

Ingredients:

- Peaches with a hint of whiskey
- 2 peaches, whole, 4 oz. whisky
- Simple syrup made with pink peppercorns
- 2 pounds of sugar
- 4 tbsp. of peppercorns (pink)
- 20 entire fresh mint leaves for the main dish, plus extra for garnish
- 4-ounce bourbon
- 2 lime wedges for garnish

Steps:

- To make the grilled whiskey peaches, cut the peach into slices and soak them in whiskey for 4 to 6 hours in the refrigerator.
- Make the pink peppercorn simple syrup, mix sugar, 1 cup water, and pink peppercorns in a small pan.

- Set the Traeger to 180°F and preheat for 15 minutes with the lid covered when you're ready to cook. If super smoke is available, use it for the best taste.

- Cook syrup for 30 minutes on the barbecue until either desired smoke taste is achieved. Remove the steaks from the grill.

- Preheat the oven to 350 degrees Fahrenheit. Cook the whiskey-sliced peaches immediately on the grill grate for 10 to 12 minutes, or until softened and grill marks appear.

- Muddle 1/2 ounce pink peppercorn simple syrup with 10 fresh mint leaves and (4 slices of grilled whiskey peaches) to create the julep.

- 20 fresh mint leaves, with a few more for garnish

- So over the rim of the glass, sprinkle crushed ice. Stir with the bourbon over crushed ice. 1 big sprig of mint and fresh lime for garnish. Enjoy!

9.38: Grilled Peach Smash Cocktail

Preparation time: 5 minutes

Cooking time: 10 minutes

Servings: 2

Ingredients:

- 2 sliced peaches, grilled

- 10 mint leaves

- 1 ½ ounce smoked simple syrup from Traeger

- Bourbon (four ounces)

- 2 mint sprigs for decoration

Steps:

- Once ready to cook, preheat the Traeger to 375°F and cook for 15 minutes with the lid covered.

- Brush the peach slices with Traeger smoked simple syrup and cut them into 6 pieces. Cook 10 to 12 minutes, or until peaches are softened, and grill marks appear, immediately on the grill grate.

- 3 grilled peach slices, 5 mint leaves, and (Traeger smoked simple syrup) in a mixing glass

- Muddle the ingredients to release the mint oils and grilled peach juices. Put in the bourbon and the crushed ice.

- Shake vigorously and strain into a stemless wine glass. Finish with a sprinkling of crushed ice. Serve with a sliced peach and a sprig of mint as a garnish. Enjoy!

9.39: Smoked Grape Lime Rickey

Preparation time: 10 minutes

Cooking time: 45 minutes

Servings: 4

Ingredients:

- Red grapes, ½ pound
- 1 tbsp. of sugar plus ½ cup
- 1 cup of water
- 2 limes, half 1 lime, sliced
- 1 tbsp. of sugar
- 1 liter of lemon-lime soda

Steps:

- When preparing to cook, preheat the Traeger to 180°F for 15 minutes with the lid closed.

- Rinse the grapes well before placing them in a wide baking tray. Stir ½ cup sugar into ½ cup water until sugar dissolves. Pour the wine over the grapes.

- Smoke the cookie sheet immediately on the grill grate for 30 to 40 minutes, or until the grapes are tender.

- Remove the baking dish from the grill and put the whole contents into a blender. Puree until smooth on high, then filter through a fine-mesh sieve.

- Place the lime slices and halves immediately on the grill grate after tossing them with 1 tablespoon sugar. Cook for 15–20 minutes, or till grill marks appear on the surface. Remove the slices from the grill and put them aside. When the lime halves have cooled enough just to handle, juice them.

- Filling a pint glass halfway with ice to start the cocktail. 1 1/2 oz. Toasted lime juice, a splash of soda, 1 ½ oz. Smoked grape syrup. Serve with a grilled lime slice as a garnish. Enjoy!

9.40: Grilled Blood Orange Mimosa

Preparation time: 5 minutes

Cooking time: 15 minutes

Servings: 4

Ingredients:

- 2 tbsp. of powdered sugar 3 oranges, divided
- 1 sparkling wine bottle
- Garnish with thyme sprigs

Steps:

- When preparing to cook, preheat the Traeger to 375°F with the lid covered for 15 minutes.
- Soak the cut side of the oranges halves in sugar and put the cut side down immediately on the grill grate once the grill is heated.
- Grill for 10-15 minutes, or till grill marks appear on the oranges.
- Remove the steaks from the skillet and set them aside to cool to room temperature.
- When the oranges are cool enough to handle, juice them and filter the juice through a fine sieve to remove any pulp.
- Fill each glass with 5 oz. sparkling wine and 1-ounce blood orange juice.
- Serve with a sprig of thyme as a garnish. Enjoy!

9.41: Smoked Jacobsen Salt Margarita

Preparation time: 5 minutes

Cooking time: 1 day

Servings: 2

Ingredients:

- Sea salt with kosher certification
- 3 cup honey from Jacobsen Co.
- Tequila, 6 oz.

- 4 oz. of lime juice, freshly squeezed
- ½ cup kosher salt (Jacobsen Salt Co.) smoked kosher salt
- 2 tsp. of liqueur orange

Steps:

- Take kosher sea salt (whatever much you wish to smoke) and lay it out on a tray if creating your smoked salt.
- Set the temperature on the Traeger to 165°F and warm for 15 minutes with the lid covered. If super smoke is available, use it for the best taste.
- Place the salt tray immediately on the grill grate and smoke for approximately 24 hours, stirring every 8 hours. Please remove it from the grill after it has cooked for 24 hours, and use it in all of your favorite recipes. Use Jacobsen salt co. (Cherrywood smoked salt) if you wish to avoid the lengthy smoking session.
- In a small saucepan, combine the 1 cup water and honey. Cook for approximately 20 minutes over medium heat, stirring occasionally.
- Ice should be added to a cocktail shaker. Combine the lime juice, tequila, lime juice, simple syrup, and orange liqueur in a mixing glass. Cover and shake for approximately 30 seconds, or until well combined and cooled.
- On a dish, sprinkle smoked salt. To rims the edge of a cold rock glass, press the rim into the salt. In a cup, drain the margarita. Enjoy!

9.42: Smoked Arnold Palmer

Preparation time: 5 minutes

Cooking time: 5 minutes

Servings: 4

Ingredients:

- Teabags (black) 4
- Lime, juiced medium 8
- Traeger smoked simple syrup 1 cup
- For garnish use, lemon cut into wheels shape

Steps:

- In a temperature pitcher or dish, place the tea bags.

- Put water to a boil, then strain it over the tea bags. Allow 5 minutes for the tea to steep.

- Erase the (tea bags) and allow the tea to cool before serving.

- Lemons should be juiced. Toss the lemon juice into the iced tea.

- In a mixing bowl, combine the lemon tea and Traeger smoked simple syrup. Refrigerate the mixture until it is totally cold.

- Put in a glass over ice after it has cooled. Enjoy! Serve with a lime wheel as a garnish.

9.43: Smoked Berry Cocktail

Preparation time: 15 minutes

Cooking time: 15 minutes

Servings: 2

Ingredients:

- A half-cup of stemmed strawberries

- Blackberries (half cup)

- Blueberries, half a cup

- Iced tea or 8 ounces bourbon

- Lime juice (2 oz.)

- Simple syrup (3 ounces)

- Water with soda

- Garnished with mint

Steps:

- When preparing to cook, preheat the Traeger to 180 degrees Fahrenheit with the lid covered for 15 minutes. If super smoke is available, use it for the best taste.

- Wash the berries well before spreading them out on a fresh cookie sheet and grilling them. 15 minutes of smoking berries

- Transfer the berries to a blender once they have been removed from the grill. Puree the berries until smooth, then filter out the seeds using a fine-mesh sieve.

- Put 2 oz. of berry puree into the bottom of a glass to make a layered drink. Then, using the back of a spoon, pour 2 ounces bourbon or iced tea into the glass, followed by ½ oz. Lime juice and ½ oz. Simple syrup, soda water, and ice. Finish with a sprig of mint or a few additional berries as a garnish.

9.44: Traeger French 75 Cocktail

Preparation time: 5 minutes

Cooking time: 10 minutes

Servings: 2

Ingredients:

- 2 finely sliced lemons
- Gin, 3 oz.
- 1 oz. of freshly squeezed lemon juice
- 1 oz. smoked simple syrup from Traeger
- Champagne, 6 oz.

Steps:

- Set the Traeger temperature to 500°F and warm for 15 minutes, lid closed, for the grilled lemon.
- Place lemon straight on barbecue grate after brushing the Traeger smoked simple syrup. Grill for 15 minutes a side or until caramelized marks emerge.
- In a mixing container with ice, combine the gin, lemon juice, and (Traeger smoked simple) syrup. Shake vigorously before straining into a champagne flute.
- Finish with a splash of champagne and a grilled lemon topping. Enjoy!

9.45: Smoke Screen Cocktail

Preparation time: 25 minutes

Cooking time: 15 minutes

Servings: 2

Ingredients:

- Lemons 4
- Ransom whiskey 4 oz.

- Traeger smoked simple syrup 1 ½ oz.

Steps:

- When preparing to cook, preheat the Traeger to 500°F with the lid covered for 15 minutes.

- To make the grilled lemon juice, cut 1 lemon in half and cook it. To make the garnish, slice the remaining lemon into 1/4-inch thick wheels and put them on the grill.

- Remove the lemon wheels and set them aside. Grill for 15 min, or until one side of the lemons has grill marks. The split lemon should produce 3/4 oz. of juice.

- In a shaking glass with ice, mix 3/4 oz. Grilled lemon juice and Traeger smoked simple syrup and ransom whisky. Shake vigorously. Delicate drain into a cooled coupe glass with a roasted lemon wheel as a garnish. Enjoy!

9.46: Seeing Stars Cocktail

Preparation time: 5 minutes

Cooking time: 0 minutes

Servings: 2

Ingredients:

- Siete leagues Blanco tequila, 4 oz.

- A half-ounce of lime juice

- Gifford blue curacao, 1 oz.

- 1 oz. of juice from a watermelon

- 1 oz. of simple smoked syrup from Traeger

- 2 slices of watermelon, to serve as a garnish

Steps:

- Combine all of the ingredients in a shaker with ice. Fine filter into a rock glass full of ice and rimmed with smoked salt.

- Serve with a slice of watermelon as a garnish. Enjoy!

9.47: Classic Daiquiri

Preparation Time: 5 minutes

Cooking Time: 5 minutes

Servings: 1

Ingredients:

- Lime juice, 1 oz.
- 2 tsp. sugar (ultra-fine)
- White rum, 2 oz.
- Lime slices (for serving)

Steps:

- To dissolve the sugar and lime juice in a cocktail glass, mix them together.
- Fill with ice, add the rum, and shake until well chilled. Pour into a coup and garnish with a lime slice.

9.48: Maui Waui Cocktail

Preparation time: 5 minutes

Cooking time: 30 minutes

Servings: 2

Ingredients:

- 4 strawberries, fresh sugar
- A single orange
- 1 tbsp. of simple smoked syrup from Traeger
- 2 oz. of water
- 1 cup agave nectar
- Pineapple juice, 2 oz.
- Orange juice, 2 oz.
- 3 kiwi fruit slices
- Ice

- Rum, 2 oz.
- Cherry from Italy

Steps:

- When you're ready to cook, fire up the grill according to the manufacturer's directions. Preheat the oven to 325°F and bake for 10-15 minutes with the lid covered.

- Half the strawberries and roll them in granulated sugar. Cooked for 15-20 minutes directly on the grill. Remove the steaks from the grill and put them aside to cool.

- Slice 1 orange into wheels for the burned orange agave. Cover the orange wheels with 1 tbsp. Traeger simple syrup and grill until the exterior has a little sear. Reduce the temperature to smoke and put aside for 10-15 minutes to cool.

- 1 cup agave nectar, thinned with 2 oz. Water for 45 to 60 minutes, steep the burned chard oranges in the agave on smoke, stirring every 10 minutes.

- Put equal parts freshly squeezed pineapple juice and orange juice onto a shallow sheet pan to make smoked juice. Put the sheet pan on the grill grate directly and smoke for 45 minutes. Remove the steaks from the grill and put them aside to cool.

- Combine the burned kiwi slices, orange agave and grilled strawberries in a mixing glass. Lightly muddle. Combine ice, rum, and smoked juice in a cocktail shaker. Shake well and strain twice over ice.

- On a skewer, skewer a cooked pineapple and an Italian cherry. Enjoy!

9.49: Smoked Hot Buttered Rum

Preparation time: 5 minutes

Cooking time: 30 minutes

Servings: 4

Ingredients:

- 2 cups of liquid
- a quarter cup of brown sugar
- ½ stick melted butter
- 1 tsp cinnamon powder

- ¼ tsp nutmeg powder
- Cloves, powdered
- Salt
- Rum, 6 oz.

Steps:

- When preparing to cook, preheat the Traeger to 180°F with the lid covered for 15 minutes. If super smoke is available, use it for the best taste.

- Stir 2 cups water with all components except the rum in a shallow baking dish and put immediately on the grill grate. 30 minutes of smoking

- Remove the steaks from the skillet and place them into a blender pitcher. Process until the mixture is foamy.

- In four glasses, put 1.5 oz. of rum each. Divide the heated butter mixture among the four glasses equally.

- Add freshly grated nutmeg and cinnamon stick to the top. Enjoy!

9.50: Strawberry Basil Daiquiri

Preparation time: 5 minutes

Cooking time: 20 minutes

Servings: 2

Ingredients:

- 4 stemmed strawberries
- 6 tbsp. granulated sugar (distributed)
- 6 leaves of basil
- White rum, 3 oz.
- Lime juice, 2 oz.
- 1 oz. smoked simple syrup from Traeger
- 2 basil leaves, to be used as a garnish
- 2 lime slices to serve as a garnish

Steps:

- Once ready to cook, preheat the Traeger to 375°F and cook for 15 minutes with the lid covered.

- 2 tbsp. Of granulated sugar, cut strawberries in half. Cooked for 20 minutes directly on the grill grate. Remove from the heat and set aside to cool.

- In a shaking pan, gently mix 1 tbsp. Of powdered sugar and basil leaves. Muddle in the strawberries once more.

- Pour in the white rum, lime juice, and simple smoked syrup from the Traeger. Ice should be added to the shaker.

- Fill a chilled glass halfway with the ingredients and garnish with sliced lime and fresh basil leaf. Enjoy

9.51: Smoked Bloody Mary with Grilled Garnishes

Preparation Time: 30 minutes

Cooking time: 1 hour

Servings: 4

Ingredients:

- 5 Roma Tomatoes, ¼ " thickly cut
- Seasoning with salt and pepper
- Traeger Beef Rub, 2 tbsp.
- 10 bacon slices
- 1 jar pickled asparagus
- 1 jar pickled green beans
- 1 pepperoncini jar
- 1 jar cocktail onions steeped with vermouth
- A few cherry tomatoes
- 1 jar olives, mixed
- 2 fresh mushrooms
- 2 grilled shrimp
- 1 grilled lobster tail
- Bamboo Skewers, 4 celery stalks

- 3 quarts of tomato juice
- 3 tbsp. Worcestershire sauce
- 5 tsp. of spicy sauce
- 2 tsp. of prepared horseradish
- 1 lemon, whole and juiced
- 2 lemon wedges, whole
- Salt Ice Traeger Bloody Mary Cocktail
- 1 ½ oz. of vodka

Steps:

- Once ready to cook, preheat the grill to 275°F with the lid covered for 15 minutes.
- Remove the stems and quarter the tomatoes. Place the tomatoes on a metal rack on top of the baking pan.
- Pepper, salt and Traeger Beef Rub to taste. On the grill, put the baking pan and rack with the tomatoes.
- For the Smoked Bacon, cook the bacon immediately on the grill grate next to the tomato for approximately 60 minutes, or until crisp. Crispy bacon will hold up to being used as a decoration in the drink.
- Remove tomatoes and bacon from the grill after 1 hour. Remove the skins from the tomatoes and put them aside to cool.
- Raise the temperature of the grill to medium and preheat it.
- Using olive oil, brush the skewers and put them straight on the grill. 5 minutes each side on the grill, or till grill marks appear. Remove the steaks from the grill and put them aside to cool.
- To make the Bloody Mary Mixture, pulse peeled tomatoes in a food processor until smooth.
- Combine tomato juice, Worcestershire sauce, horseradish, spicy sauce, and 1 full lemon juice.
- Season to taste with salt and black pepper. Pulse once more to mix
- Rub a lemon slice over the rim of a pint glass, then dip it in Traeger Bloody Mary Cocktail Salt.
- Fill glass with ice cubes, vodka, and the Bloody Mary Mixture. Gently stir

- To make the Smoke Bloody Mary, garnish with a lime and a lemon slice on each rim.
- Toss the cocktail with smoked bacon, grilled, pickled veggie skewers, and a celery stick. Immediately serve
- Have fun

9.52: Strawberry Mint Julep Cocktail

Preparation time: 5 minutes

Cooking time: 0 minutes

Servings: 4

- 2 oz. smoked simple syrup from Traeger
- 16 big stemmed strawberries
- A quarter cup of fresh mint leaves
- Bourbon, 12 oz.
- 2 big strawberries, cut vertically into 6 slices to serve as a garnish
- 6 fresh mint sprigs for garnish

Steps:

- In a medium-sized pitcher, combine Traeger smoked simple syrup, entire strawberries, mint, and bourbon.
- Muddle until the mint and strawberries are evenly distributed.
- Pour the contents into glasses in an equal layer. Fill the glass with crushed ice until it overflows.
- Put a straw in each glass and a strawberry slice on top. Enjoy!

9.53: Sunset Margarita

Preparation time: 10 minutes

Cooking time: 55 minutes

Servings: 2

Ingredients:

- Four oranges
- 2 cup agave nectar + 1 tsp. agave nectar
- 1 cup of water
- 1 oz. agave nectar (burnt orange)
- 3 oz. tequila repos ado
- 1 ½ oz. lemon juice, freshly squeezed
- Cherrywood smoked salt by Jacobsen Salt Co.

Steps:

- Preheat the Traeger to 350°F with the lid covered for 15 minutes.
- Slice one orange in half and brush the cut side with agave syrup to get the burned orange agave syrup. Grill for 15 minutes, or till grill marks appear, with the cut side down on the grill grate.
- Slice the second orange and spray both sides with agave while the oranges halves are cooking. Cook for 15 minutes, or until grill marks appear, by placing pieces immediately on the grill grate adjacent to the halves.
- Remove the orange halves from the grill grate and set them aside to cool. Juice half of them and filter once they've cooled. Remove from the equation.
- In a small bowl, whisk together 1/4 cup water and agave nectar. Remove the oranges pieces from the grill and toss them into the agave mixture, saving a few for decoration.
- Lower the grill temp to 180°F and put the agave and oranges in a shallow dish directly on the grill grate. 40 minutes of smoking Remove the pan from the heat and strain the contents. Remove from the equation.
- To make the cocktail, rim the glass with Jacobsen smoked salt. In a cocktail glass, combine tequila, grilled orange juice, fresh lemon juice, and burned orange agave syrup. Add the ice and give it a good shake.
- Over clean ice, drain into rimmed glass. Serve with a roasted orange slice as a garnish. Enjoy!

9.54: Smoked Salted Caramel White Russian

Preparation time: 10 minutes

Cooking time: 20 minutes

Servings: 4

Ingredients:

- Half-and-Half (16 oz.)
- Caramel sauce with salt
- 6 oz. of vodka
- 6 oz. Kahlua

Steps:

- When preparing to cook, preheat the Traeger to 180°F with the lid covered for 15 minutes. If super smoke is available, use it for the best taste.
- Fill a small baking dish halfway with half-and-half and put it immediately on the grilling grate. Put 2 to 3 cups of water into a shallow baking dish and put it next to the half-and-half on the grill.
- For 20 minutes, smoked both the half-and-half and the water. Allow cooling after removing from the grill.
- Refrigerate the half-and-half until ready to use. Fill ice cube pans halfway with smoked water and Place them in the freezer until fully frozen.
- Into four glasses, divide the smoked ice cubes. Pour the caramel sauce into the glass and swirl it around.
- Salted caramel sauce to taste
- Fill each glass with 1-1/2 oz. Vodka and 1-1/2 ounce Kahlua, then top with smoked half-and-half. Enjoy!

9.55: Grilled Frozen Strawberry Lemonade

Preparation time: 5 minutes

Cooking time: 15 minutes

Servings: 4

Ingredients:

- 1 pound of strawberries, fresh
- 8 lemons, halved
- ½ cup of turbinado sugar
- A quarter cup of Cointreau

- Simple syrup ¼ cup
- 2 cups of ice
- 1 c. Tito's tequila

Steps:

- Once ready to cook, preheat the grill on high for 15 minutes with the lid covered.

- Place the lemon halves immediately on the grilling grate after dipping them in turbinado sugar. Place the strawberries next to the lemons after tossing them with the remaining sugar.

- Grill until grill marks appear on both lemons and strawberries, approximately 15 minutes for lemon and 10 minutes for strawberries.

- Remove from the heat and set aside to cool.

- Using a strainer, extract the juice from grilled lemons, removing any seed or pulp. Fill a blender pitcher halfway with water.

- Remove the stems from the grilled strawberries and combine them with the lemon juice in a blender pitcher, simple syrup 2 cups ice, vodka, and Cointreau.

- Add to 4-6 glasses after pureeing until smooth. If desired, sprinkle with roasted strawberries and roasted lemon wedges. Enjoy!

9.56: Smoked Eggnog

Preparation time: 10 minutes

Cooking time: 1 hour

Servings: 4

Ingredients:

- 2-quart whole milk
- 1 quart of thick cream
- 4 beaten egg yolks
- 1 c. sugar
- Bourbon, 3 oz.
- 1 tsp. of extract de vanilla
- Nutmeg (1 tsp.)

- 4 beaten egg whites
- Cream whipped

Steps:

- Plan, this recipe requires chill time.

- Set Traeger temperature to 180°F and preheat, lid closed for 15 minutes. For optimal flavor, use super smoke if available.

- Pour the milk and cream into a baking dish and smoke on the Traeger for 60 minutes.

- Meanwhile, in the bowl of stand mixer, beat egg yolks till they lighten in color. Slowly add 1/3 cup sugar & continue to beat till sugar completely dissolves.

- After milk & cream have smoked, add along with bourbon, vanilla & nutmeg in egg mixture & stir to combine.

- Put egg whites in the bowl of a stand mixer and beat into soft peaks. (When you lift the beaters, prepare ahead of time since this dish needs chilling time.

- Preheat the Traeger to 180°F with the lid covered for 15 minutes. If super smoke is available, use it for the best taste.

- Place the milk and cream in a baking dish and smoke for 60 minutes on the Traeger.

- Meanwhile, beat the egg yolks in the mixing bowl until they soften in color. Keep adding 1/3 cup sweetener and beat until sugar melts fully.

- Add the smoked milk and cream to the egg mixture, along with the vanilla, bourbon and nutmeg, and whisk to incorporate.

- In the stand mixer, whisk the egg whites until soft peaks form. (When lifting the beaters, the whites should form a peak that curls down slightly.)

- While the mixer is still running, slowly drizzle in 1 tablespoon of sugar and beat until firm peaks form.

- Gently incorporate the egg whites into the cream mixture, then whisk everything together well.

- Allow for flavor melding by chilling the eggnog for a few hours. Finish with a sprinkling of nutmeg and a dollop of cream on top. Enjoy

- The whites should curve down slightly to form a peak.)

- While the mixer is still running, slowly drizzle in 1 tbsp. Of sugar and beat until firm peaks form.

- Gently incorporate the egg whites into the crème mixture, then whisk everything together well.

- Allow for flavor melding by chilling the eggnog for a few hours. Finish with a sprinkling of nutmeg and a dollop of whipped cream on top. Enjoy!

9.57: Zombie Cocktail Recipe

Preparation time: 5 minutes

Cooking time: 45 minutes

Servings: 4

Ingredients:

- Pineapple with smoked orange juice

- Orange juice, freshly squeezed

- Pineapple nectar

- 2 oz. rum (light)

- 2 oz. rum (dark)

- Lime juice, 2 oz.

- 1 oz. smoked simple syrup from Traeger

- Smokey orange and pineapple juice, 6 oz.

- 2 grilled orange peels (to serve as a garnish)

- 2 pineapple pieces grilled for garnish

Steps:

- Once ready to cook, preheat the Traeger to 180°F and cook for 15 minutes with the lid covered.

- In a shallow sheet pan, combine equal parts of freshly squeezed pineapple juice and orange juice and smoke for 45 minutes. Remove from the oven and set aside to cool. Take out 3 oz. of juice and store the rest in the freezer for later use.

- In a mixing glass, combine lighter and darker rums, 3 oz. of smoked pineapple juice and orange juice, lime juice, and Traeger smoked simple syrup.

- Shake with ice and pour into a tiki glass over fresh ice.

- Serve with grilled pineapple and grilled orange peel as garnish. Enjoy

9.58: The Old Orchard Cocktail

Preparation time: 5 minutes

Cooking time: 20 minutes

Servings: 2

Ingredients:

- 2 sliced apples
- 2 tbsp. of sugar (granulated)
- A pinch of cinnamon
- Rye whiskey, 3 oz.
- 1 ½ oz. smoked simple syrup from Traeger
- 1 oz. of freshly squeezed lemon juice
- 4 oz. hard cider from Angry Orchard

Steps:

- When preparing to cook, preheat the Traeger to 500°F with the lid covered for 15 minutes.
- Toss apple slices with cinnamon and granulated sugar.
- Cooking for 20-25 minutes with apple slices straight on the grill grate. Remove from the heat and set aside to cool.
- Mix the Traeger smoked simple syrup and fresh lemon juice in a shaker, whiskey.
- To mix flavors (add ice) and shake for 15 seconds.
- Strain into a beer glass over fresh ice and top with angry orchard cider.
- Serve with a baked apple-cinnamon slice as a garnish. Enjoy!

9.59: The Trifecta Cocktail

Preparation time: 5 minutes

Cooking time: 0 minutes

Servings: 2

Ingredients:

- Mint leaves 16
- Traeger smoked simple syrup 1 oz.
- Bourbon 3 oz.

Steps:

- Leaves of mint and Traeger simple syrup should be lightly muddled.
- Fill the glass halfway with crushed ice and add the bourbon.
- To make an ice dome, top with additional crushed ice. If preferred, garnish with mint leaves and bitters. Enjoy! Stir until the outside of the cup is frosted.

9.60: Traeger Boulevardier Cocktail

Preparation time: 5 minutes

Cooking time: 1 hour

Servings: 2

Ingredients:

- 4 oranges (main) 1/2 cup honey
- 1500 milliliters rye whiskey
- A half-ounce of Campari
- 1 ½ ounce vermouth (sweet)
- 2 tbsp. of sugar (granulated)
- 3 oz. grilled rye with an orange infusion

Steps:

- Once ready to cook, preheat the Traeger to 350°F with the lid shut down for 15 minutes.
- 2 oranges, sliced in half and honeyed on the cut side. Remove the peels from the remaining orange and put them on the grill. The cooking time is 20 to 25 mins.
- Remove off the grill and set aside to cool. Cook 20 to 30 minutes, or until black grill marks form, by placing orange halves cut down immediately on the grill grate. Remove the orange halves and set them aside to cool.
- Fill a bottle of rye whiskey halfway with orange halves and steep for 10 to 12 hours. The orange taste will get sweeter and more prominent as they soak longer.

- In a mixing glass, combine all ingredients and mix until diluted. Into a new coupe glass, strain and serve neat.

- Serve with roasted orange peel as a garnish. Enjoy!

9.61: Tequila Sunrise

Preparation Time: 5 mins

Cooking time: 0 hours 5 mins

Servings: 1

Ingredients:

- Ice

- Orange juice, 4 oz.

- Silver tequila, 2 oz.

- Grenadine, ½ oz.

- Garnish with an orange slice

- Garnish with a maraschino cherry

Steps:

- Ice should be added to a tall glass. Stir in the tequila and orange juice until well combined. Decorate with an orange sliced and a maraschino cherry after adding the grenadine.

9.62: Color-changing margaritas

Preparation time: 5 minutes

Cooking time: 30 minutes

Servings: 4

Ingredients:

- 2 c. purple cabbage, diced

- 4 c. water that has been brought to a boil

- Tequila, 8 oz.

- Triple sec, 4 oz.

- 3 oz. lime juice, freshly squeezed

- 1-quart lemonade

- 4 lime wedges to serve as a garnish

- For the rim, 1/4 cup salt (kosher) or coarse sea salt

Steps:

- In a big heatproof dish, place the cabbage. Put boiling water over cauliflower and set aside for 5 minutes, or until the water becomes a deep blue color. Remove the cabbage and let the water cool.

- Transfer to ice trays when the water is no longer hot. Freeze for 4 hours or until solid.

- Combine tequila, lime juice, triple sec and lemonade in a medium pitcher or measuring cup. Using a lime slice, wet the rims of the glasses and then dip them in salt.

- Divide the margarita amongst the glasses with purple ice cubes. Serve with a lemon slice as a garnish.

9.63: Margarita Watermelon

Preparation time: 10 minutes

Cooking time: 20 minutes

Servings: 16

Ingredients:

- 1 watermelon, triangularly sliced

- 1 cup of tequila

- a third of a cup of triple sec

- 1/4 cup lime juice, freshly squeezed

- For garnish, 1/4 cup margarita salt

- 1 lime zest for garnish

Steps:

- Watermelon should be placed in a big dish or baking tray. Add lime juice, tequila, triple sec over the top. Soak for 1 hour.

- Combine the salt and lime zest on a small dish.

- Serve watermelon slices dipped in salt mixture.

9.64: Classic Margaritas

Preparation time: 5 minutes

Cooking Time: 5 minutes

Servings: 2

Ingredients:

- 2 lemon wedges for rimming and garnishing glasses
- For rimming glasses, use
- ¼ cup kosher salt or coarse sea salt.
- Tequila, 4 oz.
- 1 ½ oz. Freshly squeezed lemon juice 2 oz. triple sec
- Ice

Steps:

- On a small shallow dish, sprinkle salt. Rub a lime wedge over the rims of two glasses, then dip them in salt to coat them.
- Stir together the lemon juice, tequila, triple sec in two glasses. Serve with ice and lime as a garnish.

9.65: Boozy Grinch Punch

Preparation time: 10 minutes

Cooking time: 20 minutes

Servings: 12

Ingredients:

- 1 packet (0.13 oz.) Kool-Aid Lemon Lime mixture
- 4 c. ice and water
- 3 c. soda (lemon-lime)
- Pineapple juice, 2 c.
- Vodka, 2 c.

- 1-gallon ginger ale
- Slices of lime for rimming
- For rimming, use red sanding sugar.

Steps:

- Mix Kool-Aid and water in a big pitcher.
- Add soda, vodka, ice, Kool-Aid, pineapple juice and ginger ale in a big punch bowl.
- To rim glasses, use a lime slice and sand sugar to coat. To serve, pour the punch into glasses.

9.66: Cranberry Mimosas

Preparation: 1o minutes

Cooking time: 10 minutes

Servings: 4

Ingredients:

- 2 tbsp. of sugar 1 lime, halved
- 1 cup cranberry juice, sweetened
- 1 champagne bottle
- 12 cranberries, fresh
- 4 sprigs fresh rosemary, tiny

Steps:

- Lime the champagne glasses and then roll them in sugar. Fill each glass with ¼ cup cranberry juice and top with champagne.
- Make a hole in the cranberries using a toothpick. Garnish mimosas with rosemary skewers threaded through cranberries.

9.67: White Christmas Margaritas

Preparation time: 15 minutes

Cooking time: 15 minutes

Servings: 6

Ingredients:

- 1 can of unprocessed coconut milk (14 oz.)
- Silver tequila, 12 oz.
- Triple sec, 8 oz.
- lime juice, 1/4 cup
- Ice, 4 c.
- For rimming glasses, use a lime wedge.
- Sugar sanding for rimming glasses
- Lime slices to serve as a garnish
- Garnish with cranberries

Steps:

- In a blender, mix coconut milk, lemon juice, tequila, triple sec and ice. Blend until completely smooth.
- Using a lime slice as a rim, dip glasses in sanding sugar. Serve in a glass with lemon and cranberries on top.

9.68: Santa clausmopolitans

Preparation time: 5 minutes

Cooking time: 5 minutes

Servings: 4

Ingredients:

- Rim white sanding sugar lime wedge
- 1 ½ cup cranberry juice
- 1 cup vodka
- A quarter cup of triple sec
- A quarter cup of lime juice
- A half-cup of fresh cranberries

Steps:

- Using a lime wedge, wrap each glass in sanding sugar.

- Combine the cranberry juice, vodka, triple sec, and lemon juice in a cocktail glass with ice. Shake the cocktail shaker until it is completely cold.

- Pour the beverages into rimmed glasses and decorate with cranberries.

9.69: *Jack Frosties*

Preparation time: 5 minutes

Cooking time: 10 minutes

Servings: 5

Ingredients:

- 1 cup of vodka

- Prosecco, 1 c.

- A half-cup of blue Curacao

- ½ gallon lemonade

- 6 cups of ice

- For rimming, use a lemon slice.

- For rimming, use white sanding sugar.

Steps:

- Combine Prosecco, vodka, blue curacao, lemon, and ice in a mixer. Blend until smooth.

- Soak each glass in sanding sugar after running a lemon slice over the rim.

- Serve immediately with Frosties in rimmed glasses.

9.70: *Maui Waui cocktail*

Preparation Time: 5 minutes

Cooking Time: 30 minutes

Servings: 2

Ingredients:

- 4 sugared fresh strawberries

- a single orange

- Traeger Smoked Simple Syrup, 1 tbsp.

- 1 cup agave 2 oz. water

- Pineapple juice, 2 oz.

- Orange juice, 2 oz.

- 3 kiwi fruit ice cubes

- 2 oz. Italian Cherry Rum

Steps:

- When you're ready to cook, fire up the Traeger according to the manufacturer's directions. Preheat the oven to 325°F and cook for 10-15 minutes with the lid covered.

- Half the strawberries and roll them in granulated sugar. Cooked for 15-20 minutes directly on the grill. Remove the steaks from the grill and put them aside to cool.

- For the Agave Burnt Orange: 1 orange, cut into wheels Coat the oranges wheels with 1 tbsp. Of Traeger Simple Syrup and cook until the exterior has a little sear. Reduce the temperature to smoke and put aside for 10-15 minutes to cool.

- 1 cup agave nectar, thinned with 2 oz. water For 45 to 60 minutes, steep the burned chard oranges in the agave on smoke, stirring every 10 minutes.

- In a shallow sheet pan, combine equal parts fresh-squeezed orange juice and pineapple juice. Put the sheet pan on the grill grate directly and smoke for 45 minutes. Remove the steaks from the grill and put them aside to cool.

- Combine the burned orange agave, kiwi slices, and grilled strawberries in a mixing glass. Lightly muddle. Combine ice, rum, and smoked juice in a cocktail shaker. Shake well and strain twice over ice.

- On a skewer, skewer a grilled pineapple and an Italian cherry. Enjoy!

9.71: Moscow Mule Punch

Preparation time: 5 minutes

Cooking time: 10 minutes

Servings: 8

Ingredients:

- Ice, 4 c.
- 4 cup ginger ale
- Vodka, 3 c.
- 1 cup lime juice, freshly squeezed
- 1 cup mint leaves, plus a few more for garnish
- 2 lemons, sliced, plus more lemons for garnish

Steps:

- Add ginger beer, ice, lime juice, vodka, lime slices, and mint in a large punch bowl.
- Pour the punch into glass or copper cups and top with more mint.

9.72: Dalgona Martini

Preparation time: 5 minutes

Cooking time: 5 minutes

Servings: 1

Ingredients:

- Ice
- Bailey's (2 oz.)
- Vodka, 2 oz.
- Granulated sugar (2 tbsp.)
- 2 tbsp. of instant coffee
- 2 tbsp. of cold water

Steps:

- Add ice to a cocktail glass or glass, then Baileys and vodka. Shake or stir vigorously until well cold. Fill a martini glass halfway with ice and strain it into it.
- Combine the coffee, sugar, and water in a medium mixing basin. Whisk vigorously until the mixture becomes silky smooth and glossy, then keep mixing until it hardens and retains its lofty, frothy form.
- On top of the martini, scoop and swirl the beaten coffee mixture.

9.73: *Beat the Heat Slushies*

Preparation time: 5 minutes

Cooking time: 5 minutes

Servings: 4

Ingredients:

- 4 c. raspberries, frozen
- 1 white wine bottle (750 mL)
- 2 Spindrift® Raspberry Lime (12 oz.) cans
- A quarter cup of vodka
- Lime juice (1/2 lime)
- 4 lime slices as a garnish

Steps:

- Blend raspberries, Spindrift, vodka, wine and lime juice until smooth in a blender. To serve, divide the mixture among glasses and top with a lime slice in each.

9.74: *Boozy Fishbowl*

Preparation time: 5 minutes

Cooking time: 5 minutes

Servings: 8

Ingredients:

- Lemonade, 6 c.
- A third of a cup of pineapple juice
- 1 cup rum and
- 1 cup vodka
- Lemon slices,
- ½ cup blue Curacao
- Ice

Steps:

- Fill a large fishbowl or punch bowl halfway with ice and add lemonade, rum, pineapple juice, vodka, and blue Curacao. Serve with lemon slices as a garnish.

9.75: Giggle Juice

Preparation time: 10 minutes

Cooking time: 10 minutes

Servings: 8

Ingredients:

- For rimming glasses, use a lemon slice.
- Sugar is used to rim glasses.
- 1 Moscato (750 ml) bottle
- 3 c. lemonade (pink)
- 1 lemon-lime soda can
- 1 cup of vodka
- 2 c. strawberries, sliced
- 1 lemon, cut into half-moon slices of ice

Steps:

- Lemon wedges are used to rim glasses, which are then dipped in sugar.
- Combine the soda, Moscato, pink lemonade, vodka, and fruit in a big pitcher. Toss in the ice and whisk to mix.
- Serve by dividing the mixture among the glasses.

9.76: Mojito recipe

Preparation time: 5 minutes

Cooking time: 5 minutes

Servings: 1

Ingredients:

- 1 lime's juice

- 1 tsp. of sugar (granulated)

- A small handful of mint leaves, plus a serving sprig

- White rum, 60 ml

- To taste soda water

Steps:

- In a small container, mix the lime juice, sugar, and mint leaves, crushing the mint leaves as you go — you may do this with the end of a rolling pin. Add a handful of ice to a large glass and serve.

- Pour the rum over the top and whisk with a lengthy spoon. Serve with a splash of soda water and a sprig of mint on top.

9.77: Bergamot mojito

Preparation time 20 minutes

Cooking time 10 minutes

Servings: 6

Ingredients:

- 300 g caster sugar (golden)

- 6 lemons, juiced

- 1 bergamot, zested and juiced

- 12 mint leaves (available from ocado.com)

- 150 milliliters golden rum

Steps:

- In a pan over medium heat, combine the sugar and 1 liter of water. Bring to a boil, then remove from heat and cool to room temperature.

- In a food processor, mix the mint, lime juice, and bergamot zest and juice, then added the cooled syrup and pulse until blended. Put into a plastic bottle and freeze, stirring every 30 minutes with a fork until completely frozen.

- Spoon the granite into cold glass and pour the rum over it to serve.

Conclusion

You've mastered a few of the finest smoker grill recipes, and you're on your way to being a grilling, BBQ, and general cooking expert. Seeing so many recipes in such a short period of time may be intimidating. We split the book into sections, each of which was many pages long. The results are excellent when you run a smoker correctly and use the best pellets. Taste induced is so amazing that not only you but every guest who comes will be astounded. The meal's outstanding culinary skills will certainly wow those who eat it. You have the ability to make this book; I've invested a lot of love, effort, and time in it. I'm certain that each recipe is all I dreamed it would be. To get the best results, we suggest that you follow the things. To guarantee a great dinner, stick to the details as much as possible, use this excellent guidebook, and try these recipes.

Made in the USA
Monee, IL
21 February 2022